ECONOMIC STRATEGY A

Economic Strategy and the Labour Party

Politics and policy-making, 1970–83

Mark Wickham-Jones
Lecturer in Politics
University of Bristol

First published in Great Britain 1996 by
MACMILLAN PRESS LTD
Houndmills, Basingstoke, Hampshire RG21 6XS
and London
Companies and representatives
throughout the world

A catalogue record for this book is available
from the British Library.

ISBN 0–333–67065–5 hardcover
ISBN 0–333–69372–8 paperback

First published in the United States of America 1996 by
ST. MARTIN'S PRESS, INC.,
Scholarly and Reference Division,
175 Fifth Avenue,
New York, N.Y. 10010

ISBN 0–312–16405–X

Library of Congress Cataloging-in-Publication Data
Wickham-Jones, Mark, 1962–
Economic strategy and the Labour Party : politics and policy
-making, 1970–83 / Mark Wickham-Jones.
p.   cm.
Includes bibliographical references and index.
ISBN 0–312–16405–X (cloth)
1. Great Britain—Economic policy—1945–   2. Labour Party (Great
Britain)   I. Title.
HC256.6.W49   1996
338.941—dc20   96–26643
                                                          CIP

10 9   8   7   6   5   4   3   2   1
05 04 03 02 01 00 99 98 97 96

Printed and bound in Great Britain by
Antony Rowe Ltd, Chippenham, Wiltshire

Contents

List of Tables and Figures

Acknowledgements

I have accrued many debts during the research for this book which it is a pleasure to acknowledge. Michael Artis and Martin Burch patiently provided extremely useful comments on many drafts of the thesis on which it is based. Patrick Seyd and David Howell examined the thesis and proposed many important improvements. I have also benefited from suggestions from Lewis Minkin and John Schwarzmantel. My colleague Vernon Hewitt commented perceptively on a draft. Desmond King tirelessly gave excellent general advice and offered acute and detailed revisions on numerous occasions. I am very grateful to all of them for their help and the many amendments they suggested. Responsibility, of course, is mine.

I would like to thank all those who gave up their time so that I could discuss Labour's economic policy-making with them. Tony Benn and Ruth Winstone have been especially helpful in providing access to a variety of Labour party documents and papers including Benn's unabridged diary. I am grateful to them for their assistance and for permission to quote from Benn's unpublished diary. I am also grateful to Stephen Bird and Andrew Flynn of the National Museum of Labour History, to Alan Haworth, secretary of the Parliamentary Labour Party, and to the staff and librarians of the British Library of Political and Economic Science, the Labour Party library and the TUC library. For their help and encouragement I would like to thank Charles Wickham-Jones and Prim Wickham-Jones.

I owe an immense debt to Julie Tarling. Her support and encouragement contributed towards this volume in a manner that words cannot fully express.

Mark Wickham-Jones
December 1995

Abbreviations

ACAS	Advisory Conciliation and Arbitration Service
ADP	Agreed Development Plan
AES	Alternative Economic Strategy
APEX	Association of Professional, Executive, Clerical and Computer Staff
ASTMS	Association of Scientific, Technical and Managerial Staff
AUEW	Amalgamated Union of Engineering Workers
AUEW–TASS	Amalgamated Union of Engineering Workers Technical and Supervisory Section
CAC	Conference Arrangements Committee
CBI	Confederation of British Industry
CEPG	Cambridge Economic Policy Group
CLP	Constituency Labour Party
CLV	Campaign for Labour Victory
CLPD	Campaign for Labour Party Democracy
CSE	Conference of Socialist Economists
EEC	European Economic Community
EETPU	Electrical, Electronic, Telecommunications and Plumbing Union
FEASC	Finance and Economic Affairs Sub-Committee
GMWU	General and Municipal Workers Union
HPC	Home Policy Committee
ILP	Independent Labour Publications
IMF	International Monetary Fund
IPSC	Industrial Policy Sub-Committee
IRC	Industrial Reorganisation Corporation
IRI	Italian Institute for Industrial Reconstruction
IWC	Institute for Workers' Control
KME	Kirkby Manufacturing and Engineering Company
LC	TUC–Labour Party Liaison Committee

LCC	Labour Coordinating Committee
LPACR	Labour Party Annual Conference Report
NALGO	National and Local Governments Officers' Association
NEA	National Economic Assessment
NEB	National Enterprise Board
NEC	National Executive Committee
NEDC	National Economic Development Council
NUBE	National Union of Banking Employees
NUPE	National Union of Public Employees
NUR	National Union of Railwaymen
PC	Parliamentary Committee (Shadow Cabinet)
PCC	Policy Coordinating Committee
PIDSC	Planning and Industrial Democracy Sub-Committee
PLP	Parliamentary Labour Party
PO	Public Ownership
PSG	Public Sector Group
RD	Research Department papers' classification, 1970–74, 1979–83
RE	Research Department papers' classification, 1974–79
RES	Research Department papers' classification, 1974
SDP	Social Democratic Party
SWP	Sector Working Party
TGWU	Transport and General Workers Union
TUC	Trades Union Congress
USDAW	Union of Shop, Distributive and Allied Workers
WPBI	Working Party on Banking and Insurance

Introduction: Economic Strategy and the Labour Party

In June 1973 the Labour party published a new policy document entitled *Labour's Programme 1973*.[1] The first forty pages outlined Labour's economic policies involving detailed proposals for public ownership, planning, price controls and industrial democracy alongside the more conventional measure of demand reflation. Overall the publication contained a radical and sweeping set of measures and Labour's leftwingers were jubilant at its adoption. At the core of the new document was an interventionist industrial strategy which proposed that the next Labour government nationalise 25 of the top 100 companies in the UK. Obligatory planning agreements determining output and employment levels would be concluded with the remaining large private firms. One leading member of the left, the MP Tony Benn stated: 'The party is now firmly launched on a leftwing policy.... it is a remarkable development of views that we have achieved in three years of hard work.'[2] Labour's rightwing leaders made no attempt to conceal their hostility and contempt towards the new policies. One of the party's foremost intellectuals, Tony Crosland, argued that *Labour's Programme 1973* was 'written by people who didn't live in the real world'.[3] Crosland publicly called on Labour to 'return to sanity' and abandon its economic proposals.[4]

Ten years later, in June 1983, the Labour party lost the general election on a manifesto whose economic strategy had much in common with the measures of *Labour's Programme 1973*. *New Hope for Britain* promised that a Labour government would extend public ownership into every important sector of the economy and 'negotiate agreed development plans with all leading companies'.[5] For a decade Labour's economic strategy was dominated by a set of proposals which many in the party opposed as economically impractical,

1

ideologically mistaken and electorally damaging. Through these policies, Labour committed itself to bold and far-reaching objectives: 'Our longer-term goal is to replace the bulk of private ownership by these diverse forms of common ownership.'[6] Such sweeping objectives went well beyond those Labour had adopted earlier during the postwar period. The central task of this book is to outline the new economic strategy, detail the disagreements which occurred between its advocates and many of Labour's leaders, and explain how the party came to embrace a policy package which generated such conflict. I will also examine the consequences of its adoption for Labour's fortunes more generally.

The period in which Labour advocated the Alternative Economic Strategy – as the new policies were known by the mid-1970s – was one of profound crisis and seemingly irreversible decline for the party.[7] This crisis comprised several distinct elements. In ideological terms, Labour's experience in government between 1964 and 1970 and again between 1974 and 1979 indicated to many the exhaustion of the party's Keynesian welfarist policy programme. Both governments had departed from their original social democratic trajectory and resorted to deflationary economic policies. Many party members felt bitterly disappointed by the relative lack of substantive achievement of these administrations. Indeed, for leftwingers, Labour's failure in office was the direct cause of their espousal of the new socialist policies contained in *Labour's Programme 1973*. Others in the party were as dismissive of the new strategy as leftwingers were of the more moderate measures that Labour had abandoned. The debate over policy, as examined in this book, indicated considerable uncertainty and disagreement over what should be the party's social democratic strategy and objectives. After 1979 that debate intensified into a savage dispute over Labour's internal structure.

Labour's crisis was not confined to a dispute about its ideology and policy. Perhaps even more important was its electoral dimension: the party's share of the vote at successive general elections declined from 47.9 per cent in 1966 to 43.0 per cent in 1970. By 1979 Labour's vote was down to 36.9 per cent. In only one election in this period (October 1974) did Labour's vote indicate even a slight recovery.

Moreover, it was not just Labour's vote that declined, the party's individual membership halved between 1970 and 1983.

The nadir of this crisis occurred with the general election of June 1983. The result was near-catastrophic for the Labour party. The party's share of the electorate plunged to 27.6 per cent. The Liberal–SDP Alliance came within 700 000 votes or around two per cent of displacing Labour in the popular vote. In many ways Labour was on the verge of dissolution into a regional party far removed from competition for national office. The party had lost 119 deposits, whilst the Liberal–SDP Alliance had lost just 10. In the south of England, the party had won just three seats outside of London. It was now third in 150 southern seats. To win another election Labour needed 127 gains. It was second in only 132 seats, some of which looked hopeless prospects for the party, in the immediate future at any rate, given the huge majorities enjoyed by sitting Conservative MPs.

This disastrous election result was the inevitable consequence, according to many commentators, of Labour's shift leftwards after 1979 and of the vicious civil war which had engulfed the party.[8] The debacle was associated directly with the radical policies laid out in Labour's election manifesto. In opposition, it was argued, leftwingers had moved the party abruptly and decisively leftwards and voters had given their verdict.[9] Labour's left was characterised as a group of manipulative and intolerant individuals who wanted to drive out all dissenters from the party.[10] After 1979 they seized their opportunity and plunged the party into an unnecessary and seemingly irrational dispute, one that was almost without point or reason. One historian of the period states 'Labour's response to defeat in 1979 was to press the self-destruct button.'[11] The author of one recent text concludes 'The Labour party's shift to the left, in the wake of the 1979 election defeat, created a vacuum in the ideological centre of British politics.'[12] Another notes that between 1979 and 1983 'the party endorsed a radical programme. . . . but this period. . . . was an aberration'.[13]

Aside from the difficulties of 1979–83, Labour's decline has been attributed to long-term trends within the British economy and society which have served to undermine its position within the party system. Economic developments

include deindustrialisation, the decline of large-scale units
of mass production, the decline in working class voters, and
the decrease in union membership.[14] Social changes have
meant that those remaining working class voters are less
likely to identify with Labour. As a result the party can no
longer rely on a large homogeneous working class to support it. Some commentators have concluded that structural
determinants, which the party was powerless to prevent, have
eroded its electoral base – Labour's decline, due to external circumstances confronting the party, is both terminal
and inevitable.

Whilst structural changes have played a large part in
Labour's decline, the party's failure to adapt to those external developments has also been important. Ivor Crewe concludes: 'The Labour party has failed to cope electorally with
structural changes in the Labour force. Political "agency"
as well as economic "structure" must therefore account for
part of Labour's electoral misfortunes.'[15] Crewe focuses on
the agency of successive Conservative governments in shaping an environment hostile to Labour, largely through council
house sales. But Labour's own agency has been important:
elsewhere Crewe has detailed the party's failure to develop
a policy package which met voters' policy preferences.[16] Many
observers would blame its 1983 electoral defeat, in part at
least, on the failure of its leftwingers to respond to the aspirations of the electorate. The left was too concerned with
the ideological dimensions of Labour's programme: the result was massive electoral defeat.

It is important to note that persistent ideological and electoral problems are not confined to British social democracy. Whilst Labour has experienced the most marked decline,
other European social democratic parties have faced major
difficulties over the last twenty-five years.[17] Again, external
structural factors have been emphasised as being crucial
determinants of their performance in elections and in office. In a survey of social democratic parties, Perry Anderson notes the fragmentation of their traditional working-class
electoral bases and the increased limitations placed objec-
tively upon the social democratic policy sphere through the
internationalisation of the economy.[18] It has become more
difficult for social democratic parties either to forge a suc-

cessful electoral coalition or to construct a distinctive reformist policy package. Adam Przeworski has emphasised the constraints that capitalism as an economic system places upon social democratic parties.[19] He concludes that social democracy has exhausted itself as a political phenomenon. Frances Fox Piven has stressed the decline of mass production as a central cause of social democratic dissolution: deindustrialisation 'altered the possibilities of workplace solidarity and organisation' and so weakened social democratic parties.[20] The diversified ability of different parties to respond to deindustrialisation has been an important determinant of variations in their performance. But Fox Piven lays weight upon the external environment in which social democratic parties compete for votes. More recently Jonas Pontusson has argued in similar fashion that the steady erosion of mass production units has undermined the economic base of social democratic parties. The crisis of social democracy is: 'a product of two structural-economic changes: (1) the shift to smaller units of industrial production; and (2) the growth of private nonindustrial employment.'[21] In any investigation either of the British Labour party or of social democracy more generally such arguments provide an important context.

THE ARGUMENT IN BRIEF

In this book I examine the nature of the economic strategy advocated by Labour between 1970 and 1983 and I analyse the implications of its adoption for the party. The strategy is called here by the title later taken up for it, the Alternative Economic Strategy (AES). It comprised a package of six interlocking elements. Whilst the first component, reflation, was orthodox, the others were innovative and radical. They included measures for public ownership, planning, price controls, industrial democracy and import restrictions. (The latter was added to the package a little later than the other elements.) I outline and assess the economic theory upon which the AES was based and the policy measures that it involved. I consider the developments in the strategy which occurred during the period in which it was advocated by Labour. I compare it to earlier Labour economic strategies and study in depth the opposition within the party to the AES, notably from rightwingers.

The economic strategy adopted by the Labour party after 1970 is important for several reasons and these are reflected in the themes of this book. First, the Alternative Economic Strategy is of interest because many, supporters and opponents alike, claimed that it marked a departure for the Labour party. They argued that it represented a fundamentally different economic strategy based on a new theory with fresh objectives distinct from those of its predecessor. It attracted, for a time at any rate, considerable support: by 1979 it was *the* strategy of the Labour left. The 1970s were a period of severe economic crisis throughout advanced industrial nations. The AES presented one effort by social democrats to tackle that crisis. It linked economic recovery to the social democratic objectives of equality and accountability. As an attempt to reverse economic decline through social democratic measures it is worthy of analysis.

Second, the AES is significant because it is germane to any analysis of the Labour party's social democratic commitments. Social democracy is an ambiguous political phenomenon and commentators differ over their interpretation of its nature and potential. In Chapter 1 I contrast three different perspectives about social democracy. Economic strategy goes to the heart of the *raison d'être* of social democratic parties: they lay great weight upon their economic programmes and upon their claim to be capable of organising the economy successfully. Their central goals are to be realised through economic policies and material means. The development of Labour's economic policy between 1970 and 1983 provides the basis for an examination of the kind of social democracy that Labour espoused in this period.

Third, an analysis of economic policy-making in Labour indicates what type of organisation the party was after 1970. Academics do not agree about where power lay within Labour during this period. I outline two different views in Chapter 1. In this book I examine the process by which the Alternative Economic Strategy was adopted. I detail the work of Labour's internal policy-making committees. How did the Labour party come to make such a break in terms of the economic strategy it espoused? I also consider the contribution of the TUC and of Labour's affiliated trade unions to policy development. I go on to survey Labour's performance in government during 1974–79. I outline policy-making developments within Labour on its return to opposition in 1979 and relate these to the political developments within the party, including the struggle to democratise the party's constitution.

Fourth, the AES is important because of the consequences its adoption by Labour had for the party. These consequences, notably the constitutional struggle within Labour, proved far-reaching and may go some way to explain the party's problems during the 1980s and even the 1990s. The question of why Labour followed the policy trajectory it did is of central importance in explaining the party's performance over the last twenty years – a period for much of which, as noted already, Labour has appeared to be, electorally at any rate, in decline. The Alternative Economic Strategy and Labour's policy-making experience between 1970 and 1983 is especially relevant to any analysis of the internal crisis undergone by the party after 1979. I indicated above that some commentators suggest that Labour lurched leftwards after its election defeat and that its leftwingers submerged the party in a vindictive and ultimately illogical conflict. The result of the radical policies foisted upon Labour was the electoral disaster of 1983. In this book I shall examine both aspects of this argument: did Labour move abruptly to the left after 1979 and did leftwingers immerse the party in a senseless and unnecessary conflict? An analysis of the AES and of economic policy-making within the Labour party may go some way to providing an understanding of Labour's decline and crisis. My aim is not to provide an overall assessment of the debates either about Labour's problems or about the crisis of social democracy. Rather it is to consider how far Labour's difficulties can be located within the framework of those arguments outlined above.

My argument can be summarised briefly as follows. First, I suggest that the Alternative Economic Strategy marked a radical departure in the kind of social democracy that Labour advocated. The adoption of the AES indicated a qualitative break with Labour's Revisionist past. The party had adopted a new and much more radical set of social democratic objectives. Second, I establish that, whatever the formal content of party policy documents, most of Labour's leaders did not reconcile themselves to the AES. They remained hostile throughout the period and their opposition to the AES explains the failure of the 1974–79 Labour government to implement the measures to which the party was committed. Third, I demonstrate that the institutional character of Labour and its pluralist nature were important in allowing this divergence to occur. Labour's policy-making process meant that the sub-committees of the NEC and the party's research department were exceptionally influential in the formation of policy. By contrast the coherence and plausibility of the left's ideas and the wider support that they enjoyed throughout the party were less important. It was the left's involvement in Labour's internal policy-making committees which allowed it to influence decisively the party's economic programme. Fourth, I argue that the disunity which became endemic in Labour with the failure of its leaders to accept party policy was the chief cause of the left's demands to reform the constitutional nature of the party. The policy division which occurred within Labour caused major problems for the party after 1979 and explains at least part of Labour's decline. Labour's election defeat in 1983 was as much the product of a period of disunity as of the party's extremism. I conclude that any analysis of Labour's decline must examine the internal determinants of the party's crisis as well the external causes.

A Note on Terminology and Sources

Much of the analysis of Labour's economic policy-making I undertake is presented in terms of left and right. The Alternative Economic Strategy was the creation of the leftwing of the Labour party, while many rightwingers were hostile to it. The terms 'left' and 'right' are problematic.[22] They might be taken to imply that such groups have a uniformity of outlook. They might also suggest that all members of Labour are so aligned and involved in conflict with one another. Despite these problems, such terms are commonly used both by commentators and participants. There are compelling reasons for their adoption, not least, as Patrick Seyd argues, the existence of factions corresponding to left and

right within the party.[23] Lewis Minkin concludes that the
left–right split within Labour is 'probably the most important feature of the party's internal politics'.[24] It would be
wrong to regard Labour's left and right as either monolithic or inflexible bodies. It is necessary to emphasise they
are variable groupings and do not encompass the whole party
in ideological disputes. Left is taken here to refer to those
within the Labour party who support radical policies aimed,
albeit gradually, at the transformation of society.[25] Right is
defined as those who oppose radical policies and are content with pragmatic proposals not involving a fundamental
transformation. For much of the post-war period, Labour's
right has been Revisionist and the terms will be used interchangeably here. Likewise I take social democracy to be a
generic concept which can be used interchangeably with
socialism in most contexts.

In this book I draw on a variety of sources. The substance
of the AES is taken from key Labour party documents advocating it and from the theoretical work of those who developed it, most notably Stuart Holland. I have also used
extensive archive material and private papers where they are
available. I have consulted the minutes of Labour's NEC,
the TUC–Labour Party Liaison Committee, and the sub-committees of the NEC including the Industrial Policy Sub-Committee and the Public Sector Group. I have also studied the
minutes of the PLP and the shadow cabinet (formally the
Parliamentary Committee). I have examined the background
briefing papers produced by Labour's research department,
the Liaison Committee and others involved in party policy-
making. The suffixes RD, RE and RES in footnotes indicate
the reference number of these documents. (Authored papers are the work of named individuals, unauthored papers
are by various members of the party's research department.)
On occasion interview material has been used to establish
the plausibility of an argument.

Some of these sources are problematic: they may reflect
the private desires of the author at the expense of accuracy. The veracity of unpublished diaries and other documents has been checked against official minutes and
newspaper records. For example, Benn's account of a joint
NEC–shadow cabinet meeting in 1973 has been compared

to a verbatim report of the discussions.[26] Benn's notes stand up extremely well to the comparison. He records Harold Lever as saying, 'There was no relationship at all between the remedies we proposed and the problems faced by the last Labour government.'[27] The report says Lever argued 'There is no argument to relate these solutions to the problems that afflicted the last Labour government.'[28] Benn and the report list Crosland giving the same set of seven priorities for Labour.[29] Benn's account is abridged and on occasion he uses different words but he conveys accurately the arguments made. More than that he also records the spirit and atmosphere at meetings (confirmed by newspaper reports) in a way that official minutes rarely do.

THE STRUCTURE OF THE BOOK

The book proceeds as follows. In Chapter 1, in order to provide a framework for my analysis, I discuss different perspectives of the nature of social democracy and of the organisational structure of the Labour party. In Chapter 2, I analyse the nature of Labour's economic strategy before 1970 and I examine the party's experience in office between 1964 and 1970. In Chapter 3, I outline the objectives and the theoretical basis of Labour's Alternative Economic Strategy. I also look at the developments that took place within the party's economic policy between the original formulation of the AES in 1973 and the party's election defeat in 1983.

In Chapter 4, I assess the debate which took place within the Labour party over economic strategy after 1970. My focus is on the hostile response of rightwingers to the AES. In Chapter 5, I outline how Labour came to adopt the AES in 1973 through a detailed investigation of the party's policy-making machinery. In Chapter 6, I examine the development of Labour's industrial strategy in office after 1974. In Chapter 7, I look at the conflict within the party after 1979 and I explore the links between the demands for constitutional change and policy-making in the party.

In the Conclusion I return to my central questions about the Alternative Economic Strategy, the Labour party and the nature of British social democracy. I provide an overall economic evaluation of the AES and I consider why Labour adopted such a strategy. Drawing from my examination of the AES, I analyse the nature of both British social democracy and the Labour party. I consider what role the AES may have played in Labour's decline after 1970 and its election defeat in 1983. In the Epilogue I outline Labour's attempted recovery since 1983. I consider the changes made to the party's policy-making machinery and to its economic policy commitments.

1 The Nature of Social Democracy and the Labour Party

INTRODUCTION

Since its formation in 1900 the British Labour party has been firmly rooted in the social democratic tradition. The majority of its leading members, political commentators and labour historians have taken Labour to be a social democratic party. Yet there is no agreement as to what the social democratic tradition precisely amounts and therefore no agreed 'yardstick' with which to analyse Labour's strategy and achievements. Likewise, there is no agreement about the nature of Labour itself and the distribution of power inside it. Instead academics and others have differed in their interpretation of how the party's constitution operates.

In this chapter I examine differing perspectives on social democracy and on the Labour party. I look at distinct theories of two central aspects of any social democratic organisation. First, what kind of objectives does Labour hold? Second, how do such aims emerge from within the party? I consider briefly the definition of social democracy as a political strategy. I go on to outline, in turn, three different theories about the nature of social democracy in the postwar period. Finally, I examine the nature of Labour and consider two theories about the distribution of power within the party.[1] My aim is to provide a framework about the nature of social democracy and of the Labour party within which I can analyse economic policy-making between 1970 and 1983. What kind of social democratic strategy was embodied by Labour's economic policy and what sort of party developed such measures?

There is considerable common ground amongst theorists of social democracy as to how it should be defined as a political phenomenon. According to Adam Przeworski, social democracy developed out of three inter-locking choices made by the socialist movement.[2] These choices were: first, that socialism should be promoted from within the existing institutions of capitalist society (namely parliament); second, that support should be sought for it beyond workers alone; and third, the programmatic character of the movement should be based on gradual reforms rather than an immediate wholesale transformation of society. The result of these choices was that social democracy was based on the attempt to win power through the electoral process based on inter-class alliances in order to enact reforms. Gøsta Esping-Andersen adopts a similar set of criteria to define social democracy as 'a movement that seeks to build class unity and mobilise power via national legalisation'.[3] Padgett and Paterson define social democrats as 'those who seek to realise socialist ideals within the institutions of liberal capitalist society'.[4]

These definitions are programmatically vague. They say little about the content of the policies that social democrats have put forward at any point historically or even about the objectives that they uphold. Three broad aims have dominated social democratic demands: the achievement of economic efficiency, greater equality, and accountability at all levels in society. The key goals of social democratic parties have commonly been orientated around increasing through production the economic resources available to workers (and other disadvantaged groups), organising society on egalitarian principles, and encouraging accountability by ensuring individuals can participate where possible in those decisions which effect them. Reformism usually denotes policies based on a commitment to the achievement of such objectives in a gradual fashion. These are general objectives and social democracy is open to considerable variation. Social democratic parties have offered different policies with divergent aims. Such broad definitions encompass many of the parties of the left over the last hundred years. The term reformism is itself uncertain and open to a wide range of interpretations. Nevertheless such definitions allow comparison of different social democratic parties which share advocacy of parliament, inter-class alliances and reformism. They can easily be applied to the British Labour party as a social democratic body. It has consistently advocated the parliamentary road to power and has looked for the support of nonworkers in its electoral strategy. Its policies have revolved around some ill-defined concept of reformism.

INTERPRETATIONS OF SOCIAL DEMOCRACY

Three theories of social democracy can be distinguished from each other by a variety of criteria. The aspects of each interpretation to be considered include its objectives, the view it takes of the economy, the economic theory it utilises, the policy tools it adopts and the electoral strategy it promotes. Each suggests social democracy is typified by particular policy tools and that it involves contrasting objectives. Each theory represents a divergent diagnosis of the potential that social democracy embodies. Two of the interpretations are optimistic about its prospects, the third is pessimistic. Each theory is analysed largely in terms of its economic nature. The theories lend themselves easily to such an approach. They are all dominated by economic factors, their objectives are met through economic means and economics shapes their other characteristics.

The three theories are: first, the Revisionist model as typified by the work of Anthony Crosland; second, the labour movement approach as embodied in books by Gøsta Esping-Andersen, Walter Korpi and John Stephens; and last, the structural constraints thesis as contained in the arguments of Adam Przeworski and others. (Table 1.1 presents a summary of the differences of the three approaches.)

Revisionism

The most influential perspective concerning social democracy in the UK since the second world war has been the Revisionist approach.[5] The fullest statement is found in Anthony Crosland's seminal 1956 book *The Future of Socialism*.[6] However, Crosland was by no means the only Revisionist thinker. Other texts include several of the contributions to *New Fabian Essays* published in 1952 and Socialist Union's

Table 1.1 Perspectives on social democracy

	Revisionism	Labour movement	Structural constraints
Nature	Static	Dynamic	Dynamic
Potential	Optimistic	Optimistic	Pessimistic
Objectives	Equality	Structural change	Economic security
View of economy	Competitive	Monopolistic	Capitalist
Economic theory	Keynesianism	Marx/class conflict	Neo-liberal
Policy	Demand management	Public ownership, planning	Weak Keynesianism
Electoral strategy	Moderate/ popular	Radical/popular	Moderate/ unpopular

volume *Twentieth Century Socialism*.[7] Anticipations of many Revisionist arguments were contained in Douglas Jay's volume *The Socialist Case* and Evan Durbin's book *The Politics of Democratic Socialism*.[8] During the 1950s similar themes were articulated by Hugh Gaitskell, Roy Jenkins and other rightwing Labour MPs.

The Revisionists claimed that capitalism had been changed in a fundamental and irreversible way. The term 'Revisionism' was a deliberate throwback to Eduard Bernstein's contention at the turn of the century that Marxism had to be updated in the light of developments to capitalism.[9] Crosland's claim was that postwar changes to capitalism meant that older socialist strategies based upon Marxism needed to be amended. At the heart of the metamorphosis of capitalism was the Keynesian revolution in economic policy, carried out during the 1940s and 1950s. The adoption of Keynesian techniques of demand management, namely fiscal and monetary policy, meant, according to Crosland and other Revisionists, that the state could ensure that economic activity reached a level sufficient for full employment. Socialist Union claimed 'The Keynesian revolution in economic thought had destroyed the myth of financial orthodoxy which had blocked the way to economic planning and helped to paralyse even the best intentioned Labour governments.'[10] Keynesian demand management came to be at the centre of social democratic economics.[11]

Two points followed from this transformation in the nature of capitalism. First, it was not going to collapse in an inevitable crisis and second, the power of capitalists within society was undermined by the ability the state now had to manage the economy successfully. Crosland claimed that capitalists no longer enjoyed the authority they had in the years before the war. He argued that 'the government has access to a wide variety of fiscal, physical and monetary controls. . . . they do enable the government broadly to impose its will on private industry'.[12] In *The Conservative Enemy* Crosland claimed: 'Above all, the corporation is confined by the actions of government.'[13]

Capitalists had also lost power to their own workforces because of full employment. Tight labour markets meant that workers were in a much better position to bargain with employers who could not afford lockouts and the foregone profits. In a seller's market, Hugh Gaitskell argued, 'The power of employers over workers is nowadays very seriously limited by the trade unions.'[14] The cost of strikes was reinforced by the fact that a firm's share of competitive product markets might be lost. A dual shift had occurred: capitalists had lost power nationally to the state and locally to their workforces. Crosland claimed, 'The power of those who control the state exceeds the power of those who manage the instruments of production.' He went on to suggest there had been 'a pronounced shift in the balance of political power towards the workers'.[15]

Moreover, Crosland and others suggested capitalists were no longer the exploitative ogres that socialists had taken them to be. The nature of companies had changed as ownership had become diffused and separate from management. Crosland claimed that business leaders 'owe their power to their position in the managerial structure and not to ownership'.[16] Having undergone a 'managerial revolution', those in positions of authority did not have a cohesive class identity.[17] They were not motivated by profit maximisation alone, as proprietal capitalists had been, but also by such non-economic factors as prestige, professional pride and stability. They accepted some social responsibility and responded to a range of incentives other than crude profit levels. Profit was not unimportant, but managers had 'a considerable range of choice' in making decisions.[18] It was inappropriate to conceive of industrial relations as antagonistic between different classes: workers and managers could cooperate towards shared objectives.

Crosland argued that because of these changes it was wrong to characterise the UK as capitalist. He used the term 'post-capitalism' to denote a new set of structures based on a mixed economy.[19] These changes were permanent. Such was their structural impact and their entrenchment by the 1945–51 Labour government, they could not be reversed. Socialist Union argued: 'Whatever theoretical arguments may be adduced against it [planning for full employment] there is no turning back on what experience has proved.'[20] The fact that the Conservatives accepted much of the Keynesian revolution and adopted policies within the new framework reinforced this sense of permanence. The economic success of the UK economy during the 1950s was further evidence of the durability of the new arrangements.

The emergence of Revisionism marked a shift in the trajectory of British social democracy. Traditionally social democrats had highlighted public ownership as the central objective of economic policy. Whilst he accepted that the mixed economy was important, Crosland emphasised demand management as the active element of any policy package. It was through manipulation of the aggregate level of demand – indirect interventions within the existing framework – that the state would influence economic decision-making and so ensure full employment. Provided there was sufficient purchasing power in the UK's economy, firms would produce goods and services to meet that demand. The beauty of the Keynesian system was that it allowed the state to impose its will upon capitalists without the need for direct intervention. Taxation and public spending were the most relevant policy tools. Accordingly, the traditional emphasis of social democrats upon public ownership as a key objective was misplaced. If ownership was separate from control, then public ownership was not needed – control would suffice. Crosland stated 'ownership is not now an important determinant of economic power'.[21] Socialist policies could succeed in a society where private ownership remained predominant and it was simply wrong to equate socialism with public ownership.

A constant theme of Gaitskell was that public ownership was simply a means to socialist ends, and not a particularly useful one at that.[22] Socialist Union stated, 'What has been achieved is due not to the abolition of private ownership, but to all the various controls by which the rights of ownership have, piecemeal, been eliminated.'[23] In *The Conservative Enemy* Crosland wrote: 'A determined reforming government can now generally get its way without a change in ownership.'[24]

Large-scale monopolistic public ownership created a host of problems as to how decisions should be made and what criteria should guide them.[25] Nationalisation was bureaucratic and restricted freedom and competition. It improved neither efficiency nor industrial relations nor the distribution of income and wealth. Rita Hinden, editor of the predominantly Revisionist journal *Socialist Commentary*, noted after Labour's 1959 election defeat, 'The experience of public ownership has been insufficiently successful or inspiring to arouse a desire for more.'[26] The Revisionists also pointed out that nationalisation was electorally extremely unpopular.[27]

Crosland did not rule out public ownership altogether. It might be used to bring about improvements in efficiency or where other measures would not meet a specific goal. Each individual case had to be justified and nationalisation should not take the form of the old monopolistic model. Crosland proposed that the government nationalise single companies which would compete with the remaining private firms within the industry. It was unlikely that such 'competitive public enterprise', as Crosland called it, would be needed often.[28] It should be used only as a 'power of last resort'.[29]

Revisionists were equally critical of planning policies which involved direct controls over the economy. Crosland felt that planning had become an empirical issue – judgements could only be made about it on an *ad hoc* basis.[30] It should take a very moderate form – one far removed from the proposals made by many social democrats before 1945. Most Revisionists were lukewarm about proposals for worker participation in running firms.[31] Socialist Union concluded that 'these ideas have now lost their appeal'.[32] Given the managerial revolution, most employers could be trusted and such measures were unnecessary. Workers' power had increased through full employment and collective bargaining – not through industrial democracy. It was, Crosland felt, unsurprising that workers were apathetic towards direct participation in decision-making: it was 'remote from the vicissitudes of life on the factory floor'.[33]

Labour's commitment to public ownership and direct planning was symptomatic, Revisionists claimed, of how the party's economic strategy was trapped in the past. They argued that social democracy had to modernise its strategy and image. British society had changed dramatically in the postwar period: the number of working class voters had declined and those that remained had changed in outlook. Crosland claimed that developments had made 'society as a whole less and less proletariat' while those who remained working class 'subjectively are seeking to acquire a middle-class status in life'.[34] Revisionism adopted an electoral perspective very similar to that mapped out by Anthony Downs in his 1957 book *An Economic Theory of Democracy*.[35] Downs suggested that a successful party had to offer a policy platform designed to win over the middle ground, more precisely to capture the median voter. Likewise Crosland argued, 'Typically the marginal vote will be in the centre and this is the vote for which both parties are competing.'[36] Labour had to meet the transformed aspirations of a moderate electorate.

The Revisionists adopted a new set of policy aims. The Labour party in the UK should, they claimed, be concerned with promoting equality, fellowship and social justice.[37] Socialists need not focus on matters of production, which were relatively unproblematic, but on distribution. Social democratic objectives shifted away from narrowly economic or material ones. In 1960, writing the forward to the Japanese edition of *The Future of Socialism*, Crosland concluded, 'Under these conditions a mainly economic orientation will be increasingly inappropriate for Socialist parties.'[38] By contrast, the welfare state was central: access to housing, to health services, to social security were the immediate goals that Revisionists adopted. Keynesian economics allowed for the extraction of a surplus from the economy, taken through taxation, which could be re-allocated through the welfare programmes now at the centre of social democratic objectives.

Crosland's Revisionism is a static model of social democracy.

It assumes that the necessary structural changes to society and the economy have taken place and it accepts the existing framework of institutions. It further asserts that the necessary tools to manage the economy in a desirable fashion are available. This does not mean that no further changes at all are required. But future developments will be neither economic nor involve transformations. Social democracy adopts an essentially managerial role in such circumstances. The Revisionists' central objective is to secure a more equal society. They are largely unconcerned with either economic efficiency or accountability because the transformation that has taken place has rendered such objectives irrelevant. Socialist aims can be achieved by stabilising what had previously been regarded as an inherently unstable system. Moreover, Revisionists claim that their approach is electorally popular and represents a viable set of policies on which to win office.

The Labour Movement Model

A more dynamic approach towards social democracy is presented by the labour movement model typified by the work of Gøsta Esping-Andersen, Walter Korpi and John Stephens.[39] This approach argues that the ability of social democracy to develop and become entrenched within a society will depend upon the relative power resources that the labour movement has at its disposal. A strong labour movement will be able to promote radical social democratic objectives.[40] This approach concludes that structural changes to society are still needed beyond any Keynesian-style evolution of the economy. It goes on to claim such a structural transformation is possible.

Labour movement theorists contest several Revisionist arguments. They reject the claim that the state has secured the power to control economic activity and the ability to impose its will on private firms. Any authority that the state has to promote social democratic ends will be conditional. Stephens writes that the state 'is highly dependent on the distribution of power in civil society'.[41] Labour movement theorists disagree that capitalists have lost power to their workers because of full employment. Korpi writes, 'Wage earners generally have less power resources than those who control the means of production.'[42] They do not conclude that the managerial revolution has altered the incentives of employers. Stephens argues that the aims of private enterprise do not coincide with those of society.[43]

The labour movement model suggests that class struggle remains central as a determinant of economic and political outcomes. The balance of power between capital and labour is an important factor shaping the nature of those outcomes. Korpi states: 'Changes in the distribution of power resources between different collectivities or classes can thus be assumed to be of central importance for social change.'[44] In this view capitalist development is the result of political class relations and state policy outcomes reflect coalitions within society.[45] Capitalists continue to have considerable economic power and ability to effect outcomes. By contrast, the political power of workers is their main asset.[46] For Esping-Andersen, 'Labour's power advantage lies in its numbers; its disadvantage in the scant and unevenly distributed resources among wage earners.'[47] Overall, society remains typified by class antagonism and conflict.[48]

In contrast to Revisionism, the labour movement approach regards neither the Keynesian revolution nor the welfare state as the bases for a stable social democratic society.[49] The Swedish labour economist Rudolf Meidner claims, 'Experience has taught us that the free market forces guarantee neither full employment nor equality. To give the highest priority to these goals means challenging the principles of the capitalist system.'[50] Social democrats must be prepared to seek further structural change through prolonged struggle. Jonas Pontusson states, 'In contrast to Crosland and other revisionists, the authors [Korpi and others] conceive the transition to socialism as a change of economic systems and a product of class conflict.'[51] As the relevant power resources change, labour movement theorists believe that the promotion of social democracy requires the development of new policies. They claim that the economic crisis of the 1970s indicates the need for radical interventionist measures. Esping-Andersen argues, 'much more drastic steps [to control investment] will have to be taken in the future if full employment and more equality are to be achieved.'[52] Indirect tools, such as demand management and taxation, will not suffice and far-reaching policies, including forms of public ownership, remain relevant. In this approach social democracy remains concerned with productive as well as distributive issues. Social democratic objectives are not confined to equality but also issues of control within both the enterprise and the state. Stephens stresses the importance of what he terms 'production politics' in the realisation of social democratic objectives.[53] Esping-Andersen emphasises the significance of 'economic democracy'.[54] Given the dynamic class conflict that evolves between capital and labour, workers' participation within the firm in promoting economic efficiency and greater accountability is at the centre of social democratic goals. Labour movement theorists, in contrast to Revisionists, argue that direct control must be exerted on the decision-making processes of firms.

Labour movement theorists are optimistic and argue that social democracy is a viable political programme for the transformation of capitalism. It is possible for social democrats to be elected on a radical programme and for them to implement it. The support for radical policies and their success in office is seen potentially as a 'virtuous circle' or a feedback mechanism promoting further achievements.[55] A labour movement government can 'institutionalise' social democracy.[56]

In the UK, the work of the Labour MP John Strachey comes close to the arguments of the labour movement theorists.[57] Strachey is often typified as a Revisionist, yet he asserted that Britain remained capitalist and emphasised the need for social democrats to advocate radical policies including public ownership.[58] His first biographer noted that 'Crosland's arguments seemed moral or ethical, while Strachey's were rooted in economics'.[59] The leftwing Labour MP Nye Bevan's short volume, *In Place of Fear*, and the work of some members of the New Left in the UK also echo some of the themes of labour movement theory.[50]

Overall, the labour movement model suggests that social democracy will adapt and shift away from Keynesianism in a more radical direction. This dynamic and optimistic approach stresses the importance of struggle in determining outcomes and rejects the managerial role ascribed to social democracy in economic matters by Crosland. Structural reform of the economy remains paramount and possible. The objectives of the labour movement theorists go beyond equality. They promote a fundamental transformation aimed at increased economic efficiency and greater accountability as well as equality. Labour movement theorists view the economy as dominated by conflict and stress the growing concentration of firms. They draw heavily from Marx in the economic theory they adopt and they propose a range of interventionist policy tools including public ownership and planning. They claim that such a radical package is electorally viable.

The Structural Constraints Model

A pessimistic analysis of social democracy is embodied in the structural constraints model represented by the work of Adam Przeworski.[61] Przeworski typifies postwar social democracy as being characterised by an extremely moderate Keynesianism. Social democracy has developed but, rather than becoming more radical as Esping-Andersen and Korpi claim, it has become more moderate. It has lost any distinctive quality and does not promote any specific social democratic aims, whether they are equality or accountability.[62] Przeworski proposes several interlocking factors that are behind this shift to moderation. First, in the search for electoral victory and a wide coalition of popular support, social democrats must dilute their class appeal and make limited and bland national proposals. The effect of this strategy is to alienate workers from the party to the extent that social democrats find it difficult to win office at all.[63] Second, many workers reject radical socialist measures because they feel capitalism meets their material needs, especially in the short term.[64] Last, and most importantly, Przeworski concludes that such is the nature of capitalist society that it imposes major constraints on the freedom of action of any social democratic government. It is from this factor that the term 'structural constraints' comes.

The economic well-being of society depends, according to Przeworski, upon the investment decisions of private capitalists. As a result capitalists enjoy a very special position which gives them immense power. Any government, social democratic or not, requires material growth and a prosperous economy. Przeworski asserts that any policies which might damage economic well-being because capitalists would respond to them with disinvestment must be avoided. Such policies include not just nationalisation but also much more limited measures of redistribution. Social democracy, trapped by the structural constraints of capitalism, must become very moderate. Capitalist opposition, coupled with the practical difficulties of orthodox public ownership, led social democrats in the 1930s to embrace redistributive Keynesianism. Prior to Keynesianism, social democrats 'did not have any kind of an economic policy of their own'.[65] Przeworski sides with Crosland in arguing that gradual reformism – the progressive transformation of society – is abandoned. With Keynesianism, social democrats guarantee private property and promote capitalist efficiency: 'The current policy of social democrats by its very logic no longer permits the cumulation of reforms.'[66] Unlike Crosland, Przeworski does not see this position as a distinctive social democratic one: 'When in office they [social democrats] are forced to behave like any other party, relying on deflationary, cost-cutting measures to ensure private profitability and the capacity to invest.'[67]

The dilemma that social democratic governments face is summed up by Przeworski's stark conclusion:

> The very capacity of social democrats to regulate the economy depends upon the profitability of the private sector and the willingness of capitalists to cooperate. This is the structural barrier which cannot be broken: the limit of any policy is that investment and thus profits must be protected in the long run.[68]

Przeworski presents a seemingly unyielding logic as the trajectory of social democratic choices has unfolded. He further suggests that social democrats are aware of such choices and the constraints upon their freedom of action. They accept the dilemma in which they are placed and moderate their policy stance accordingly.[69] Far from offering either successful redistribution as Crosland suggested or the transformation of society as the labour movement model proposes, social democracy is extremely limited. Social democratic leaders 'offer the compromise, they maintain, and defend it'.[70]

Przeworski is not alone in his account of social democracy. Criticising Crosland, Charles Taylor argued that the requirements of capitalists remained predominant despite the apparent success of Keynesianism. Redistributive taxation was extremely limited because 'at a certain point we will tax the private sector so heavily, that we will affect its capacity (or more importantly its willingness) to invest'.[71] Many of Labour's critics have adopted similar arguments whilst focusing on a variety of reasons for the party's failures including its parliamentarianism.[72] Ralph Miliband spells out the economic constraints that any government must face: 'The task of the state has been to ensure that the requirements of capital (which does not mean its every demand) are met, but not so as to create conditions of dangerously explosive alienation of the working class.'[73]

David Coates argues that Labour governments have faced 'severe constraints on their freedom of manoeuvre' as 'capitalist imperatives' dominate policy formation.[74] Like Przeworski, he argues that social democrats are aware of their dilemma and claims, 'It is this repeated experience of the limits of the possible for the state in a capitalist system that has been one major factor pulling the Labour party leadership away from radical programmes.'[75] Miliband maintains that Labour politicians have ended up 'pursuing policies which corresponded with the purposes of capitalist interests'.[76] David Howell completes his study of British social democracy by concluding: 'Labour's commitment to social transformation became translated into a commitment to rationalise and modernise an ailing industrial structure.'[77] Leo Panitch provides a functional account of the Labour party where its central task in the postwar period has been to restrain wages so as to promote profits. Labour has been 'a highly effective agency of social control'.[78] Panitch views the development of corporatism as an attempt to integrate workers into the political and economic system in a way beneficial to capitalism. He claims: 'The integrative functions of the Labour party, in terms of their precise content, are not determined by the party alone, but by the capitalist system within which it is content to operate (and, to be

fair, change somewhat from within) and its needs at a particular moment.'[79] Social democracy performs an important
role in maintaining the existing economic order. Nearly twenty
years earlier Miliband raised themes similar to Panitch's argument and suggested that Labour engaged in 'political
brokerage between labour and the established order. This
is a function which is of crucial importance to modern capitalism.'[80]

Przeworski's conclusions are straightforward: social democratic parties will find it hard to win office; they will find
workers reject radical proposals; and they will be forced by
the structural logic of capitalism to moderate their policies.
Furthermore social democrats know and accept these realities: they abandon wholesale reform and they abandon
redistribution.

THE NATURE OF THE LABOUR PARTY

Debate about the Labour party does not concern just its
social democratic goals and policies but also the nature of
its organisation. Scholars have been interested not only in
the party's objectives but in the process by which those aims
have been adopted. There is considerable disagreement over
who controls the party and who dominates its policy-making
process. The most important debate about Labour's structure, between Robert McKenzie and Lewis Minkin, predates
recent changes to the party's constitution introduced by
successive leaders Neil Kinnock, John Smith and Tony Blair
over the last decade. In outlining differing views of the structure of the party here, I do not address these reforms. My
aim is to establish a framework within which I can examine
the institutions of the Labour party and its policy-making
process during the 1970s and 1980s. For an analysis of the
changes see the epilogue below. Until recently Labour's
constitution appeared to vest power with the annual conference, which in turn seemed dominated by the unions affiliated to Labour.[81] Labour's National Executive Committee
(NEC), situated outside parliament, was stated by the constitution to be 'the Administrative Authority of the party'.[82]
By contrast to these extra-parliamentary institutions, the

Parliamentary Labour Party (PLP) and its leaders appeared to be weak and lacking in power.

The Leadership Domination Thesis

In 1955 Robert McKenzie claimed that, whatever the formality of Labour's constitution, effective power rested with the leadership of the PLP.[83] In practice, far from being constricted by their relationships with other constituent elements of the party, they were able to dominate it. McKenzie concluded: 'The mass organisation of the Labour party outside parliament cannot and does not play the role so often assigned to it in party literature.'[84] He identified (indirectly) three features which underpinned the Labour leaders' autonomy. Interestingly and ironically, much evidence of these features is to be found in the work of Lewis Minkin, one of McKenzie's most trenchant critics.[85] Minkin strongly qualifies any support he gives to McKenzie's claims.

The first feature was the loyalty and respect that PLP leaders were able to extract from the mass membership and from the trade union leadership.[86] McKenzie's argument drew on Michels' claim that there was a psychological dimension to leadership.[87] Conference was content to be led. The trade unions, which controlled most of the votes at conference, were especially supportive of the leadership. McKenzie asserted that the leaders were helped by 'the bond of confidence' which existed between the senior union figures and the PLP leadership.[88] The PLP leaders dominated this bond of confidence and were assured of winning votes at conference. While the process by which union delegations decided how to vote at conference differed, McKenzie's claim was that the union leaders were crucial. In the early 1950s, the largest union held as many votes as the constituency Labour parties put together. The six largest unions controlled over half the conference votes. An informal alliance of moderate unions, namely the Transport and General Workers Union, the National Union of Mineworkers and the General and Municipal Workers, was able to swing most votes behind the NEC. McKenzie called this alliance 'the Praetorian guard', comprising the leaders of those unions.[89]

The second feature which explained the central role of

Labour leaders was the powers that go with their positions and the skills that they were able to develop. McKenzie was unclear about exactly what form these powers took. They appeared to be similar to the technical division of labour that Michels claimed underpinned leadership in an oligarchy.[90] Minkin provides considerable (but qualified) detail of the organisational procedures with which leaders are able to dominate Labour. Central is the ability of the Conference Arrangements Committee (CAC) and the NEC as the platform to manipulate the party conference.[91]

The third and last feature which indicated the dominance of the leadership was that the NEC has been supportive of the PLP. Trade unions dominated the voting for most of the places on the NEC. They effectively choose the twelve union delegates, the five women members and the party's treasurer (out of a total of 29). The Standing Orders of Labour prevented members of the TUC General Council sitting on the NEC as well so influential trade unionists were kept off it. Many MPs served long periods on the NEC, giving the party a continuity and stability in leadership and policy. These MPs insisted on the autonomy of the PLP and the non-MP members supported them. The membership and decisions of the NEC were dominated by leaders of the PLP.[92]

The kind of policy-making process within Labour which emerged from McKenzie's argument was, unsurprisingly, a hierarchical one which its leaders dominated. The PLP made important choices on policy matters and could act independently of the wider party in such matters. Within the NEC it was MPs who originated policies – union members followed their lead. Party leaders controlled the sub-committees of the NEC: 'The views of these committees are unlikely to be at variance with those of the majority of the PLP itself.'[93] Labour's head office had a role in preparing policy and the research department drafted proposals but the content of such drafts was dictated by the wishes of the NEC and its sub-committees. Members of staff were ultimately 'servants of the NEC and its sub-committees'.[94] Given that the NEC and its sub-committees, in turn, were controlled by the PLP, this relationship meant that the research staff enjoyed a subordinate position to the leadership.

Divided and Balanced Power

An alternative theory of the distribution of power within the Labour party is contained in the separate work of Lewis Minkin and Samuel Beer.[95] Minkin does not deny that Labour's leaders have considerable power but he suggests that there are severe limitations on them.[96] They cannot take the conference and the trade unions who affiliate to the party for granted. If the PLP leadership does not respect the conditional nature of the support received, it will lead to a re-assertion of influence by the unions and the extra-parliamentary party. The pattern for authority within the Labour party which emerges from this analysis is a contingent one. Union leaders will frequently endorse the party's political leadership but they expect the PLP not to intervene in some areas of labour politics, especially the internal organisation of unions, industrial relations and wage bargaining policies. In exchange unions will not get involved in internal party matters. The support each side gives to the other can be rescinded. Custom, tradition, patterns and norms are all important and union leaders expect political leaders to follow established practices.[97] PLP leaders must anticipate union reaction if they are to avoid conflict and ensure the support from the party conference that they require. If the PLP leaders attempt to assert their independence, they may well be successful – but only for a period. Minkin claims that McKenzie generalises too much from such incidences and produces a theory which is too dogmatic. Demonstrations of independence will produce a reaction as the conference and extra-parliamentary elements of the party respond.

McKenzie's critics question the three central mechanisms of the leadership domination thesis. First, Minkin disputes the notion that union leaders give an unquestioning loyalty to the party leadership. Loyalty is conditional. Union leaders cannot always deliver the block vote of their union, regardless of its political views. The loyalty that Labour leaders receive will reflect a particular alignment of unions which will change over time. The support Labour leaders enjoyed in the 1950s reflected an arrangement of trade unions which gradually unravelled. Changes in the relative sizes of unions were important. Over time leftwing unions such as the Transport and General Workers and the Engineers became larger and more influential. Rightwing unions such as the NUR fell in numbers, while new radical unions such as NUPE and ASTMS grew in size. The 'Praetorian guard' proved to be much more fragile than McKenzie had suggested.[98]

Second, Minkin suggests that there are strict limits to the skills and procedures open to the PLP to dominate the conference and the party. A popular issue cannot be kept unremittingly off the agenda. The ability of the CAC to use the compositing process to manipulate resolutions is also limited. Given the thirteen defeats suffered by the NEC between 1966 and 1969, the CAC did a poor job if it were trying to fix the agenda. Minkin concludes that by 1970 the CAC 'was operating as fairly as such clumsy mechanisms could'.[99] Moreover the CAC takes its lead not from the PLP but the NEC.

Last, Minkin challenges the notion that the PLP leadership can be certain of NEC support. The constituency representatives on the NEC are usually leftwing MPs.[100] They will often oppose the proposals of the PLP leadership and it is wrong to regard the NEC as always speaking with a united voice. Minkin indicates that the PLP may be unable to rely on the support of the union representatives on the NEC (and those elected by union votes as well). Union representatives expect party leaders to respect traditions about policy proposals and the role of conference. If these conditions are not met then the ability of the PLP leadership to count on the support of the NEC may well be jeopardised.

In Minkin's and Beer's view of the Labour party, power is divided and balanced between its different constituent elements. The PLP has considerable influence. But so too do union leaders, although much of it is discrete, covert and even negative. No one element of Labour is able to dominate the party. The themes of divided authority and multiple centres of power occur frequently throughout the literature criticising McKenzie. Samuel Finer wrote: 'The important thing to note here is the incompleteness of the leader's control of the party.'[101] The MP Richard Crossman likened Labour to the mythological Cerberus with its two heads. Each head (PLP and unions) was a centre of authority.[102] For Beer, Labour is 'boisterously pluralistic'.[103]

Shifts in relationships within Labour have often mirrored the shift between government and opposition. In government, party leaders have been more independent and able to ignore the party conference. In opposition the conference has re-asserted itself. Such changes took place in the 1960s. The Labour government was able to ignore a hostile conference and proceed with its own policies. The result was a divergence within the party. By the late 1960s the NEC, senior union leaders and party research staff were all taking, on one issue or another, positions critical of the Labour government. In opposition the conference once again asserted itself. A further point which emerges from Minkin's work is that it is misleading to regard Labour as inevitably split into two monolithic factions of left and right. While factions exist, there is also a 'large and amorphous' centre in the party which is not committed to either side.[104] The position taken by those within the centre varies from one issue to another and over time.

Trade unions exert an important influence on policy-making. Minkin concludes that Labour has exhibited 'an unusual power situation in which the overt dominance of the parliamentary leadership over policy formulation was constrained and checked by the often covert presence of the trade unions'.[105] On some policy issues, unions exert a negligible influence. But on others they are much more important. They delineate the boundaries of policy on certain matters and close off other issues altogether. For example, the legal status of unions and their internal operation are not areas open for discussion. For collective bargaining and wages policy, Minkin claims that unions can determine the parameters of policy discussion and have, in effect, a power of veto over party policy. Thus on a variety of issues party policy has to meet the desires of unions and on occasion proposals are vague in order not to jeopardise their support. If the unions feel that PLP leaders are not paying enough attention to their views then they may change the boundaries of policy-making and support moves to democratise the process.

Unions have less importance in initiating policy. Minkin notes: 'Many of them [unions] felt little incentive to take a positive role in determining Labour party policy.'[106] They are content to set boundaries and influence proposals. By contrast, other elements of the party are important in developing policy. The NEC brings a variety of policy documents (some jointly with the TUC) and statements to the party conference. These documents are rarely rejected and through them the NEC effectively controls the immediate and medium term policy-making of the party. Also important within this policy process are the sub-committees of the NEC and the party's research department. The NEC controls various policy committees and study groups and coopts individuals onto them. The research department has a significant role: 'Normally the initiation of draft policy proposals came from research department staff in the form of memoranda and information papers.'[107] These drafts are amended by committees – especially after discussions with unions. Finer claims that the research department is not controlled by the PLP: 'It is the creature of the NEC, which is not necessarily the cat's paw of the parliamentary leadership and at the present time is its rival.'[108]

Minkin does not deny that Labour's political leaders are important figures in policy-making. He writes, 'One feature of this policy process which stands out was the considerable role played by those members of the parliamentary leadership who were on the NEC – and particularly the party leader himself.'[109] But it is important to note that the PLP influences the policy process largely through their control of the NEC. If PLP domination of the NEC is qualified – as Minkin suggests – then their influence on the policy process is also circumscribed.

CONCLUSIONS

Although many accounts of social democracy share a broad and rather vague definition of it, there is considerable difference about its nature. The accounts of social democracy discussed here differ about its objectives and the potential it represents. Revisionist social democracy is an optimistic and static theory based on a Keynesian transformation of the economy. The labour movement model is a dynamic theory which argues that social democracy must struggle to entrench its achievements. It is however optimistic about the capacity for social democracy to do that through the adoption of radical measures. By contrast the structural constraints model is a pessimistic approach which argues social democrats must accept limited scope for action and adopt very moderate policies with extremely diminished objectives. Just as there is a lack of agreement over social democracy, scholars also differ over the nature of the Labour party. A central focus for debate has been the relationship between Labour MPs and the extra-parliamentary party. McKenzie saw the PLP as the dominant force within the party. Minkin, by contrast, has argued that authority within Labour is divided and balanced between its different constituent elements.

In later chapters I will examine the economic strategy of British social democracy after 1970 and I will consider which social democratic theory Labour's strategy most closely resembles. I will also analyse economic policy-making and internal politics within the Labour party. This examination will provide the basis for an assessment of the nature of Labour politics and the strengths and weaknesses of the two theories of the party's organisation. First, I will outline the nature of Labour's strategy and policy before 1970 – a period in which, as will be indicated, it was dominated by the ideas and values of Revisionism.

2 The Revisionist Ascendancy

INTRODUCTION

Writing in 1962, the former Labour MP and ex-cabinet minister, Hugh Dalton gave high praise to Tony Crosland's *The Future of Socialism*: 'This is a most important book, brilliant, original and brave. It has already had much clarifying influence on current thought, both inside and outside the Labour party. And its influence will grow.'[1] Five years earlier when Labour had published *Industry and Society*, the *New Statesman* had reflected on Crosland's influence on the party alongside that of Hugh Gaitskell and Socialist Union: 'The policies bear the imprint of the "new thinkers" rather than of any other group within the movement.'[2] The new document was hailed as a major development in socialist thinking. *The Spectator* commented, 'Their intention is not to end capitalism but to become capitalists too.'[3] One group of socialist MPs lamented it as a 'policy of retreat'.[4] During the 1950s Revisionism became firmly established as the basis of Labour's social democracy.[5]

After six years in power, Labour had lost office in October 1951 and spent the next thirteen years in opposition. In this chapter I examine the rise of Revisionist thought within the party in terms of its strategy and objectives. I consider the opposition to Revisionism within Labour from the Bevanites and, from the late 1950s on, from the New Left. I go on to detail the developments that took place within Revisionist strategy prior to the party's election victory in 1964. I conclude with an analysis of Labour's performance in office from 1964 to 1970. My focus is on the development of economic strategy within the Labour Party and its relation to social democratic objectives.

REVISIONISM WITHIN THE LABOUR PARTY

Revisionism became the dominant force within the Labour party during the mid-1950s.[6] Arguably, the shift towards Revisionist ideas began even earlier, during the last years of the Labour government. The administration's enthusiasm for public ownership and planning had waned as it had become more reliant on Keynesian techniques of economic management. The new doctrine appeared to build on the Morrisonian concept of 'consolidation.' Herbert Morrison, Labour's Deputy Prime Minister between 1945 and 1951, advocated a breathing space, but for Revisionists consolidation meant that the necessary structural changes to society and the economy had been made and that few, if any, further radical measures were needed. Denis Healey later remembered, 'What Tony [Crosland] did was produce a rationale for the approach which Attlee had taken [in office].'[7] Labour's objectives and economic strategy could be adjusted accordingly. By the summer of 1950 the party had no specific candidates for nationalisation (several had been dropped from a 1949 document). Although Labour stated some general criteria for public ownership, it stressed the different forms that it could take other than outright nationalisation. The party placed more emphasis on the ability of controls to manage industry. Its manifesto for the 1951 election was moderate and backward looking with no firm commitments for the extension of state ownership.

In opposition, Revisionist ideas were discussed within Labour publications, especially *New Fabian Essays* where Tony Crosland's forthright argument stands out. Such ideas had less impact on party strategy and between 1951 and 1955 there was some uncertainty over the future direction of Labour's policy. An ageing leadership dominated by Attlee and Morrison did not provide the party with a clear strategic direction. It was not apparent exactly what Morrison's term 'consolidation' implied for Labour and the party was dominated by political events, namely a bitter dispute between rightwingers and the Bevanites.

Hugh Gaitskell's election as Labour's leader in December 1955 marked the beginning of the Revisionists' ascendancy within the party. Labour had lost a second successive general election in May 1955 and afterwards Attlee retired. It was now that a detailed analysis by Labour of the changes that had taken place in economy and society and of the implications of those changes for social democracy took place. The defeat confirmed to many the need for new policies. The Revisionist arguments contained within *The Future of Socialism* were taken up by the new Labour leader and many of his close associates.

As a result, from the mid-1950s a string of Labour policy documents reflected Crosland's social democracy.[8] The most straightforward in its adherence to Revisionism was *Industry and Society*. It claimed that ownership was separate from control: 'In the large companies, it is the managers who now undertake the functions once performed by capitalist owners.'[9] It went on to argue that the managerial revolution had had a decisive impact: 'Their concern [managers] is with production as much as with profits and with expansion far more than dividends. Salaries, pensions, status, power and promotion – these rather than wealth are their operating incentives.'[10] There might even be conflict between managers and shareholders over the retention of profit for investment rather than its distribution in dividends. It was apparent that Labour regarded public ownership as a limited and problematic policy tool. The party's only precise commitment was to renationalise steel and road haulage. Beyond that Labour was vague in its intentions: 'We reserve the right to extend public ownership in any industry or part of industry which, after thorough enquiry, is found to be failing the nation.'[11]

Where nationalisation was used, it should be at the level of the firm. The idea of nationalising individual firms, termed competitive public enterprise by Labour as well as by Crosland, dated from the party's 1949 document, *Labour Believes in Britain*.[12] Morrison told the party conference that year that Labour would 'revitalise private enterprise with its own techniques of competition'.[13] An internal party document argued that state enterprises should 'compete on equal terms with private firms'.[14] The proposal was reiterated in 1953's programme *Challenge to Britain*.[15] *Industry and Society* did not rule out this form of public ownership but it emphasised an even weaker position: the state should largely confine itself to buying the shares of firms so that the whole nation could benefit from their success. Labour proposed to set up a public trust under independent trustees which would invest in firms. It would not intervene in the running of companies.

Labour suggested that the standard tools of Keynesian demand management would largely suffice in handling the economy. One draft document stated: 'The major instrument of Labour economic planning is the Budget.'[16] *Plan for Progress* in 1958 was confident: 'There is little reason to doubt that the return to power of a Labour government, pursuing policies of expansion and full employment, will in itself do much to create an expansionist mood in British industry.'[17] This document emphasised the use of fiscal policy in economic management. There would be some planning to coordinate the economy, but it would take a very weak form, similar to that proposed by Crosland in *The Future of Socialism*, and would not mean a return to wartime controls. Similarly, just as Crosland rejected a formal wages policy, so too did Labour in this period.

Labour's policy documents were supportive of the private sector. They accepted the morality of the market and rejected the idea that socialism must involve changes in ownership. *Industry and Society* went so far as to claim that 'under increasingly professional managements, large firms, are as a whole serving the nation well'.[18] *Signposts for the Sixties* argued that 'in terms of efficiency, these vast, centralised concerns are often, but by no means always, justified'.[19] (It went on to criticise the unaccountable nature of such power.)

Industry and Society, passed overwhelmingly by the 1957 party conference, was perhaps the highpoint of Revisionist influence within Labour. Many saw the document as a substitute for any extensions of public ownership. W. A. Robson wrote of 'the abandonment of public enterprise'.[20] Later documents were also largely Revisionist in orientation. *Signposts for the Sixties,* produced in 1961, was extremely vague about public ownership. Earlier, Labour's manifesto for the 1959 election was very much in line with Revisionist thought. It attacked inequality and offered improved pensions, education and health. The section on economic policy and public ownership was brief. Steel and road haulage would be taken over but that was it, unless after thorough enquiry an industry was found to be failing the nation: 'We have no other plans for further nationalisation.'[21] It also reflected the Revisionist's claim that electoral considerations should be paramount. Socialism was mentioned only three times. Labour appeared to have taken on the Downsian-type electoral strategy that Revisionists advocated.

OPPOSITION TO REVISIONISM

It would be wrong to over-emphasise the dominance of Revisionism within the Labour party. Lewis Minkin disputes the extent and intensity of support for it. He claims that the large vote for *Industry and Society* represents a mixture of tactical manipulation by the leadership, contingent support from union leaders and pragmatic acquiescence by the party.[22] Other commentators argue that the success of Labour's leadership in getting such documents endorsed by the party was due to more than the machinations of a few well-placed individuals.

The Bevanites

Some Labour MPs, alongside many grassroots activists, did attempt, throughout the 1950s, to articulate an alternative strategy to Revisionism. Their loosely knit group was termed either 'Bevanite' because of its association with the leading leftwing MP, Nye Bevan, or 'fundamentalist' because it continued to uphold the need for fundamental transformation and public ownership.[23] The origin of the Bevanites was in the 'Keep Left' group formed in 1947 to articulate criticism of the Labour government. Its immediate concern was with foreign policy and defence issues: Keep Left members were reasonably satisfied with the economic policy performance of the Attlee government in its first years.[24] After 1951 this orientation towards foreign policy remained the distinctive element of the Bevanites' pronouncements.

The economic ideas of the Bevanites lacked the coherence of Revisionism and seemed to be rooted in the past. Fundamentalists lacked a theoretical perspective and were negative in their orientation. They continued to uphold the need for sweeping public ownership and detailed planning measures but with little apparent justification. Unable to reconcile their support for further intervention with the ascendancy of Keynesianism, the Bevanites appeared bewildered by the success of the economy in the 1950s and the shift in party policy. In calling for a return to wartime economic controls, the leftwing MP Barbara Castle stated in 1952 that 'Labour must turn back the clock'.[25] In 1952 a *Socialist Commentary* editorial asked, 'What after all is Bevanism? The extraordinary fact is that there is *no* distinct policy which can be attached, like a placard, to this name.'[26] Susan Cros-land aptly captures the anachronistic nature of Bevanism in her comment: 'The fundamentalists were fighting battles already won.'[27] One distinctive element of Bevanism was its rhetoric. Bevan's *In Place of Fear* was a polemical volume and contained few substantive policy proposals. The *Fabian Journal* was scathing: 'Those who like arguments to be logical and coherent, or who seek intelligent discussion about future Labour policy will be disappointed.'[28] In the late 1950s Bevan made his peace with Gaitskell as he became Party Treasurer and took a senior shadow cabinet appointment.

One critic of Revisionism often associated with Bevanism was Richard Crossman.[29] But his work was variable and he had little impact on party policy. At times he made concessions to Revisionism and at others his arguments were blurred and unclear. Some of his ideas, including his acceptance of Keynesianism, echoed Crosland's theories. John Strachey also criticised Revisionist theory.[30] He claimed that society remained capitalist and that conflict was an endemic feature of it. It was up to workers and others, using democratic processes, to maintain pressure continually through radical policies to advance socialist objectives.[31] Like Crossman, Strachey had limited impact on debate within the Labour party. He was recognised by some as an important critic of Revisionism but his attempts to develop a middle ground between the Bevanites and the Revisionists came to little. He toned down some of his more radical policy proposals especially on capital controls – possibly not to alienate the Labour leadership.

As a group the Bevanites were disorganised and focused very much on personalities – with Bevan at the centre – rather than a theory. They received limited support from within the PLP and outright hostility from many union leaders: more backing came from constituency Labour parties. The ideas of Bevanism are closer to the labour movement perspective of social democracy than to Revisionism. But, theoretically undeveloped and negatively articulated, fundamentalism neither challenged the intellectual leadership that Revisionism enjoyed within Labour nor greatly influenced party documents. Bevanism was unable over economic issues to mobilise a sustained alternative to Revisionism.

The New Left

A further source of opposition to Revisionism came in the late 1950s from the 'New Left' and especially the work of Michael Barratt Brown and John Hughes.[32] Although a major manifestation of the New Left was in terms of cultural disaffection, its members also challenged Revisionist economic arguments.[33] In 1957 the journal *Universities and Left Review* produced a pamphlet, *The Insiders*, as a direct rebuttal of *Industry and Society*. It argued that shareholders remained important and that their interests were not divergent, either from each other or from managers. Managers were still motivated by profits: most of their benefits 'can only be derived through the profits of corporate enterprise'.[34] Moreover, through interlinked holdings, shareholders were able to exercise considerable influence across the economy. Michael Barratt Brown argued that directors of firms, rather than managers, made overall policy decisions and that many directors were nominated by banks and other important shareholders.[35] He suggested that there was an interlocking network within British capitalism made up of an elite group holding multiple directorships.

Revisionism was far too generous in its attitude to private industry. Barratt Brown attacked Labour's *Plan for Progress* for not examining the pricing policy of monopoly firms. He concluded: 'Yet there is hardly a word of criticism of the role of giant corporations in our economy.'[36] Another economist, John Hughes claimed that the economy was dominated by large monopoly firms which generated inflation, did not invest, promoted inequality, were inefficient and exploited the public sector.[37] In the early 1960s, as economic problems in the UK became more apparent, New Left critics of Revisionism became more vocal. Hughes argued that the concentration of large firms in the economy was leading to stagnation.[38] The economy was trapped in a pattern of short-lived booms followed by recessions. Such a pattern was inequitable as well as inefficient: firms and property increased prices to increase their share of national product and sustain high profits.

This diagnosis of an economy dominated by large and unaccountable corporations whose actions were neither efficient nor equitable placed public ownership firmly on the New Left policy agenda. It was presented an indispensable means of controlling private firms. A central focus was on the steel industry – the most contentious piece of nationalisation carried out by Labour in office and one that had been denationalised by the Conservatives. Hughes argued that public ownership for steel was necessary to make power accountable, to meet long-term national interests, and to coordinate the rest of the economy in terms of investment.[39] Many New Left authors accepted Crosland's arguments that public ownership had not been a success. They claimed that this outcome simply reflected the nature of the nationalisations that Labour had carried out.[40] *The Insiders* attacked Labour's vague and limited justification for further public ownership. Michael Artis and Peter Sedgewick argued that Labour's plans should be based on wider and more precise criteria including the needs of the community and anti-monopoly measures, and not just on economic efficiency. They proposed several industries as candidates for nationalisation including financial institutions, arguing, 'Unless these concerns are nationalised, proper government control of the scale and direction of investment becomes impossible.'[41]

Alongside nationalisation, the New Left proposed a plethora of policy tools. These included import and exchange controls and trade agreements to protect the balance of payments and maintain full employment. Planning would also be required: private firms should submit their investment plans to the government for approval.[42] The state should introduce price controls and redistributive taxation. Another feature of the economics of the New Left was support for industrial democracy and workers' control. Ken Coates talked of 'a very real rebirth of interest' in this area.[43] The argument for industrial democracy was often couched in rather abstract terms. It was seen as means of promoting an efficient economy and an accountable set of relationships.

The New Left was responsible for one other major economic policy proposal. In 1959 Ken Alexander and John Hughes co-authored *A Socialist Wages Plan*. They argued for a planned growth of wages as a necessary part of a more radical package, including public ownership, which would 'probe the limits of reform within capitalism'.[44] The national wages plan involved redistribution, stable prices and controls on profits and prices alongside a steady growth of wages. It needed a strong alliance between the unions and the government.

The New Left was divided in its attitude to the Labour party. Some writers, notably Ralph Miliband, remained trenchant critics of the Labour party having any potential and adopted a position in line with the structural constraints model outlined in the last chapter.[45] Others, who were in effect close to the labour movement approach, felt that Labour had the capacity to transform society through radical policies.[46] But they had little impact on the party. Crosland devoted one chapter in *The Conservative Enemy* to refuting *The Insiders*, whilst Gaitskell apparently regarded them as 'pretty lunatic'.[47] The only area where the New Left may have had influence concerns the socialist wages plan which bore some similarity to Labour's early 1960s proposals for planning incomes.[48] The New Left had little success in building links with older leftwingers within the Labour party. Many of its members were scathing towards the Bevanites who they felt had failed to counter the Revisionists' arguments. A *New Reasoner* editorial, angry about the large vote for *Industry and Society* at the 1957 Labour conference, stated: 'The victory of the right at Brighton is rooted in ten years of research, publication and propaganda. . . . It is futile to counter this work merely with denunciations or with policies derived from the study of society in the Thirties or in the First Great

War.'[49] Peter Sedgewick concluded: 'Only the right and centre of the party (through the work of Crosland, Strachey and various Fabian essayists) could claim any attempt at a pondered overview of British society or world economics.'[50]

By the late 1950s, Labour was a Revisionist social democratic party. Although elements of the party upheld different views and the depth of support for Revisionism can be questioned, it was the ideas of Crosland and Gaitskell which dominated Labour. With few exceptions Revisionists monopolised the debates over theoretical proposals and the arguments about practical economic policy and social democratic objectives. Two factors account for Revisionism's success within the party: first, its intellectual dominance and second, the support that external circumstances gave to it during the 1950s. The economic climate was especially favourable towards Revisionism. Its critics appeared out of touch with reality during the 1950s as economic developments (historically impressive growth and rising living standards) appeared to uphold many of Crosland's arguments. Older strategies with emotional appeals to public ownership looked anachronistic.

Such economic success led, according to many commentators including Crosland, to social change. The working class was getting smaller and what remained represented a qualitatively different kind of working class. Such social change, in an affluent society, meant that people would no longer vote on class ties and, if Labour was to win, it needed to appeal to a wider audience. The electoral theory of Revisionism tied in with its economic theory. Labour had to offer policies that were popular. The party's defeat in 1959 seemed ample evidence of the Revisionist case for further moderation. Crosland claimed: 'The essential condition of socialist parties winning elections is that such parties adapt themselves to the new society.'[51]

THE ADAPTATION OF REVISIONISM

Hugh Gaitskell did not reap any benefits from the Revisionist policies Labour had developed. He died suddenly in 1963 and was replaced by Harold Wilson. Partly as a result of

Wilson's succession, but more importantly in reflection of certain persistent economic problems, developments to the Revisionist economic strategy did take place. Although the 1950s had seen impressive economic growth by historic standards, in comparison to the rest of Europe the UK's performance was not so striking.[52] Many of the economic problems which occurred – inflation, pressure on sterling, balance of payments crises – occurred repeatedly. Governments were often forced to resort to (albeit quite mild) deflation and the economy seemed to be bogged down in cycles characterised as 'stop/go'. There was a growing recognition that such cycles were damaging long-term growth.

The shift in Revisionist strategy was facilitated and given direction by Harold Wilson's accession to the Labour leadership. Wilson, who had not been closely associated with Revisionism, adopted a more pragmatic approach aimed at unifying the disparate elements of the party and building up electoral support. His central concern was to weld the party together and so win office; he was far less bothered about the actual content of strategy. The strategy Wilson devised involved the addition of a strong element of technocratic thinking to existing policy. The aims of Revisionism remained largely intact but new technological means were added alongside the standard tools of economic policy to achieve them. Labour developed a 'technocratic-Revisionist' strategy.[53]

Wilson's arguments were shrouded in rhetoric. He laid out a seemingly attractive set of ideas without providing either the detailed theory or the practical commitments of earlier approaches. Many of his ideas were weak in content and vague in detail. For example, he stated, 'Socialism, as I understand it, means applying a sense of purpose to our national life.'[54] Elsewhere he claimed that, through extensive modernisation, Labour would promote a 'new Britain' and he identified socialism directly with science.[55] Alan Warde's conclusion captures the limited substance of his ideas as 'one of the most minimalist definitions of socialism ever defined'.[56] Institutional reform, rather than the content of policy, was the central means by which the UK would be modernised.

Keynesian demand management remained central to Wilson's strategy, supplemented by planning mechanisms. Such planning would not be direct or command based and it would not involve major structural changes to the economy. It would be indicative and would aim to coordinate the economy in order to allow steady growth to take place. A social democratic government would set aggregate levels of demand and monitor the responses of private companies. There would be no direct intervention in decision-making at the level of the firm and it would be up to individual employers to respond. It was assumed that firms would react to such incentives.

Alongside poor growth, inflation and rising wages were seen in the early 1960s as major recurring problems. The 'discovery' of an inverse relationship between unemployment and wage increases by A. W. Phillips was taken to provide an explanation of wage inflation.[57] Full employment allowed workers to achieve higher pay which led in turn to rising inflation. By contrast unemployment led to lower wages and less inflationary pressure. The Phillips curve (which illustrated this relationship) might have appeared to be a problem for any party committed to full employment as it suggested that low unemployment could be achieved only at the cost of high inflation. Revisionists had recognised earlier the effect that full employment and tight labour markets could have on wages and prices.[58] They argued that a precondition of economic success was that unions should exercise restraint and responsibility. Within the technocratic variant of Revisionism, however, a solution to the Phillips curve was provided. An incomes policy would be used to limit wage increases and control inflation. The effect of the incomes policy would be to move the Phillips curve closer to the origin thereby making the trade-off between inflation and unemployment less severe. Full employment need not prove so costly in terms of inflation and, through the incomes policy, rising wages could be planned. Wilson stated that the UK would be unable 'to achieve a sustained expansion programme unless we have a national incomes policy based on social justice'.[59] Not only would such a policy tackle inflation, it would also, advocates claimed, help promote the Revisionists' central aims of equality and redistribution.[60]

Wilson was prepared to make gestures in favour of nationalisation, arguing that it might be needed to promote economic efficiency – a justification similar to Crosland's. Whereas Crosland had felt it was unlikely to be necessary, Wilson now suggested that extensions of public ownership might be required for a better economic performance. Any difference between the two was therefore an empirical rather than a theoretical or doctrinal matter. Wilson's speeches were vague about the exact nature of public ownership and contained far more on the need for changes to taxation and the development of planning.

Revisionists such as Tony Crosland accepted many of Wilson's arguments. There were similarities in their goals and policy proposals. Wilson's stress on increased social opportunities was reminiscent of Crosland's advocacy of equality. Wilson's conception of planning as a practical response to problems was close to Crosland's view on the matter. In the early 1960s Crosland modified his economic arguments and accepted he had been too confident.[61] In a new preface to the abridged version of *The Future of Socialism* published in 1964, Crosland said he wished to alter only one proposition. Making a rather fine distinction, he claimed that, while he had not been too optimistic about the capability of the mixed economy for growth, he had underestimated the problems of the UK economy in delivering it.[62] In fact Crosland made several changes to the shortened version of his book. He edited much of a rather complacent chapter entitled 'How Much Do Economics Matter?' and dropped the title altogether. He also removed the chapter on wages and inflation which rejected the need for a wages policy. He adapted the conclusion so that some more sweeping and self-contented claims were eliminated. The Revisionist position now accepted that growth could not be taken for granted. Despite such changes Crosland's emphasis on Keynesian economic policy and the demand side of the economy remained.

Given the dominance of Keynesian demand management and the emphasis placed on welfare objectives, Labour remained a Revisionist party. Wilson's contribution to policy development was neither distinct from nor independent of Revisionism. It is an open question how far removed he was from Revisionism: he had been shadow chancellor under Gaitskell and many of his economic arguments reflected a Revisionist-type package of policy, albeit a slightly more interventionist one.[63] The modernisation of Labour under Wilson echoed the electoral arguments of the Revisionists that the party had to adapt.[64] Some of the technocratic developments to policy had taken place before Wilson's accession to the leadership. The stress on the scientific revolution had begun earlier in 1960 with *Labour in the Sixties* drafted by Morgan Phillips, Labour's general secretary, and Peter Shore, then head of the research department.[65] *Signposts for the Sixties* also referred to the need for Labour to make full use of science.[66] Terry Pitt, who later took charge of the party's research department, had drafted for Hugh Gaitskell an early version of Wilson's famed speech about the technological revolution to the 1963 conference. Revisionists remained important within the party after Gaitskell's death and continued to take many of the senior places in the shadow cabinet.

Wilson was successful in uniting his party and in October 1964, Labour won the election with modified Revisionist policies. Central themes of the Labour manifesto included the need to exploit the scientific revolution and to plan economic expansion.[67] The document lacked detail and was vague as to what the proposed national plan would involve. The only firm commitment to public ownership remained the perennial one for steel.

REVISIONISM IN PRACTICE 1964–70

After its election victory, the new government found its economic strategy under immense strain from the start.[68] Labour inherited a huge balance of payments deficit and a currency which was almost certainly over-valued. Revisionism was ill-equipped to deal with such circumstances, arguably all the more so when the government decided not to devalue to try to restore competitiveness. Instead the government resorted to a series of moderate deflations from November 1964 aimed at cutting imports, taking the pressure off the balance of payments, and restoring confidence in sterling.

The hope was that such deflations would provide a short term solution to the external deficit while longer term and more institutional measures such as the National Plan, incomes policy and tax changes promoted a major expansion of growth.

However, the deflations served to undermine the longer term policies and the government ended up resorting to the very policies that it had attacked when in opposition. By protecting sterling and not devaluing, the government's economic strategy began to unravel and its claim that it would end cycles of 'stop/go' appeared ironic as it embarked on a prolonged 'stop'.[69] The culmination of the deflations came in July 1966. Labour had been returned at an election in March 1966 with an increased majority. But a few months later matters were brought to a head by a seamen's strike. It indicated the fragility of the balance of payments as the pound came under massive pressure. Wilson refused to devalue and the government was forced to cut planned spending increases, raise taxation, increase interest rates, tighten credit restrictions and introduce a wages freeze. All these policies were anathema to social democrats: the spending cuts involved many of the policies upon which social democratic objectives depended.

The deflation derailed the National Plan. Vague and ambitious, it contained no discussion of how to meet the targets it laid out. There was no consideration about what might be done should problems or obstacles occur. It lacked teeth and there was no question of intervening in the decisions made by firms. By the time of the July deflation, the plan's targets were hopelessly unachievable. The deflation also damaged the government's attempt to foster a voluntary agreement for planned wage rises with the unions. Rather than creating a virtuous circle where incomes policy revolved around high growth, rising productivity and real wage increases, the government resorted to a six month wage freeze in 1966 and a period of severe restraint afterwards. Unsurprisingly, the unions came to associate incomes policies with straightforward restraint and lower real wages.

With the failure of planning, the government's economic and industrial strategy became more micro-orientated. Labour reformed company taxation, introduced a variety of allowances (especially for depressed areas), and launched several new measures including the Selective Employment Tax and the Regional Employment Premium. The main innovation to modernise the economy concerned the foundation in 1966 of the Industrial Reorganisation Corporation (IRC) to promote mergers and increase the size and efficiency of British companies. The only piece of public ownership carried out by Labour was the renationalisation of steel. It did little to generate demands for further state ownership. The relationship of this industrial strategy to social democratic ends was ambiguous.[70]

Another sterling crisis in November 1967 meant that devaluation could no longer be avoided. In order to satisfy the IMF (from whom credit had been obtained) and to offset inflation, further deflationary measures were made at the same time and subsequently. Such a tough deflationary approach (coupled with tight monetary policy) meant that by late 1969 the balance of payments was in surplus. But the improvement had been achieved at a very high price in terms of the objectives held by Revisionists. The economic growth and many of the social policies for which they hoped, in order to promote greater equality and social justice, had not materialised. Unemployment had doubled under Labour to over 600 000 by January 1968. There were major political consequences for the Labour party from the measures undertaken by the government as relations deteriorated markedly between the two.

Tension between the government and the labour movement was furthered by the attempt to introduce legal reforms to the framework in which trade unions operated. Barbara Castle, the Secretary of State for Employment and Productivity, published a White Paper, *In Place of Strife*, which proposed cooling off periods before strikes, government powers to call ballots, and government policing of certain disputes. Compliance in these matters would be legally enforced by fines. The unions felt that they had been scapegoated for the government's own economic failures. The PLP revolted against the proposals – as did members of the cabinet – and Wilson and Castle were forced to drop them. Not only were relationships with the unions worsened, the authority of the government was damaged.[71] By the time

Labour left office in 1970, the government was barely on speaking terms with the unions, while party activists openly attacked their leadership for its performance. At the Labour conference, the leadership suffered eight defeats concerning economic policy in the late 1960s. Perhaps the surprise is that Labour had been expected to win the election of 1970 at all.

Labour's left was critical of the government's economic strategy throughout its time in office. But, once again, they were compromised by their failure to develop a theoretical alternative to Revisionist social democracy.[72] Michael Foot stated in 1968: 'It is foolish to under-rate the economic consequences of Keynesian techniques.'[73] Many Leftwingers tended to focus, as the Bevanites had before, on non-economic issues such as the Vietnam war and arms sales to South Africa. In 1967, one year after the 'July Crisis', a May Day manifesto attacking the Wilson government was published by several members of the New Left.[74] Much of it was taken up in an attack on the social measures and foreign policy of the Labour government. The manifesto criticised the power wielded by large corporations and the inequality of capitalism but developed neither a detailed economic analysis nor policy conclusions. It was followed a year later by an extended book-length version, packaged as a popular paperback. The volume harkened back to some earlier cultural themes of the New Left: it attacked the values of capitalism and its reliance on advertising.[75] It focused on the dominance of the economy by large companies and the lack of accountability and the inequality generated by capitalism. Much of the May Day Manifesto remained couched in rather general terms and had little impact on Labour policy.[76]

Labour remained a largely Revisionist party in its economic policy during this period. In 1969 *Labour's Economic Strategy*, endorsed the contents of *Industry and Society* and *Signposts for the Sixties*.[77] It was defensive in many parts, stressing the obstacles the government had faced. In other areas it was more radical, though its proposals were not based on any original or detailed analysis. It emphasised the social policy achievements of Labour and proposed a strategy based around increases in public expenditure and redistributive taxation, combined with the use of other specific tools. These included measures to promote regional development, better training facilities and the monitoring of price increases. There was a proposal to set up a state holding company as part of the process of regional development. Labour also endorsed industrial democracy but went on to say it was 'a long-term process'.[78] A general policy document, also published in 1969, *Agenda for a Generation*, was more moderate.[79] It accepted the existence of large companies within the economy and came close to endorsing their activities. It contained little by way of proposals for further public ownership and endorsed the need for an incomes policy. It did not advocate either sweeping intervention or greatly increased control within the economy.

The continued dominance of Labour by Revisionism was apparent in its 1970 election manifesto, *Now Britain's Strong – Let's Make It Great to Live in*.[80] It was moderate and general, supported continued industrial modernisation and endorsed the proposal for a state holding company to help the regions. There were no firm commitments for public ownership or indeed other interventionist measures. Additional policies would be used on *ad hoc* basis to tackle specific problems, most notably to encourage regional development. The commitment to a wealth tax from *Labour's Economic Strategy* was considerably toned down.

CONCLUSIONS

In this chapter I have examined the nature of the Labour party's social democracy between 1951 and 1970 in terms of its economic strategy and objectives. Four central themes have emerged. First, that Labour was during this period a Revisionist party. The social democracy that the party embodied, in terms of its objectives and the policy tools it adopted, was very close to that laid down by Crosland in *The Future of Socialism*. Additions were made to the Revisionist armoury in the early 1960s, but the party's economic policy remained focused on the use of Keynesian demand management.

Second, Labour's left, while unhappy with Revisionism, did not develop either a theoretical alternative or a different set of policy proposals in this period. For a variety of reasons, they were unable to challenge the Revisionist orthodoxy. The response of Labour's left consisted for the most part of negative reaction, rhetorical statements, and appeals to the past. Those that did try to confront Revisionism, mostly from the New Left, had little impact on the Labour party.

Third, in practice Revisionism did not live up to expectations. Harold Wilson's government had included many Revisionists, including Tony Crosland and Roy Jenkins, amongst its senior ministers. Most verdicts on Labour's economic record in office, both immediate ones and those passed since, have been negative.[81] The high hopes of 1964 had come to little: 'stop/go' had not been replaced by smooth growth and the expected surplus for the social plans of the Revisionists had not been generated. Staggering from crisis to crisis, the government had little conception of what social democracy meant in practice. Social spending had increased and economic equality had improved – but not on the scale the Revisionists had intended.[82]

Fourth, by 1970, Revisionism was beginning to be questioned as the basis of Labour's economic strategy. There was considerable concern over the nature of the party's programme and its lack of achievement in office. Labour activists felt especially let down. They concluded that the government had put the interests of capitalists before those of its own supporters. The kind of argument made by Adam Przeworski, that social democracy must accept the structural constraints of capitalism, appeared borne out to many of them. Alasdair MacIntyre talked of 'the strange death of social democratic England'.[83] Between 1964 and 1970 Labour membership fell from 830 000 to 680 000. At the very least, there were major problems with implementing a Revisionist strategy.

3 Labour's Alternative Economic Strategy

INTRODUCTION

In early 1973 Richard Clements, the editor of *Tribune*, celebrated euphorically the development within the Labour party of a new set of policy proposals: 'For the first time Labour has a comprehensive answer to the ills of our society. . . . it provides a real basis for challenging society.'[1] A few months later when *Labour's Programme 1973* was published, *Tribune* pronounced with pleasure that Labour was 'now in a position where public ownership has become the crux of its policies'.[2] Tony Benn called it 'the most radical programme the party has prepared since 1945'.[3] By 1975, with the adoption of import controls, the new strategy came to comprise six distinct but inter-related elements. While one of these, reflation, was conventional, the others were original and radical. They included public ownership, economic planning, price controls, industrial democracy and import controls. They were presented together as an economic strategy aimed at regenerating the British economy and providing the basis for a society built on socialist values. Proponents claimed that economic efficiency was compatible with socialist aims such as equality and accountability. So far-reaching were the objectives of the strategy that they would amount to a fundamental transformation of the UK. These proposals were at the heart of the Labour party's economic strategy in its 1976 and 1982 policy programmes.

In this chapter I examine the substance of the Alternative Economic Strategy (AES), the name given to Labour's economic proposals by its supporters in the mid-1970s. In the first sections I outline the economic theory of the strategy and the nature of its objectives. I go on to look at the central different policy proposals it entailed and consider the elaboration of each area between 1970 and 1983. I analyse the overall development of Labour's strategy in this period.

Finally, I assess the social democratic nature of the AES with regard to the different perspectives outlined in Chapter 1. I contrast Labour's new economic strategy with the party's Revisionist orthodoxy.

A variety of sources provide the detail for this analysis of the AES. The most complete account of its theoretical underpinnings is Stuart Holland's The *Socialist Challenge*.[4] Holland's other work also contains a wealth of detail about the AES – unsurprisingly, given that he was one of its principal architects within Labour's policy-making committees.[5] He was a seemingly tireless publicist for the strategy, producing a deluge of books and articles supporting it.[6] Between 1970 and 1983 three major Labour party programmes, as well as many shorter publications and internal party memoranda, advocated the AES as the centre of the party's economic plans. The TUC–Labour Party Liaison Committee endorsed it in several documents, most notably in *Economic Planning and Industrial Democracy*.[7] Alone, the TUC provided support for a version of the AES, albeit a moderate one, in many of its economic publications. Many newspaper articles by those involved in constructing the strategy, such as the leftwing MPs Tony Benn, Judith Hart, Michael Meacher, and Brian Sedgemore, also made the case for the AES.[8] Other published accounts laid out the new proposals. For example, the Tribune group of MPs produced a detailed overview of economic strategy in January 1975.[9] Another group within the party, the Labour Co-ordinating Committee published its version of the AES in 1980.[10] Similar arguments for the AES are to be found outside the Labour party. After 1979 there was an explosion of literature outlining the AES.

Not all the arguments advocating the AES were consistent. It would be surprising, given the voluminous literature, if there was uniformity. Different points were put forward at various times and individuals differed over their own interpretations of the AES. These differences were most marked in the academic versions of it.[11] My objective here is not to examine critically this literature. It is to outline the substance of Labour's Alternative Economic Strategy through a consideration of its policy documents and the ideas of those close to the party. There is a substantial degree of agreement about the nature of the AES among those within the Labour party who developed it.[12]

THE THEORY OF THE ALTERNATIVE ECONOMIC STRATEGY

The central reason, according to architects of the AES, why the Labour party needed a new economic strategy after 1970 was that the economy had undergone a fundamental transformation.[13] Stuart Holland argued that in virtually all areas of the economy, a few giant firms, usually multinationals, now controlled production.[14] This view was taken up forcibly by Labour policy documents in the early 1970s: for example, *Labour's Programme 1973* pronounced that 'the economy is completely dominated by a hundred or so giant companies'.[15] In the UK the top one hundred manufacturing companies increased their share of output from one fifth of the market in 1950 to one half by 1970. Another document stated that the five top firms in each sector of the economy accounted for almost three quarters of production in that sector.[16]

Monopolistic firms (more technically olipolistic ones) were able to control the markets in which they operated. Holland spoke of a 'mesoeconomy' because multinationals were above the standard microsize of firms and nearer to the macroeconomic level of government policy.[17] Crosland's argument assumed that the economy was a competitive one. Holland stated: 'There is nothing wrong in principle with Keynesian demand management techniques in a market economy composed of small national firms of the old competitive model.'[18] But, with the rise of giant firms, the Revisionist model no longer accorded to reality. Holland concluded: 'The analysis of capitalism put forward by Anthony Crosland in the 1950s was no longer valid – not least because of the sharp growth in the degree of concentration in manufacturing.'[19] Judith Hart argued that Keynesian policies 'are becoming increasingly undermined by the trend to monopoly in the new capitalism of the seventies'.[20]

Labour leftwingers claimed that power now lay with large firms, often multinationals, which were able to extract the

policies they desired from weak governments. In 1972 a
motion at the TUC Congress stated bluntly that multinationals were 'undermining the national sovereignty of democratically elected governments'.[21] Holland suggested that the
1964–70 Labour government had lacked the necessary instruments to control them. The problem was not Labour's
intentions but 'its capacity to control the economy'.[22] Multinational companies transfer-priced goods to avoid paying
taxes in the UK.[23] They created unemployment by relocat-
ing production elsewhere and weakened the balance of payments through capital transfers. Overall they reduced the
economic power of the national government in an unaccountable fashion. The Tribune group stated: 'Above all it
is the development of these multinational companies which
has led to the downfall of conventional Keynesian economics.'[24] Holland spoke of the 'new producer power'.[25]

Revisionists assumed an economy where no single firm or
group of firms dominated. They presumed that firms were
price-takers and that prices, although sticky, were set by forces
other than the firm alone. Increased demand meant that
firms had to increase production to benefit. But under either
monopolistic or oligopolistic conditions, firms could become
price setters rather than price-takers.[26] They could achieve
abnormally high profits by setting higher prices than would
be brought about in a competitive economy. This use of
market power would exacerbate inflation. Holland argued
forcefully that firms were either setting prices collusively or
simply following the price leadership of other firms.[27] Either
way, they enjoyed super profits far above what a competitive
market would deliver. Such competition as did occur between firms was not through price but brand attachment.[28]

Keynesian demand management relied largely on fiscal
and monetary policies to secure full employment. But in-
jections of money into the economy through fiscal policy
might not lead to increased production because firms might
respond with increased prices rather than greater output.
Firms might not increase investment simply in response to
what could be a short-term rise in aggregate demand. The
timescale on which they made decisions was much longer
than the standard fiscal cycle. Higher taxation, to generate
government revenue, could have the effect of pushing pro-

duction abroad and damaging employment in the UK. Firms wanted to avoid taxation and their transnational nature provided them with the means to do so. Multinationals were able to wring major tax concessions from governments anxious to sustain investment. Monetary policy was equally ineffective. The rate of interest had little impact on investment because firms financed expansion from retained profits. Regional policy did not work because firms traded off the incentives that different governments offered.[29]

Some radical commentators went so far as to argue that the rise of multinationals had completely eroded the power of the nation-state.[30] By contrast, Holland accepted that multinationals had considerable power without concluding that national governments had lost all authority.[31] He claimed that new policy tools, distinct to those of the Keynesian orthodoxy, would be sufficient to control the activities of multinationals. Proponents of the AES continued to advocate economic policy at the level of the nation state and they rejected international cooperation as the basis for economic policy.

It was not only on economic grounds that the trend towards monopoly amongst UK firms was attacked. Advocates of the AES repeatedly noted that such authority was undemocratic and unaccountable. Power lay neither with the state nor with the electorate but 'in the boardrooms of the handful of giant firms in the mesoeconomic sector which have come to constitute the commanding heights of the economy'.[32] Labour concluded that 'economic power must be transferred from a small elite to the mass of the people'.[33] Holland challenged Revisionist ideas about the managerial revolution and harmonious relationships within the workplace. Profits, rather than any wider criteria such as prestige, remained the central motivation of managers. Labour stated that 'the interests of these huge companies cannot be expected to coincide with the interests of the national economy'.[34] The AES reinstated antagonistic class relations into Labour's strategy and developed a considerable hostility towards private firms. Earlier economic research about takeovers and corporate raiders had suggested that there were limits to managerial discretion. Managers were forced to maximise profits to retain control and avoid takeovers.

Revisionists saw inflation largely as a consequence of rising wages. The left's theory stressed, in contrast, the monopolistic pricing decisions of companies.[35] Workers were an innocent party to this process and wage increases reflected the steps that they had to take to maintain their living standards. The first draft of Labour's 1972 policy document stated: 'We have rejected today's conventional wisdom that there is a direct and almost exclusive link between prices and incomes.'[36]

It was the monopolistic state of the economy, according to Holland, which was responsible for Britain's economic decline. Such an economic structure with limited competition made it easy for firms to realise high profits. There was little incentive for them to invest in new products. That firms did not need to inject capital into production to maintain profits provided an explanation of poor investment rates in the UK and of declining competitiveness with other countries. One result of such endemic low investment was that British industry was trapped, according to a phrase of Benn's, in 'a spiral of decline' as its manufacturing sector got smaller and smaller.[37] The failure to achieve sustained growth and with it the pressures on full employment stemmed from the structure of the economy. Holland argued that the monopolistic economy led to stagnation. When firms increased prices to protect profits, they eroded real wages. This erosion in turn caused a lack of demand. The extraction of high profits through pricing undermined real wages and led to underconsumption and unemployment. It was therefore the structure of the economy which explained the UK's poor economic performance – a further contrast to the Keynesian theory which the Revisionists held.

The AES marked a theoretical departure from the analysis of Revisionism. The main theoretical influence for the argument about monopolisation was not Keynesian economics but Marxist in orientation. Elements of the theory such as the focus on the concentrated structure of the economy, the pressure on firms to maximise profits, and the role of classes and class conflict drew on Marxist economic analysis. It was not an orthodox Marxism but one which stressed the monopolistic nature of capitalism. Keynesian analysis was not rejected completely and the adequacy of levels of effective demand was regarded as a central part of economic strategy. Holland also drew from the postwar industrial policies of several European countries, notably Italy and France. It is interesting that the British Labour party had come to adopt a strategy which relied so heavily on a variant of Marxism. Most Labour leaders had, since 1945, been dismissive of Marx. Other Labour politicians had seen his importance largely in emotional or historical terms. His ideas were now a central theoretical basis of Labour's economic strategy.

This theoretical justification for the AES was repeated over the next ten years and remained remarkably consistent.[38] Leftwingers continued to argue that it was the monopolistic nature of the economy which had undermined Keynesianism and necessitated public ownership. The rise of large firms in the economy was responsible for stagnation and Britain's economic plight. *Labour's Programme 1982* argued that the British economy was dominated by a few multinational firms. It blamed decline on the private sector: 'British capitalism has failed equally to create a successful industrial base.'[39] Economic decay was 'a consequence of the way industry is organised and run'.[40] Likewise the 1982 TUC–Labour Party Liaison Committee document, *Economic Planning and Industrial Democracy*, argued: 'Successive governments have been unable to counterbalance the concentrated and unaccountable power of large companies.'[41] This document also suggested undemocratic decision-making by large firms was undesirable and ought to be reformed.

THE OBJECTIVES OF LABOUR'S ECONOMIC STRATEGY

With the Alternative Economic Strategy, Labour had adopted a very radical set of objectives: *Labour's Programme 1973* proposed to transform the economy and society away from private towards public ownership.[42] Such fundamental goals were repeated in subsequent documents: *Labour's Programme 1976* re-iterated the need for far-reaching change whilst *Labour's Programme 1982* restated the aim made in 1973 and 1976 that the party's priority 'was to bring about a fundamental and irreversible shift in the balance of power and wealth in favour of working people and their families'.[43] Labour's ultimate objective was nothing short of a 'steady but decisive transformation in the economy – from one that is unregulated, unaccountable and dominated by the private sector, to one that is subject to planning, characterised by a wide range of socially owned industries and enterprises'.[44] One draft had been even more strongly worded, twice describing capitalism as evil.[45]

The first sections of *Labour's Programme 1982* outlined in more detail than previous documents the principles and beliefs for which Labour stood. This emphasis reflected a view within the party that not enough attention had been given to its philosophy rather than a substantive shift of policy. The programme stated bluntly that Labour rejected the 'selfish, acquisitive doctrines of capitalism'.[46] The party claimed that markets did not work and that planning, social control and democracy were needed in their place. Sweeping intentions for a future government were spelt out. Economic regeneration would require radical policies: 'Our social and economic objectives can be achieved only through an expansion of common ownership substantial enough to give the community decisive power over the commanding heights of the economy.'[47] Public enterprise would eventually displace private ownership.

In terms of immediate economic objectives, Labour's central aim in all three programmes was full employment. Its first documents after 1979 were vague about what full employment involved but with *Labour's Programme 1982* a precise target was given.[48] Labour would reduce unemployment to under one million within the five years of its term of office. There was also a qualitative aspect to Labour's proposals: the party wanted greater justice, democracy, accountability and equality. The arguments that Labour made in favour of industrial democracy after 1979 included a claim that it was held to be 'a matter of principle that key decisions which affect the future of society should not be taken in private by unelected bodies'.[49] These qualitative goals were regarded as complimentary with full employment as part of a wholesale transformation. The measures of the AES would achieve not just full employment but the greater accountability and equality that Labour sought as power was shifted within society:

'We need a strategy, not just for recovery, but for socialist transformation of the economy.'[50] In an interview with the historian Eric Hobsbawm, Benn captured aptly the dual nature of the AES: 'I don't say that that is a comprehensive transformation strategy, but at least its got the twin goals of running it and changing it.'[51]

Reflation

Reflation remained an important element of the left's economic strategy after 1970. *Labour's Programme 1973* stated: 'A Labour government will be always ready to take action on the level of demand.'[52] It went on to claim that such a measure alone would be unsuccessful. The TUC's Economic Review in 1972 concluded: 'Policies relying on management of overall demand. . . . will be ineffective.'[53] In 1975, *Labour and Industry* asserted, 'The government cannot simply reflate the economy through major tax cuts and consumer spending.'[54] The Liaison Committee also spelt out the need for an integrated set of measures: 'Expansion will not be enough on its own; it must be backed by imaginative new policies on trade, industry, manpower and finance.'[55] The question of obstacles to growth was a particular theme of the 1981 document *Economic Issues Facing the Next Labour Government*. A year later a draft for *Economic Planning and Industrial Democracy* stated bluntly: 'This policy goes beyond traditional "Keynesian" policies of demand management.'[56] More radical policies would be needed alongside conventional reflation.

Public Ownership

Holland and others concluded that, if it was going to control monopolistic enterprises and boost investment, then a Labour government would require new policy instruments. These needed to focus on the structure of firms and their decision-making processes. Labour stated, 'We cannot, therefore afford to rely on indirect measures to control the economy. . . . instead we must act directly at the level of the giant firm itself.'[57] One way of changing decision-making processes of firms was to transfer ownership from the private sector to the public. Labour's analysis of monopoly power made public ownership a decisive and relevant policy tool. The state needed 'to control the basic levers of economic planning and power'.[58] The Tribune group argued, 'Unless there is public ownership and control of some of these multinational companies, the government will find it more and more difficult to deal with the others on an equal footing.'[59]

The new analysis gave a theoretical justification for public ownership which it had not had since 1945. The party's focus was now on profitable manufacturing firms.[60] *Tribune* argued that Labour must make absolutely clear that it was 'the commanding heights of the economy which are to be captured and not the lame ducks which are to be bolstered'.[61] The objective of public ownership would be to give the state control over the investment, pricing, employment and production decisions of a profitable firm. Especially important was that, under public ownership, competitive pricing would replace monopolistic pricing. Nationalisation would provide 'healthy competition'.[62] The state-owned firm would cut prices as low as possible. Such decisions, rejecting collusion and price setting, would re-inject competition into that sector. Together with Richard Pryke, Stuart Holland claimed that state firms would increase investment leading to 'lowered costs and better quality products. . . . They could transmit these lower costs through to lower prices and therefore act as price leaders for their sector.'[63] The remaining private firms would be forced to reduce their prices in order to hold onto their market shares. The trade union leader, Alf Allen, talked of public ownership 'in direct competition with private ownership'.[64] As Holland wrote, 'The state should itself become an entrepreneur.'[65] Increased public ownership would promote steady growth over the long term as profits would be re-invested rather than dispersed to shareholders. Decisions taken for publicly owned companies would not be liable to uncertainty and wild fluctuations. The result would be higher investment leading to higher employment, especially in disadvantaged regions.

Profitable firms were to be taken over but future decisions would be made on a range of criteria, including social factors. Some advocates of the AES envisaged public ownership (and planning) as being based on a 'social audit'.[66] However, although decisions would not be taken on a strict profit-maximising basis, the Labour party assumed that investment would be profitable eventually. Holland wrote: 'The policy would not aim to prop up every failing concern indefinitely. It would be undertaken in an entrepreneurial manner, with the aim of phasing down clearly uneconomic concerns.'[67] The left assumed that such was the state of a stagnant economy, profitable public ownership would be able to promote simultaneously greater competition through lower prices, more stable growth, and the use of wider criteria in making decisions. Greater efficiency and social benefits went hand in hand. The profits generated would fund investment and a surplus for social spending. Holland claimed that the state would end up 'both making internal company profits and [generating] external social and regional benefits'.[68] Public ownership was also beneficial on grounds of equality and accountability.

A substantial degree of public ownership would be required. At least one leading firm in each sector of the economy would have to be taken over in order to re-inject competition into that sector. This argument was the basis for the proposal in *Labour's Programme 1973* that around 25 of the top 100 firms should be nationalised. Holland argued that there were twenty-two industrial and service sectors in the UK economy. Each sector was dominated by between four and five firms. The extension of public ownership to around twenty-five leading firms would therefore provide the state with 'genuine leverage'.[69]

A state holding company would be set up to carry out and coordinate the new public enterprises. The idea of a state holding company had been floated in Labour party documents in 1969 largely as a means of promoting regional regeneration. Within the AES the proposal was much more far-reaching.[70] The National Enterprise Board (NEB), as it became called, would take the equity in the 25 leading private companies to be nationalised and then promote investment, employment and industrial democracy. Where public assistance was given to companies, it would only be in exchange for equity so the government could control the future direction of the firm. This conception for the NEB went well beyond the Industrial Reorganisation Corporation of the late 1960s (although not in Labour leader Harold

Wilson's view of it). For a time Labour proposed resurrecting the IRC alongside the NEB.[71] Labour drew on the experience of Italy and other countries with state holding companies but the NEB was conceived as a more radical vehicle for intervention.

The necessity of nationalisation remained central to subsequent party documents. In *Arguments for Socialism* Benn claimed that the mixed economy had failed and as a result public ownership was essential because private firms would not invest on the scale required for economic recovery. Michael Meacher argued that Labour would 'counter the massive concentration of unaccountable power in ever fewer hands through the injection of more publicly owned and democratically run enterprise'.[72] The focus for public ownership remained profitable individual firms. Labour made less, after 1979, of the benefits that such public ownership would produce in terms of competitive pricing. At a time of economic crisis and uncertainty over profit levels, such a shift of emphasis was not surprising. Instead the focus of Labour's case was that firms did not invest adequately and only public ownership would give a government the means to boost investment. Later Labour documents did not commit a future government to a specific target for nationalisation but the party's objectives remained sweeping. The extent of intervention amounted overall to at least 25 large profitable companies. *Labour's Programme 1976* talked of 'a significant public stake' in each sector of the economy and mentioned a total of 32 sectors.[73] *Labour's Programme 1982* re-affirmed Labour's commitment to extend common ownership to include profitable firms in each major sector of the economy.

The Financial Sector

In the original AES, little was said about the financial sector. *Labour's Programme 1973* noted that work was still underway in this area and stated that the power of financial institutions was unacceptable.[74] In 1973 the TUC voted in favour of public ownership for the banking sector – as did the Labour conference in 1971 – but such votes had no immediate impact.[75] By 1974 policy remained unresolved.

During the early 1970s Labour considered the possibility of state investment funds and capital sharing as a solution to the problem of industrial finance.[76] One proposal was that Labour would set up a National Workers' Fund into which most firms would transfer shares each year.[77] Such capital sharing was designed primarily as a redistributive mechanism but in other conceptions such funds were seen as ways of increasing investment.[78] There was mixed support for such schemes within Labour even amongst leftwingers, many of whom were opposed to anything resembling profit sharing.[79] However, in 1975 *Labour and Industry* advocated a Swedish-style investment fund.[80] A new National Investment Bank was advanced by later party documents, though the extent to which it was linked to capital sharing remained ambiguous and it was not emphasised by all supporters of the AES.[81]

Banking and Finance, produced in 1976, proposed nationalisation for the big four clearing banks, for seven large insurance companies and for one merchant bank: 'There is no substitute for public ownership when it comes to engineering a radical change in attitudes to investment priorities.'[82] Though passed by the 1976 conference, many leftwingers had doubts: they felt that such sweeping measures were unrealistic and the banking unions resolutely opposed public ownership. As a compromise the NEC proposed that the relevant unions should be consulted.[83] Most were hostile.[84] USDAW felt the proposals were of 'dubious value'.[85] APEX said *Banking and Finance* was 'unacceptable'.[86] Despite this opposition, members of Labour's Working Party continued to endorse nationalisation as an essential policy objective. However, they suggested that, because of union opposition, Labour should not proceed immediately with its plans.[87] The party's policy on banking had reached something of an impasse.

Labour's first documents after 1979 supported nationalisation in the banking sector, although not to the extent of *Banking and Finance*. In 1980 *Labour's Draft Manifesto* included the banks and insurance in its proposal for public ownership in each sector of the economy.[88] A late addition to the final version promised that the relevant banking unions would be consulted.[89] The research department noted in December

1980: 'As yet we have no policy on how to deal with the various crises in the financial markets; and our policies on the financial institutions are clearly unacceptable, as they stand [nationalisation] to many of our major affiliates.'[90] The unpopularity of banking nationalisation was difficult because of the importance that so many supporters of the AES placed on it. Benn argued, 'The public ownership of banking is an essential ingredient of a viable public policy.'[91] It was unclear how the desires of the party could be reconciled with those of the workers in banking. Benn claimed that people would come to support public ownership provided Labour gave a firm lead. In July 1982 the Home Policy Committee voted to restore Labour's commitment to nationalisation for the big four banks. The representative of ASTMS, the main banking union, Doug Hoyle, voted against any public ownership.[92] The union's leader Clive Jenkins wrote to Jim Mortimer, Labour's general secretary: 'I should point out to you that this [policy] is contrary to the policies of the unions with membership in the finance industries.'[93] The proposal for nationalisation was later rejected by the NEC and, at the 1982 conference, it presented a more moderate stance.[94] It called for tougher controls on banks and the foundation of a National Investment Bank to channel capital into industry. Labour also stated that should these measures not work then one or more clearing banks should be taken into public ownership. More sweeping proposals for nationalising the clearing banks were rejected.

Planning Agreements

The AES envisaged exercising control over companies through planning agreements.[95] The left argued that company plans should be influenced by the government in order to coordinate expansion and social objectives. The proposal was that agreement should be negotiated between the top 100 remaining private companies and the government laying out each firm's employment, investment and production targets for the next five years. The agreement would be formalised in writing and rolled forward in a re-appraisal each year. One of the advantages of this approach was that relatively few agreements were needed for the government to exert considerable influence on the economy. Such planning need not be bureaucratic, although a powerful department would probably be needed.[96]

Planning agreements would change decision-making within firms and they would lead to substantially increased investment. They would allow governments to shape the strategic decisions of private companies in the medium term. If the agreed targets were not met, a government would have a range of measures at its disposal with which to entice, persuade or even force shifts in company decisions. If firms did not cooperate they would face penalties and possible nationalisation. Holland argued that the government should indicate 'to leading private companies that they may be nationalised through the State Holding Company if they do not cooperate'.[97] Public contracts would only be available to firms which participated. Many leftwingers conceived of these planning agreements as compulsory and binding.[98] A new Industry Act would be required to give the government the strong powers it would need and to allow it to place an Official Trustee in charge of any firm should the need arise. Firms would be obliged to release a wide array of information to governments so that politicians had the necessary data at their disposal to frame an agreement.[99] Some leftwingers favoured a more radical conception of planning agreements where workers would draw up alternative proposals for their companies. Such workers' plans were associated with the initiatives at two companies, Lucas and Vickers.[100]

The term 'planning agreements' was dropped during the drafting of *Labour's Programme 1982* as being too coercive. It was proposed that they be termed 'Development Contracts'. More leftwing supporters, such as Benn, regarded this term as too voluntaristic. At one stage the phrase 'Planning Agreements/Development Contracts' was used reflecting uncertainty over the proposal.[101] Labour finally settled on the term 'Agreed Development Plan' (ADP). It was a change in name only and ADPs covered the same areas as earlier proposals. The tough powers of government and the obligatory nature that the left wanted remained. It was unquestionably intended that all large companies (the top 100 or so) would enter into agreements with the state. ADPs would be aggregated, in effect, into a national plan. Labour also proposed an elaborate (and not entirely consistent) set of new institutions with which to plan the economy.

Supporters of the AES argued that planning would promote socialist values in terms of more egalitarian relationships, give workers more control over their lives and weaken the power of private firms: one draft Liaison Committee document concluded, 'Planning is about making the economy more democratic as well as making it more efficient.'[102] The final version of *Labour's Programme 1982* included a preamble which was more hostile to industry than earlier drafts and stressed the need for greater democracy and accountability in decision-making.

Agreed Development Plans were a central feature of the Liaison Committee document *Economic Planning and Industrial Democracy*. They were seen as the main way of controlling corporate action which was 'the key area of decision-making in the economy'.[103] ADPs were of great importance because they were the means of linking national planning, company decision-making and industrial democracy. One drafting meeting noted that 'greater emphasis than in the past was given to the pressure workforces could exercise on management in the drawing up of the "development contract"'.[104] Plans were presented as the linchpin of the economic strategy both at a national and local level.

Industrial Democracy

Proposals for industrial democracy to give stronger rights to workers were an integral part of the left's strategy to transfer power from private firms.[105] Such a transfer would promote greater accountability and equality. In the original development of the AES by the Labour party there was, however, a vagueness about these measures and many of its advocates accepted that such ideas needed further development. This vagueness reflected, in part, the view that proposals for industrial democracy should be based upon pressure from the shop floor. Some leftwingers wanted Labour to place much more emphasis on workers' participation.

There was already support within Labour and unions for industrial democracy before the emergence of the AES. The arguments of the New Left had some impact in this area and in the early 1960s resolutions had been passed supporting industrial democracy at the Labour conference and the TUC congress. Since 1964 the Institute for Workers' Control had produced a large number of publications. Few of these, however, made links with other areas of economic strategy and they had limited impact on Labour, though some ideas did seep into documents by the late 1960s.[106] The TUC produced two reports in 1973 and 1974 calling for extended collective bargaining and joint decision-making.[107] Again, such proposals were not related to wider aspects of economic strategy.

In the AES industrial democracy was integrated into a broader economic package.[108] *Labour's Programme 1973* stated that industrial democracy was under consideration including proposals for democratic company boards, joint control committees and improved access to information. It accepted that industrial democracy was an 'uncharted continent'.[109] In two documents published in 1982 the imprecision about what industrial democracy would involve within the AES was partially rectified. *Labour's Programme 1982* proposed a range of statutory rights for workers, including rights for information, consultation, and representation.[110] *Economic Planning and Industrial Democracy* argued that industrial democracy was an important policy objective, not only in its own right, but also as a central means of planning the economy (through worker input into Agreed Development Plans). The Liaison document stated, 'Planning can *only* succeed if the priorities of national and sectoral strategies are reconciled with the aspirations of trade unionists transmitted upwards through an extension of industrial democracy.'[111]

Industrial democracy would involve a range of new rights and responsibilities for unions. These rights would include access to information and requirements of consultation so that workers would be given 90 days notice of any decisions affecting an enterprise. Management would have to discuss any alternative proposals made by workers. The exact framework within which a workforce made use of these new rights was left open to the workers themselves to decide. Such involvement might take the form either of joint control committees made up of unions and management or through worker representation at all levels of decision-making in the enterprise up to and including the boardroom.

There remained uncertainty over industrial democracy. One central difficulty was how the different decisions made by workers could be reconciled with one another and with the objectives of national planning. Discussions during the drafting of *Economic Planning and Industrial Democracy* recognised that conflicts – either between groups of workers or between workers and national objectives – could occur. One meeting noted: 'Reference should be made to the possibility of friction between levels and geographical areas of decision-making and the need to establish machinery and procedures to reconcile them.'[112] One draft stated: 'We cannot assume that, in every case, trade unionists will necessarily have an agreed view on particular areas of negotiation, for example, an investment location, or if they do, they will always support the views of the central planners.'[113] This problem was flagged but little progress was made in coming up with a solution.

Price Controls

The original version of the AES envisaged the control of inflation largely through price controls and what became known as the 'Social Contract'.[114] Such controls would be an integral part of planning agreements. Holland claimed, 'The current inflation stems fundamentally from the classic capitalist mechanism of monopoly power and pricing.'[115] The decisions of monopolistic firms were the root cause of rising prices. Consequently free collective bargaining was compatible with the rest of the strategy and wage increases could be financed from profits. In contrast to Revisionists, most advocates of the AES claimed that an incomes policy was not required. This rejection of incomes policy was useful in getting trade unionists to offer support, albeit qualified, for the AES.

Labour did suggest that there was a need for a partnership between unions and the government. The economist Thomas Balogh called in 1970 for a *'contrat social'*.[116] This theme was taken up by Labour leaders such as Harold Wilson and James Callaghan as well as by Stuart Holland.[117] Such a partnership was termed a 'new social contract' in *Labour's Programme 1973*.[118] The government would provide a variety of policies which would create the right climate for voluntary moderation in wage claims by workers. Within the Social Contract, as it came to be called, great emphasis was laid on price controls to limit increases in the cost of living: 'The key to any alternative strategy to fight inflation is direct statutory action on prices.'[119] At the launch of the Liaison Committee document spelling out the new proposal, *Economic Policy and the Cost of Living*, the TUC general secretary, Vic Feather, said, 'If you get prices right, the rest will follow.'[120] Provided price controls were effective, workers would not need to demand large wage increases and there was therefore no need for organised wage restraint.

Any possibility that the Social Contract was an incomes policy – either through a fixed norm or through national negotiation – was formally rejected.[121] Some Labour leaders wanted such a policy and interpreted the Social Contract as the basis for such a development. As will be seen in the next chapter, interpretations within the party differed widely as to what was the actual nature of the deal. Its exact form remained ambiguous: for example, it was unclear whether employers were directly involved in it. *Labour's Programme 1973* referred to it as a partnership between unions and Labour, but went on to include employers as a party to it in another reference.[122] Unsurprisingly Holland saw it in radical terms as an 'agreement on the main strategy for the transformation of capitalism, negotiated between government and unions'.[123]

Labour's first few documents after 1979 were hazy about its anti-inflation policy. They suggested that economic expansion, through greater utilisation of resources, coupled with some unspecified price controls, would be sufficient to prevent high inflation.[124] Anti-inflation proposals were often noted as a gap in party policy. The research department noted in November 1980 that 'at present, however, the NEC has no particular view on this subject at all'.[125]

In 1981 the Liaison Committee published *Economic Issues Facing the Next Labour Government* which attempted to come up with a solution. It proposed general discussions between a future Labour government and the TUC:

> There is a need for a national economic assessment of the prospects for the growth of the economy, involving

such key issues as the use of resources between personal consumption, public and private investment, public services and the balance of trade. Such an assessment, to be comprehensive, has to embrace such issues as the share of national incomes going to profits, to earnings from employment, to rents, to social benefits and to other incomes.[126]

The concept of the National Economic Assessment (NEA) was taken from the last days of the Callaghan government and an attempt made then to end the 'Winter of Discontent' – the outbreak of strikes, mainly in the public sector, which had crippled the economy in 1978–79. The 'St. Valentine's Day pact' of 14 February 1979 between the TUC and the Labour government had agreed that a national assessment of economic prospects (also called an agreed economic assessment) should be held each year before Easter involving both sides of industry and the government.[127]

Little further detail was given about the NEA in 1981. Unlike the 1979 version there was no direct mention of employers being involved. Much remained ambiguous about the new proposal: the status of the discussions and the form that conclusions would take. Both Labour and the unions denied that the NEA was a formal incomes policy. One member of Labour's research staff said later that 'nobody had the faintest idea what it meant'.[128] Callaghan described the 1979 version as being 'written in Delphic terms'.[129] A further Liaison Committee document, *Partners in Rebuilding Britain*, published in March 1983, attempted to clarify some of the ambiguities about the NEA. It outlined how the NEA would be built into the planning process and spelt out the series of discussions and meetings which it would involve between unions, employers, the Labour party and the government.[130]

Tension developed between the NEC and the party's research department over Labour's anti-inflation policy. The NEC remained hostile between 1970 and 1983 to anything resembling wage controls. Research department staff were more cautious about rejecting incomes policy altogether and about the effectiveness of price controls. In 1972 the research department pointed out that price controls could have major implications for profit levels.[131] Tight controls might

limit the availability of funds for investment. Nearly a decade later, *Economic Issues Facing the Next Labour Government*
also noted that effective price controls could squeeze profits
'almost out of existence – with obvious dangers to investment'.[132] Moreover if price controls determined the costs
that were added on in pricing, and wages were a major cost,
then controls would, in effect, become a *de facto* incomes
policy.[133] Alternatively, if wage increases were passed on freely,
price controls would not work. In May 1981 a research department document concluded: '*Any* serious method of controlling inflation means intervening, directly or indirectly,
in the process through which incomes are determined.'[134]
The research department warned that price controls could
be 'a disguised and unfair incomes policy'.[135] These concerns about price controls were not resolved and such measures remained a central part of the AES as the basis of its
anti-inflationary strategy.

Research department staff wanted Labour to address the
relationship of wages and inflation directly.[136] One paper
stated: 'A price freeze on its own could not be sustained,
while price regulation could well leave the rate of inflation
unchanged. This suggests we need to confront the question
of intervention in incomes determination.'[137] Unlike some
leftwingers, members of the research department accepted
wages were a cause of inflation. The original draft for the
NEA had been much closer to presenting it as an incomes
policy. It had argued that:

> As a part of a comprehensive National Undertaking and
> Agreement – on economic expansion, the creation of em-
> ployment and the achievement of greater social justice –
> the Labour Party and the TUC will need to discuss and
> agree a strategy for collective bargaining by the time Labour
> returns to office.[138]

Such a conception was more than leftwingers on Labour's
policy committees could stomach. The Home Policy Committee and the NEC called for a revised version.[139] As if to
convince themselves they were not advocating an incomes
policy, leftwingers always referred to the NEA in lower case.[140]

Many advocates of the AES remained categoric in their
denial that Labour would resort to incomes policy. They

rejected either formal bargaining or the use of norms. Benn told the 1981 conference, 'We are never going back again to the old policies of wage restraint as a means of saving capitalism.'[141] Holland continued to emphasis price controls: he 'supported the Social Contract approach of using price controls among other policies, to influence the climate of pay bargaining without specific norms for pay settlements'.[142] Leftwingers amended drafts of *Labour's Programme 1982* to make explicit the party's hostility to wage restraint.[143] The final version was unequivocal: 'We have also made clear our opposition to any policies of wage restraint.'[144]

Import Controls

Labour's strategy in 1973 did not advocate import controls. Within a few years, however, protection became a central part of the AES, although some leftwingers, including Stuart Holland, had doubts about it.[145] Labour's research department gradually became convinced by the case for some sort of control: during 1975 the department advocated protection in progressively stronger terms. In February it stated controls 'may now become necessary'.[146] In March it concluded that they 'may now be inevitable'.[147] A few months later the research department claimed, 'There is now an overwhelming case for temporary import controls.'[148] In November the argument was put even more forcibly: 'Import controls must play a major part in rescuing the British economy.'[149] The NEC produced *Labour and Industry* for the 1975 conference which proposed selective protection.[150] The TUC had called for controls several years earlier than Labour but they had been regarded largely as a defensive measure to protect jobs and not as an integral part of an economic strategy.[151]

Two arguments were made in favour of import controls. The first was a general argument made by the Cambridge Economic Policy Group in a series of annual reviews from 1975 onwards. These suggested that import controls were needed to prevent reflation resulting in a balance of payments crisis – as increased demand led to a flood of imports. The Cambridge group stated: 'There now seems to be no way of allowing simultaneously an improvement in the current balance and keeping unemployment below one million other than by introducing some form of import restrictions.'[152] The second argument, often emphasised by the TUC and unions, was specific. It advocated controls to protect individual sectors of the economy. Temporary trade barriers would allow the regeneration of firms within those sectors.

Labour's policy documents adopted both arguments. *Labour's Programme 1976* stressed the specific argument: 'Where such factors [causing economic decline] affect any key sector of British industry, import controls must provide a temporary period of protection to give time for those industrial measures of restructuring and modernising which alone can give us a base for export success.'[153] The same document outlined the general argument that import controls would help reflation. TUC documents also supported import controls for both reasons though the emphasis was on the specific.[154] *Labour's Programme 1982* restated both arguments as justifications for import controls.[155] In some cases import penetration would have to be reversed.

Advocates of the AES claimed that import controls were feasible. They argued that retaliation would be unjustified because imports would not be cut and some restraint was acceptable under the rules of GATT.[156] Given that the overall level of demand for imports would not fall, other countries would not be worse off. The UK's trading partners would realise that retaliation would prove self-defeating. A further claim was that controls would not breed inefficiency ('featherbedding') when linked to an industrial strategy. Some advocates of the AES suggested planning agreements should incorporate detailed arrangements for foreign trade.[157]

One problem faced by supporters of the AES was that demands for import controls, especially by some trade unions, might be detached from other policies. The Cambridge Economic Policy Group was also vague about any other measures required.[158] However, Benn was firm, insisting 'the policy of managing our trade is seen as a necessary part of a socialist economic strategy including an expansion of public ownership – and not a substitute for it'.[159] For the most part this argument was successful and most of the calls for import controls recognised that such measures had to be part of a wider package. In 1973 the TUC had noted that import restrictions 'need to be accompanied by other measures'.[160] At a Liaison Committee meeting in December 1979 union leaders recognised that import controls were not an alternative to Labour's other policy proposals.[161] The Liaison Committee document *Trade and Industry* concluded: 'Protection must be associated with measures of industrial modernisation and restructuring, involving the negotiation of planning agreements with key companies.'[162] TUC general secretary Len Murray argued, 'The dangers of *ad hoc* protectionism in deepening the recession were all too clear.'[163] In 1980 Geoff Bish, Labour's research secretary, accepted that there were some differences over import controls between Labour and the unions. But he stated, 'Nevertheless many of the conclusions reached by the party were similar to those in the TUC statement.'[164]

The European Community

In its 1973 programme the Labour party was hostile to the EEC for a variety of reasons but the restrictions that Europe might place on economic strategy were not mentioned. Labour proposed that the UK's membership should be renegotiated. Not all leftwingers were uniformly antagonistic to the EEC: Holland argued that the Common Market could under certain circumstances help Labour's industrial strategy.[165] On other occasions he was more critical.[166] By 1976 Labour's hostility had not abated, though the party accepted the result of the 1975 referendum in favour of the UK staying within the EEC.[167] By 1977 Holland concluded that Labour's industrial policy was 'substantially handicapped' by the EEC.[168] At the 1980 conference it was decided that once in office Labour should leave the EEC as soon as was possible. *Labour's Programme 1982* reaffirmed that decision and argued, 'The single most important advantage of withdrawal will be the ability of the next Labour government to determine its own economic and industrial policies.'[169] The NEC argued that membership of the EEC was not a separate issue to that of Labour's economic proposals.

THE DEVELOPMENT OF LABOUR PARTY ECONOMIC POLICY 1970–83

Two themes stand out in the development of Labour's economic policy between 1970 and 1983. The first is the radical nature of the strategy the party adopted in 1973. The second is the continuity of its policy proposals between 1973 and 1983. With the exception of the addition of import controls during 1975, the AES was, as one party research official stated, 'remarkably consistent' in this period.[170] Labour had adopted an extremely radical strategy. Advocates of the AES argued continually that fundamental changes were required. Benn told the 1982 conference: 'We have learned that tinkering with the problems will not work. It is no good speaking as if a little more reflation or a touch of devaluation or a few more subsidies to private industry will solve our problems.'[171] Michael Meacher argued that Labour would 'transform a discredited economic system that is patently subject to continuing, and indeed accelerating economic decline'.[172] Holland proposed a shift 'from the primacy of the private economy, to a new public, social and cooperative economy'.[173]

In a stream of policy documents after 1973, Labour reaffirmed its commitment to the original proposals. Leftwingers on Labour's Industrial Policy Sub-Committee repeatedly endorsed the initial strategy. In 1978 its members concluded, 'the main elements of party policy on industry were still relevant and their implementation by the next Labour government was essential to an effective attack on Britain's industrial problems'.[174] The continuity in policy was especially clear after 1979 when leftwingers focused on reforming the structure of the Labour party rather than developing new policies. Policy documents at this time simply upheld existing commitments. For example, one commentator, Malcolm Rutherford called Labour's *Peace, Jobs and Freedom* in 1980 'a rag-bag of old ideas stitched together without any kind of intellectual distinction'.[175] The foreword for *Labour's Draft Manifesto* noted that 'this first Draft contains few surprises'.[176] In the summer of 1981 when the Liaison Committee published *Economic Issues facing the Next Labour Government, The Times* termed its contents, 'a lot of paraphernalia of the past'.[177] The introductory note accompanying the first draft of *Labour's Plan for Expansion* in 1981 stated that 'it goes little beyond our existing policy framework'.[178]

The proposals in *Labour's Programme 1982* were very much in line with those of Labour's earlier documents of 1973 and 1976. It repeated the case for the AES and contained the same aggressive attitude to employers who were blamed for economic decline. The final draft of *Labour's Programme 1982* made apparent the continuity in policy: the source for policy commitments from existing documents was written into the margin.[179] There were over eighty attributions to existing economic policy commitments and the party's general objectives. Most of these commitments went into Labour's manifesto for the 1983 election, *New Hope for Britain*.

There were differences of emphasis in policy documents. *Labour's Programme 1982* contained less about the theoretical underpinning of planning and public ownership and more on the actual apparatus that would be involved. It also placed more stress on industrial democracy and was more explicit about the party's objectives. Some of the developments that did take place in Labour's economic strategy were not far-reaching. The National Economic Assessment appeared to be a new mechanism to control inflation. It could be interpreted as a step towards corporatism whereby unions (and employers) would be drawn into the formation and implementation of policy at a national level. However, the NEA closely resembled the Social Contract. Both strategies shared an emphasis on general discussions and voluntary agreement. The NEA was open to different interpretations in much the same way as the Social Contract had been. The role of employers in both schemes was never resolved. Labour still relied on price controls as the basis for tackling inflation. After 1980, Michael Foot as Labour leader often harked back to the Social Contract.[180] One TUC official said later, 'Despite the changes in terminology there was no change from the underlying approach of 1973's Social Contract.'[181] Stuart Holland later argued that the National Economic Assessment 'is the Social Contract by another name'.[182] One journalist, Keith Harper stated the NEA 'will be seen by critics as the social contract in new clothes'.[183]

Advocates and commentators alike noted the similarities of *Labour's Programme 1982* with earlier Labour documents. One researcher, Roy Green claimed: 'In the result, the proposed planning machinery is little different from the mid-1970s industrial strategy.'[184] Likewise Geoff Bish maintained that the policy conclusions of *Economic Planning and Industrial Democracy* 'had not advanced beyond *Labour's Programme 1973*'.[185] The journalist, John Lloyd, noted that the same document was 'the most fully fleshed-out expression of the backroom work begun in the late 1960s and early 1970s by Labour party drafters'.[186] At the 1982 Labour Conference, Stuart Holland responded to criticisms from ex-leader Harold Wilson that these were 'the same policies, the same strategies' that Wilson had claimed to support a decade earlier.[187] It can be concluded that there was a remarkable continuity in the economic policy to which the Labour Party *formally* adhered between 1970 and 1983.

Labour did not affirm its support for the AES uncritically. The Liaison Committee noted the problem of reconciling the demands of workers through industrial democracy with the objectives of national planning. Tensions over the hierarchical relations between the new planning institutions were unresolved. Price controls, Labour's research department noted, might inhibit investment and become a form of wage restraint. Import controls might lead to retaliation. Nevertheless, supporters of the AES did not view such difficulties as insoluble but as problems which could be tackled in practice.

CONCLUSIONS: THE AES AND REVISIONISM

After 1970 Labour developed an economic strategy that was in marked contrast to Revisionism. The objectives of *Labour's Programme 1973* went well beyond the Revisionist's central goal of increased equality. The need for public ownership and structural change was paramount. *Tribune* argued: 'You cannot make any progress towards the sort of equality he [Crosland] wants before you gain control of the levers of economic power.'[188] Revisionists did not accept these arguments. For example, *Socialist Commentary* declared: 'We have moved beyond the objectives of earlier generations when socialism meant primarily the nationalisation of key industries or the establishment of the welfare state.'[189] Tony Crosland had asserted that a dual transfer of power had occurred in society away from employers and to their workforces and the state. Stuart Holland challenged both shifts. He claimed that the economy was dominated by large firms run by an oligarchy of managers solely concerned with profit maximisation: 'Profits are as important in modern capitalism as ever before. The survival of the company and its management depends on them.'[190]

The AES was based on this distinct analysis of the economy. Labour had adopted a very different view of capitalism to Crosland's. The Tribune group stated, 'We do not live in a society governed by competitive liberal economic capitalist principles. We live in a society dominated by multinational companies.'[191] The theory Labour used to explain economic developments owed more to Marx than Keynes. Holland proposed a new package of radical and interventionist policy tools which would allow the state to impose its will on firms. These policy instruments were at odds with those proposed by Labour's rightwingers. The two approaches took a very different view of electoral strategy: advocates of the AES claimed that radical policies could win elections. They firmly rejected the Revisionists' advocacy of a Downsian median voter approach to strategy formation. Table 3.1 indicates the differences between the two approaches. In the next chapter I will examine the debate which took place within Labour between 1970 and 1983 over economic policy.

Despite these differences between the AES and Revisionism, it has been suggested that aspects of Holland's approach find their origin within Revisionism. In fact Crosland advocated competitive public enterprise only tentatively and as a weapon of last resort – not as the basis for a transformation of society. It has also been argued that the proposal for the NEB is essentially the same as that made in *Industry and Society* in 1957 for a National Superannuation Fund to invest in companies.[192] However, any similarities are limited. First, the AES was explicitly intended to transform society, while the proposals in *Industry and Society* were about benefiting from the capital gains of firms. Second, the AES was

Table 3.1 *Comparing Revisionism and the AES*

Element of strategy	Revisionism	AES
Objectives	Equality	Transformation
Empirical view of the economy	Competitive	Monopolistic
Basis of economic theory	Keynesianism	Modified Marxism
Policy tools	Demand management	Supply side interventions: planning, PO
Electoral strategy	Moderate	Radical

extremely hostile to industry. Firms were to blame for economic decline. *Industry and Society* endorsed the work done by the private sector. Third, the NEB was designed to control firms. The National Superannuation Fund was not. Its trustees 'will be guided solely by investment considerations and will not be aimed at securing control'.[193] Fourth, the NEB was just one part of a wide-ranging package of economic controls. By contrast, the National Superannuation Fund was the central part of a limited set of measures. Fifth, the NEB was designed to have an immediate impact by taking over one firm in each sector of the economy. The National Superannuation Fund was aimed at limited sharebuying.

The content and the objectives of the AES were far removed from those of earlier Labour documents such as *Industry and Society, Signposts for the Sixties,* or *Agenda for a Generation.* In these documents Labour had sought to promote equality within a predominantly private economy. Any changes to ownership would have little impact on the balance between private and public sectors. The level of state intervention in the economy would be restricted. By contrast, the AES made an explicit commitment to public ownership and a transformation of the economy. *Labour's Programme 1973* was written in a very different and much more aggressive language than *Industry and Society.*[194]

The new strategy also marked a departure from the traditions of the Labour left as represented by the 'Keep Lefters' in the 1940s and the Bevanites in the 1950s. They had emphasised a much more complex package of measures including public ownership of complete industries, detailed planning of individual sectors, tight physical controls on the economy (including allocation of raw materials) and manpower budgeting. They also wanted a wages policy. Overall, the economy would be subject to considerable state direction. Decades earlier Oswald Mosley in his Memorandum to Ramsey MacDonald's Labour government had focused on the demand side of the economy and on unemployment in particular. Mosley especially wanted to reform the decision-making process of the government. The Alternative Economic Strategy, based around competitive public enterprise and planning agreements, marked an original economic strategy for the Labour left.[195] Some leftwingers regarded it as a watering down of the party's historic commitment to common ownership.

Holland's proposals drew on many sources including Labour's experience in office, the lessons of other European countries, the growth of multinationals, and the development of radical economic theories. Some of his ideas are to be found in the work of the New Left economists, Michael Barratt Brown and John Hughes. They had noted the monopolisation of the economy and criticised the notion of the managerial revolution. They had called for increased public ownership, planning, import and price controls as well as industrial democracy. The New Left had also been hostile to the EEC – before the UK joined.[196] However, the New Left had not provided as coherent an account of the consequences of the concentration of capital for the economy as Holland's. It had focused on the oligarchical side of monopolisation rather than the lack of price competition and other economic dimensions. They had not developed a coherent theory of competitive public enterprise ranging throughout the economy. John Hughes had touched on something like planning agreements when he suggested that firms should agree investment projects with the state.[197] But he had not given any detail or coherence to the idea. Thus aspects of the AES, for example, the use of new public enterprise and planning agreements throughout the economy, were innovative. Most importantly, Holland's achievement was to develop such a package in an original and cohesive form.

The contrast drawn between the AES and the Revisionist policies of earlier Labour documents indicates that Labour party policy documents after 1970 embodied a different kind of social democracy. The ideas and objectives of the Alternative Economic Strategy are closer to the arguments of the labour movement perspective than Revisionism. In the AES, socialism involved a transformation of society based on the development of new relationships involving accountability and industrial democracy. The objectives of the labour movement approach are similar, being based on economic democracy. In both perspectives social democracy involves a commitment to accountability and a concern with efficiency as well as the promotion of equality. The AES and the labour movement perspective contain a similar analysis of the economy and society. They both suggest that employers remain powerful, that the economy continues to be a capitalist one, that class distinctions remain and that class conflict is an important determinant of policy outcomes. The adoption of the AES therefore suggested that the Labour party had abandoned one kind of social democracy for a qualitatively different and more radical version.

The links between the AES and the ideas of the labour movement theorists should not be overstated. Some Labour movement theorists, such as Walter Korpi, come close to adopting a form of structural analysis which suggests that a strong working class will automatically be successful. They downplay the content of economic strategy and stress the power resources available to workers. Exaggeration of the similarities between the policies of the AES and the wage-earner funds of the Swedish social democrats could also be misleading. Labour's transformation of the economy was based on direct ownership and the control of firms. The argument here is simply that the kind of social democracy embodied within the AES is close to that found in the labour movement approach.

The adoption and advocacy of the AES suggests that policy-makers within the Labour party did not accept the structural constraints model as embodied by the work of Adam Przeworski. Przeworski argues that any kind of radical reformism must be abandoned in order to meet the requirements of a prosperous capitalist economy. He claims that social democrats know and accept this situation. Jonas Pontusson suggests, 'Within his [Przeworski's] theoretical framework it is incomprehensible that social democratic leaders should push radical reforms once they recognise the choices available.'[198] Yet Labour's adoption of the AES does not resemble the moderation of reformism. Przeworski states that reformism 'always meant a gradual progression towards structural transformation'.[199] Yet the AES proposed such a reformulation of capitalism through a shift in ownership. Unlike many other strategies based on nationalisation, it was grounded on a coherent and detailed theoretical base. The adoption of the strategy suggests that Przeworski exaggerates the limits of social democracy and claims too strict a logic to which its supporters must adhere.

Labour's leaders were far less committed than leftwingers to the new proposals. Many opposed the new economic strategy and, in the face of economic crisis during the mid-1970s, they adopted arguments which reflect Przeworski's claims about the limits of social democracy. By contrast, leftwingers within the Labour Party felt they could circumvent the kind of impasse that Przeworski argues social democratic parties must encounter. They did not recognise the unyielding domination of the economy by capitalists. They asserted that, with strong policy tools, socialist aims could be achieved. Supporters of the AES claimed that profits could be taxed, the balance of ownership altered and so on without the kind of economic disaster that Przeworski predicts occurring. Social democrats did not abandon their radical policies and far-reaching intentions. At the very least, the experience of the AES throws doubt on Przeworski's claim that social democrats come to accept moderate strategies. It seems that social democrats in the UK did not perceive their strategic choice in the way that Przeworski presents it. For a period, at any rate, Labour was committed to a radical social democracy.

4 The Policy Debate Within Labour

INTRODUCTION

By 1973 the Labour party had adopted an original and radical economic strategy. Its contents marked a break with the Revisionist ideas that had dominated party documents since the mid-1950s. However, the endorsement of these ideas by Labour did not mark a conversion on the part of the party's largely Revisionist leadership. Many leaders were deeply opposed to the new proposals. The result was a prolonged debate over the kind of economic strategy to which the party should adhere. After 1970 this debate went through three distinct phases.[1]

In the first phase of the policy debate, during 1972–74, Tony Crosland and other Revisionists mounted a counter-attack against the left's Alternative Economic Strategy. They challenged the theory it was based upon and criticised the policy tools it comprised. In this phase, although leftwingers dominated policy-making, the right attempted to present an alternative policy. The result was a major gulf within the party over its economic strategy. Labour was able, for the most part, to patch over these policy differences during the February 1974 general election. But the debate continued in a second phase when the party was returned to office in March 1974. Revisionists, now dominant within the government, persisted in criticising the AES and leftwingers found themselves on the defensive. The intellectual debate entered a third phase in 1979 when Labour returned to opposition. Rightwingers again faced a strategy with which they largely disagreed. More than that, they were confronted with extremely unfavourable political circumstances as the left within the party was ascendant. In this phase rightwingers took a less positive attitude to policy-making than they had during 1972–74.

In this chapter I examine the debate within Labour over

the nature of the party's economic strategy between 1970 and 1983. I consider each of its three phases in turn. First, I look at the Revisionists' response to the arguments contained in *Labour's Programme 1973*. I go on to outline the disagreements within the Labour government before assessing the discussions over policy which took place in opposition after 1979. My aim is not to consider the process by which Labour's policy emerged but to examine the arguments that were made within the party and against the AES.

THE FIRST PHASE: THE ORIGINAL REVISIONIST RESPONSE

In *Socialism Now*, published in 1974, Tony Crosland restated the Revisionist case and directed considerable criticism at the AES. He regarded Holland's mesoeconomics as 'bogus intellectualism'.[2] Crosland rejected the idea of a growing trend to monopolisation in the economy and claimed that the public sector, the government, and unions all still had considerable power. He stated that the strength of multinationals was 'grossly over-estimated'.[3] Globalisation meant that domestic companies now faced competition from firms elsewhere. Competition remained a central characteristic of the economy. Crosland concluded, 'It is therefore hard to discern a massive shift of power to the private corporation nor is any concrete evidence for it ever advanced.'[4] A former economic adviser of Crosland's, Wilfred Beckerman launched a bitter attack against Holland, claiming that he had over-emphasised multinational power and the irresponsibility of private enterprise.[5] Firms could not easily switch production around the world because different types of labour were non-substitutable. The rise in mergers was indicative of competitive pressure from abroad.

The Revisionists rejected the left's animosity towards the private sector. Crosland felt there was 'not that great a conflict between multinational companies and the national interest'.[6] Roy Jenkins, another leading Revisionist who became Labour's deputy leader in 1970, argued, 'Individual firms, like individual workers, are the agents of economic forces they cannot control.'[7] The MP John Mackintosh concluded: 'Labour must have policies that give industry stability and continuity.'[8] Crosland insisted that firms were often unfairly blamed for the poor economic performance of the 1960s which owed more to the actions of governments. He maintained, 'I see no reason to alter the Revisionist thesis that government can generally impose its will on the private corporation.'[9]

Crosland suggested profits were not as abnormally high as Holland claimed. He drew on the analysis of two Marxists, Andrew Glyn and Bob Sutcliffe, to argue that the share of profits in national income had halved during 1964–70.[10] Beckerman claimed that wages and international competition had squeezed profits, reducing what was available for investment. Revisionists held that profits were essential for economic prosperity and governments must take account of the impact of their policies on the rate of return and on economic confidence.[11] Crosland argued, 'No policy which does not take account of the need for an adequate profit for investment will achieve its objectives.'[12] He did not believe it was possible 'to attain the high investment we want if profits show so dramatic a decline'.[13] In 1973 Denis Healey asserted that it was not possible to increase corporation tax greatly without damaging investment.[14] Holland disputed this analysis of profit levels. He claimed that profits were under-reported and siphoned-off overseas to countries with lower taxation rates.[15] The Glyn and Sutcliffe data did not accurately reflect the distribution of national income. Labour's research department also queried the extent of the profits crisis: 'During the investment slump of 1970–73, both profits and company liquidity were rising quite sharply.'[16]

Most Revisionists continued to hold a Keynesian analysis of economic problems. Commenting on the draft of *Socialism Now*, one academic wrote to Crosland, 'Your economic strategy, much oversimplified, amounts to better demand management of a fairly traditional kind.'[17] Crosland thought that macro-policy, Keynesianism and incomes policy were 'vastly more important than industrial policy'.[18] Beckerman claimed: 'Many of the weaknesses of the free market can be corrected by the appropriate general fiscal policies without the need to intervene all over the place.'[19] Crosland stated, 'The reason why the economy did not grow up to the limit of this higher productive potential was that the final demand was not there.'[20] Jenkins adopted a similar argument: 'At the root of the matter [unemployment] is inadequate demand, particularly on the investment side.'[21]

These arguments led to the paradox of the Revisionists blaming their own actions in office for the disappointing economic performance of the 1964–70 Labour government. It was their lack of will-power and their policy errors (especially the failure to devalue sooner) which explained the poor outcomes. By contrast, the left's argument acquitted members of the government of responsibility. The problem, they argued, was not the intent of Labour ministers but the economic strategy and policy tools available to them. The solution of this paradox lies in the fact that, by adopting such a stance, Revisionists were able to argue that their strategy remained relevant and viable. Crosland claimed that a government with a clearer sense of priorities would have more success and suggested that Labour should float sterling and be explicit about the necessity of a formal and institutionalised prices and incomes policy.[22] Revisionist objectives remained largely orientated around equality and social justice.

Revisionists had become more cautious. In one downbeat speech, Crosland stated frankly, 'The true answer is that we have no panacea for our economic difficulties.'[23] Denis Healey, the shadow chancellor, told colleagues, 'We must warn everyone against expecting too much. We might have to cut public expenditure.'[24] Revisionist pessimism was fuelled, partly at any rate, by their dissatisfaction with Labour's leftwing policies. Crosland said later, 'In opposition we built up hopeless expectations of how far and fast we could hope to progress.'[25] Jenkins argued, 'It is vital the next Labour government should not arouse hopes which it cannot fulfil and not take on commitments it cannot make.'[26]

Labour's right rejected the practical proposals of the left's strategy. In early 1973 Crosland declared bluntly, 'We lack credibility on the central and dominant economic issues of the day.'[27] Revisionists were especially hostile to further nationalisation. Crosland's assistant, David Lipsey, remembered that he 'was probably more hostile to public ownership than he ever let on'.[28] If fair compensation was paid there would be no redistribution in income and wealth.

Crosland maintained that there was 'no link between public ownership and equality, no link between powers and control'.[29] Revisionists challenged the claim that changing ownership would improve efficiency and increase investment. Why should the actions of the state lead to higher profits? Crosland noted his 'reservations about ambitious ministers and ambitious officials just thinking they can do the job on their own successfully'.[30] He saw public ownership as bureaucratic and unaccountable. In any case, public ownership was unimportant: 'The explanation [of economic developments] does not lie primarily in the British pattern of ownership.'[31] A Whitehall briefing paper in 1976 stated: 'Crosland believes that the Keynesian revolution has made nationalisation unnecessary for the purpose of managing the economy.'[32] Jenkins argued, 'It is no good pretending that the transfer of ownership in itself solves our problems.'[33] Mackintosh called on the left to 'give up the outmoded obsession over ownership'.[34]

Labour's new proposals for public ownership were a departure from the party's traditions and echoed suggestions made earlier by Crosland for competitive public enterprise. Holland cited Crosland's work as an influence on his own – apparently much to Crosland's chagrin. Holland later remembered that Crosland might have come to terms with the new strategy and even acted as a 'godfather' to it. On occasion Crosland did claim an association with Labour's plans, but his motive in doing so appeared to be to convince the public of the party's moderation.[35] The similarities between Crosland's proposals for public ownership and those of *Labour's Programme 1973* are limited. Crosland envisaged competitive public enterprise as an occasional tool, used sparingly to improve the performance of inefficient firms. Lipsey felt, 'His ideas had not really changed from *The Future of Socialism.*'[36] The extensive scale of Labour's new policy, the way that public companies would operate, and the attitude to the private sector were very different from Crosland's plan. The leftwing MP Eric Heffer doubted Crosland's commitment even to limited nationalisation: 'Crosland was not serious about even these ideas because he came out against any NEB development at all.'[37] Lipsey concluded: 'Crosland did not support the taking of profitable private companies into public ownership. He argued that the key was taxation not ownership.'[38]

Revisionists opposed the plans for the NEB and wanted to confine it to acting as an agent for regional regeneration. Roy Jenkins supported the idea of a state holding company for this purpose, but he was horrified at plans for the NEB to control so much of the economy and to take over profitable firms.[39] Crosland made a series of pragmatic criticisms of it: under what criteria would it act; how would it be funded during its first years of existence; who would carry out its management tasks and how would it generate profits?[40] The Revisionist MP David Marquand wrote: 'A British IRI [the Italian state holding company that had influenced Holland]: What form could it take? How would you solve the problems of accountability and control?'[41] In its proposal that the NEB should takeover 25 companies, Crosland felt that the left had elevated dogma out of all proportion: 'We risk deceiving the public. Nationalisation is not an end in itself. . . . Nationalisation is one possible means of furthering these aims [equality, justice and democracy].' Crosland went on: 'What we cannot justify is a threat to every large firm in Britain, good or bad, socially responsible or not, progressive or reactionary, based on the misleading assumption that a change in ownership will produce miraculous results.'[42]

Other leading Revisionists criticised the practical elements of the left's strategy. Harold Wilson, Edmund Dell, James Callaghan, Harold Lever, Shirley Williams, and many other MPs within the shadow cabinet attacked aspects of Labour's proposals.[43] The proposals for the NEB and to takeover 25 of the top 100 companies were their central targets. Criticisms voiced included: the extent of state powers for the new agency; the proposal for an Official Trustee; the timeframe for the takeovers; the criteria for nationalisation; the role that management would play; the effectiveness of state control; the impact of the policies on inflation; and the level of compensation which would have to be paid. Roy Jenkins stated: 'It is no good taking over a vast number of industries without a clear plan as to how and by whom they are going to be run.'[44] In *The Guardian*, Edmund Dell described the NEB as a monster.[45] At the PLP he felt that vast claims were being made for the NEB 'when a more moderate role would be of greater value'.[46] Beckerman said Labour had adopted 'potentially naive and muddled proposals'.[47] The MP Roy Hattersley suggested the public ownership proposals were based on leftwing dogma alone: 'Such a policy appears unrelated to the real needs of real people.'[48]

Rightwingers claimed they did not oppose all public ownership. They accepted a case for some nationalisation in specific areas. But such intervention had to be justified on a case-by-case basis. By and large control – rather than nationalisation – would suffice. The idea that Labour should take over one firm per sector of the economy went far beyond their position. They regarded this proposal as a 'numbers game' which 'elevated theory above practice'.[49] They did not accept the argument that monopolisation necessitated such a measure. Crosland rejected Holland's claims: 'No sound social or economic case for a massive nationalisation programme has been made out. And certainly such a programme in Britain would not cure the underlying weakness of British industry.'[50] The rightwing MP Bill Rodgers called the left's plans 'an emotional spasm designed to please the faithful'.[51]

Revisionists opposed other aspects of the strategy including planning agreements and price controls. Lipsey remembered that 'Crosland was at least as hostile to planning agreements as to public ownership'.[52] Such an extension of state interference would hinder the ability of private firms to make decisions and so to compete with foreign companies. He disliked their use as the central focus of the state's relationship with private firm and felt they would undermine the work of the Monopolies and Mergers Commission.[53] Members of the shadow cabinet were especially opposed to obligatory arrangements. Dell argued later, 'Planning agreements were a farce. We hadn't the faintest idea what they meant.'[54] Crosland claimed that the only result of price controls 'would be a disastrous further squeeze on profits'.[55]

The left's economic strategy would be, Revisionists claimed, 'electorally disastrous'.[56] Such policies allowed the Conservatives to generate considerable fear amongst voters. Shirley Williams claimed that the rise in Liberal votes was a reflection of the lack of support for Labour's proposals.[57] Roy

Hattersley claimed such commitments made it 'immeasurably difficult' for Labour to win an election.[58] An added criticism was that the controversy engendered by the strategy diverted attention from mistakes of the Conservative government and from the more attractive policies that Labour had developed.

Judith Hart defended the proposals for nationalising the 25 companies and for the NEB, arguing that 'to be effective it must be on a substantial scale'.[59] The *New Statesman* noted, 'Even the 25 companies proposal itself, though arguably a tactical error in electoral terms, arises naturally out of the statement of a convincing case for the establishment of a National Enterprise Board.'[60] Leftwingers also denied that the policies were so unpopular. Benn asked, 'Do the British people really want a society in which industrialists and bankers have more power over Britain's economic future than the governments they elect.'[61] If Labour provided a clear lead, the electorate would respond positively. Holland denied that the commitment to the 25 would lose votes.[62]

With *Labour's Programme 1973*, Labour had adopted a strategy about which most of the leadership were extremely uneasy. Peter Shore later called it 'a virtually impossibilist programme'.[63] Leftwinger Barbara Castle wrote later, 'The more timid Labour politicians had their private reservations.'[64] Another leftwing MP Stan Orme said, 'There was a feeling at grassroots level that the PLP was not firmly committed to the programme.'[65] Crosland appeared determined to make it apparent that the Labour leadership would not be bound by the new strategy. He attacked the idea that Labour would in office introduce wide-ranging nationalisation: 'This is a wild fantasy. It [such radical measures] would imply that ministers, most of whom served from 1964–70 in a moderate majority Labour government have been converted to a militant Marxism.'[66] Harold Wilson later made similar scornful criticisms, stating that in opposition 'sub-committees and sub-sub-committees had produced grandiose proposals for nationalising anything and pretty nearly everything'.[67]

What had emerged within Labour during 1973 was a huge gulf between left and right over the party's economic strategy. It would be wrong to suggest that all members were on one side or another of this dispute. Many, including trade union representatives on the NEC, were not involved. Furthermore it would be mistaken to ascribe complete unity to the Labour left. Some leftwingers did not give the new economic strategy priority. Michael Foot felt that Labour's central aim should be to get the UK out of the EEC.[68] A few leftwingers did not grasp the detail of the new proposals and saw them, if anything, as a dilution of Labour's commitment to public ownership.[69]

Rival Interpretations of Party Policy

Despite such differences, a superficial unity was preserved by two factors during the February 1974 election campaign. First, arguments between the Revisionists and the left were blurred by the fact that Wilson and others were prepared to make some concessions, albeit vague ones, towards radical policies. In 1973, Wilson's central concerns were to dump the proposal to nationalise the 25 companies and to avoid being tied by precise commitments. To do that he was prepared to adopt a radical gloss. Wilson made plain his hostility to the nationalisation of profitable companies and he criticised the left's proposals at shadow cabinet and NEC meetings. But at the same time he presented sweeping intentions in his speech to the 1973 Labour conference. Indeed one commentator noted that Wilson's advocacy of public ownership might amount to 2,500 companies, let alone 25.[70] Such plans were general and timeless but they went some way to placating Labour activists. Some rightwingers were concerned by the concessions that Wilson offered. Reg Prentice and Shirley Williams wanted Labour to make specific and limited proposals for nationalisation.[71] Ironically, some leftwingers were also perturbed by Wilson's imprecise proposals. Judith Hart noted that 'vague commitments can and do mean all things to all people'.[72]

Second, it was possible for the party's factions to interpret the same policy in very different ways because aspects of Labour's proposals remained ambiguous. The main focus for different interpretations of party policy was the Social Contract. It had been developed during 1973 as a partnership between unions and a future Labour government but the precise form that it would take was extremely vague.[73] Wilson and others used this nebulous formula to play down many of the specific points of the left's industrial strategy and stress instead the need for reconciliation between government, employers and the unions. The Labour leader saw the Social Contract as a forum where economic and social problems could be discussed and a social wage developed which the unions would then take into account when bargaining for pay increases. In September 1974 Wilson said the contract was 'a way of life based on economic and social justice, aimed at replacing conflict and confrontation with cooperation and conciliation'.[74]

Tony Benn's definition was much more formal and radical: 'A joint commitment to social, industrial and economic reform.'[75] Benn said later, 'I conceived it [the Social Contract] as a resumption of our common programme but for him [Wilson], it was the route that led back into *In Place of Strife* and a pay policy.'[76] Leftwing MPs described the Social Contract as 'a contract for a socialist industrial programme'.[77] One trade union official later remembered: 'the Social Contract meant all things to all men. It was a piece of imagery.'[78] The vagueness of the Social Contract allowed the right to distance themselves from the left's radical measures. Labour's industrial strategy was also open to interpretation. The NEB was conceived by Wilson as a re-incarnation of the Industrial Reorganisation Corporation, the 1960s body to promote mergers and regional aid. He did not see it in radical terms and said on one occasion, 'I do not agree with the role given to it.'[79] Eric Heffer and Ian Mikardo separately complained that Wilson was distorting the functions of the NEB when the Labour leader had claimed that it was not a means of nationalising industries.[80]

Some rightwingers were unhappy about the vague formula of the Social Contract. They doubted it would control inflation and they wanted Labour to adopt a more explicit commitment to some form of an incomes policy. The February 1974 manifesto contained an imprecise formula over incomes policy and *The Times* reported that a majority of the shadow cabinet were not happy with this form of the Social Contract.[81] Jenkins and Crosland, amongst others, wanted a tougher version with sanctions. However, unity came first during the election campaign. Labour's leaders placed considerable emphasis on the Social Contract during the election campaign of February 1974 and depreciated more radical areas of party policy. Leftwing MP Michael Meacher concluded later: 'They [the leadership] may have seemed to be [united]. . . . There's no question now that they never agreed with it [the Manifesto], never wanted it and made no attempt to implement it.'[82] Wilson's biographer, Philip Ziegler, talks of him 'ignoring' Labour's radical manifesto about which he was unhappy.[83] In their account of the election, David Butler and Dennis Kavanagh note, 'A large segment of the parliamentary party and Mr Wilson were far from happy about fighting the election on a programme that was radical because of its socialist dogmatism rather than its rational empiricism.'[84] Barbara Castle concluded that Labour was a party 'held together only precariously'.[85]

THE SECOND PHASE: THE DEBATE IN OFFICE

The second phase of the policy debate began when Labour returned to office in March 1974 as a minority government. At a second election in October the party secured the barest of majorities (three seats). Two distinct strategies emerged within the government to deal with the perilous economic situation it had inherited. Rightwingers presented a Revisionist approach based on reflation and redistribution, while the left looked to Labour's industrial strategy. The right, focused around Denis Healey as Chancellor of the Exchequer, was strong within the government: Crosland was at the Department of the Environment and Jenkins at the Home Office. The left was represented by Tony Benn at the Department of Industry and a few other Ministers. Numerically the right was predominant and exerted considerable influence upon policy formation.

Labour had, nominally at any rate, been elected on a radical manifesto. Benn at the Department of Industry began work on implementing its proposals by setting up the NEB for profitable public ownership and developing planning agreements. But the hostility of rightwingers to what was formally the party's strategy re-emerged, as the unity patched together for the election campaign began to fray. Bernard Donoughue, one of Harold Wilson's policy advisers, claimed that, from the start, Wilson wanted the Downing Street policy unit to work on popular policy ideas that would contrast those Labour had developed out of office.[86] Rightwing ministers frequently attacked Benn's proposals. Subsequent memoirs have made apparent their hostility, even at the time this opposition became public as details of cabinet disputes were leaked.[87]

In May 1974 Benn took his plans to the Liaison Committee but received an antipathetic reception from other ministers.[88] *The Times* claimed, 'Strenuous efforts are now being made to limit the damage of these public ownership proposals.'[89] Even the leftwing Barbara Castle regarded Benn's ideas as 'most lurid'.[90] On another occasion, cabinet member Harold Lever emphasised that Labour was not against industry and that he 'thought it important that industry should have the prospect of profitability to invest'.[91] In several speeches Denis Healey made explicit the important role that he felt the private sector fulfilled.[92] He told the CBI in the summer of 1974, 'I can assure you that the government has no intention of destroying the private sector or encouraging its decay.'[93] Roy Jenkins stated, 'I am also in favour of a healthy, vigorous and profitable private sector,' a phrase that Wilson later inserted into the White Paper on industrial strategy. Dell later remembered that throughout this period 'reassuring the private sector was important'.[94] These speeches confirmed press leaks about the hostility of rightwingers to the left's proposals.

Benn lobbied publicly and directly for the left's strategy, generating a series of conflicts with his colleagues. He irritated fellow ministers who saw his speeches as an attempt to railroad policies through the government. Benn, in contrast, felt it was important to rally support for his proposals.[95] His arguments, both outside and inside, the cabinet had little impact on the trajectory taken by the government. Early in 1975, Benn presented a paper to the Ministerial Committee on Economic Strategy laying out the full Alternative Economic Strategy. Co-authored with his research assistants Francis Cripps and Frances Morrell, the proposals included import controls and was one of the first full statements of the AES.[96] Benn claimed that the government was faced with a choice between two strategies. The first involved spending cuts, taxation increases, pay restraint and help for the corporate sector while the second comprised the standard measures of the AES. Benn's claim was that Keynesian-style Revisionism was no longer a viable option.

Although rightwingers rejected Benn's dichotomy of the strategic choice open to Labour, his argument proved prescient and the government was forced into spending cuts in April 1975. At the time Benn's own proposals for import controls and sweeping intervention were rejected. Shirley Williams challenged his data and suggested his conclusions were 'premature'.[97] Jenkins said that Benn's plan was 'not a remotely viable alternative. It would take us into a siege economy.'[98] By the spring of 1975 the course the government was to take had been established. It was subject to frequent criticism from Benn, along with other elements of the Labour party such as its research department and the Tribune group of MPs.

One reason for public debate within the government was the question of the UK's membership of the EEC. Rival sections of Labour held strongly opposing views on Europe. The party's formal policy, decided at a special conference in 1975, was that the UK should leave – despite the renegotiations that the new Labour government had carried out. Many MPs, especially on the Revisionist side of the party, were enthusiastic supporters of the EEC and could not countenance such action. The solution to this dilemma that Labour had come up with, originally proposed by Benn, was that the government should not make the final decision. Instead it should delegate the choice back to the electorate and hold a referendum on the issue.

As part of the campaign over the referendum, the doctrine of collective responsibility was dropped as cabinet colleagues argued publicly against each other. Overall, the cabinet voted to stay in the EEC but seven 'dissenting' ministers campaigned for a rejection of the new terms. Given the emphasis that was placed on the role of the EEC in determining the UK's economic future, the whole economic strategy of the government was dragged into the discussion. Benn claimed that because of EEC membership, 'We are no longer masters of our own fate in industrial and regional policy.'[99] Benn and Brian Sedgemore stated that the EEC would cost the UK 450,000 jobs.[100] By contrast, rightwingers claimed that the UK benefited economically from membership and that sovereignty was not a major issue. Healey said caustically that those who blamed foreign scapegoats 'for our shortcomings were escaping from real life by retreating into a cocoon of myth and fantasy'.[101] Jenkins said bluntly that he found it 'increasingly difficult to take Mr Benn seriously as an economic minister'.[102] Crosland dismissed the arguments about the EEC costing the UK jobs as 'nonsense'.[103] The resolution of the EEC question with the vote to stay in the Community ended, partially at any rate, such public debates.

The IMF Crisis

Argument within the government over the course of its economic strategy continued after the referendum. On many occasions Benn called in cabinet for aspects of the AES such as protection or state intervention. These discussions followed well-established patterns with Benn unable to convince colleagues of either the feasibility or the desirability of his proposals. Given the positions they had articulated in opposition, the hostility of most of the cabinet to the AES was unsurprising. Benn remained the focus for the debate around the AES, but he had little impact as arguments were simply repeated. Rightwingers in the cabinet continued to argue that his policies were impractical. Import controls would provoke retaliation and further state intervention would be likely to damage investment.

The resignation of Harold Wilson as Labour leader and Prime Minister in March 1976 gave Benn the opportunity once again to make the case for the AES as part of his campaign for the leadership of the Labour party. He had little hope of winning but the election provided him with the chance to articulate his radical proposals. During the brief campaign Benn claimed, 'The British public has got to realise that our manufacturing industry is so weak that unless we protect it and then invest behind a wall of protection this country could be on its way down in a very serious way.'[104] The contest made plain just how far removed Benn's own views were from those of the government. He received 37 votes and came fourth in the first round. He withdrew, and it was James Callaghan who won, defeating Michael Foot in the third ballot.

At two further points during 1976 the cabinet undertook a fundamental discussion about economic policy.[105] The first occasion was in July during a prolonged sterling crisis. Benn's proposals were rejected as the cabinet opted for spending cuts and tax increases. The problem for Benn was that the sides in this dispute were by now well drawn.[106] At an earlier discussion Joel Barnett, Chief Secretary to the Treasury, claimed, 'Benn. . . . was never able to convince a single one of his colleagues (other than the few already convinced) despite his scintillating exposition.'[107] The July spending cuts were as anathema to Revisionists as to leftwingers. Crosland despaired of the course taken by the government but he continued to regard the left's strategy as impractical, noting 'the absurd Benn–Holland–Bish strategy is dead as a dodo'.[108]

The chancellor, Denis Healey, was blunt about the cuts. As early as May 1975 he argued, 'What we have to do is to shift more people from the public to the private sector.'[109] In 1976 he claimed there was simply no alternative.[110] Public spending could not be funded by further tax increases or increased borrowing. Healey appeared much influenced by the argument of two economists, Roger Bacon and Walter Eltis, that the private sector was being effectively crowded out by the public sector. They claimed that a large public sector constrained the resources available to private firms and imposed punitive tax burdens.[111] Healey apparently regarded their arguments 'as the most stimulating and comprehensive analysis of our economic predicament which I have yet seen in a newspaper'.[112]

Two radical Labour policy documents produced during 1976 were indicative of the gap between party and government. When *Labour's Programme 1976* was published in May, *The Times* reported that it would damage 'the government's patient efforts to build a working relationship with industrialists and City interests' because of its radical intentions.[113] Healey described the economic package as 'totally unrealistic'.[114] When *Banking and Finance* was publicised, Harold Lever acted quickly to distance the Government: he stated that the government had 'no intention of nationalising the banking, insurance or pharmaceutical manufacturing industries'.[115]

The July cuts did not restore stability to sterling and once again in September the pound came under pressure. Healey decided that the government would have to approach the IMF for a loan. The IMF crisis provided Benn with another opportunity to present the AES to the cabinet as part of the extensive discussions surrounding the terms of the loan. He received limited support from leftwingers in the cabinet such as Albert Booth, Michael Foot, Stan Orme, Peter Shore and John Silkin, though they had doubts about aspects of his proposals.[116] A majority of the cabinet remained hostile to his plans. Healey criticised import controls as promoting inefficiency and leading to a siege economy. Two commentators claimed: 'Without a Treasury Minister behind him, Benn was pulverised. Even non-economic ministers, primed with briefs from No 10, joined in to expose the weakness of his assessment for import controls, direction of investment and a siege economy.'[117]

Just as he had resisted the July cuts, so Crosland opposed the application to the IMF because of the demands that he realised it would make for further spending reductions. But the Revisionists did not have an acceptable alternative policy. For a time Crosland considered supporting a modest form of the AES based around limited import controls.[118] Peter Shore had made some suggestions along these lines for a much watered-down version of Benn's strategy. Ultimately, this scheme was unacceptable to Crosland and the other Revisionists.[119] Most Revisionists opposed any protection and they found accepting the IMF's terms a lesser evil than endorsing a limited version of the AES.[120] Crosland decided to support Callaghan and he acquiesced in the cuts that the IMF deal involved. Many parts of the Labour party, including the research department, attacked these cuts.[121] *Tribune* newspaper, which had continually lobbied for the AES, called on the government to reject the IMF loan. Leftwing MPs had no impact on the government: twenty-eight voted against the IMF loan but the government was saved from defeat in the House of Commons when the Conservatives abstained.

The Demise of Revisionism

The IMF crisis was of great symbolic importance: the spending cuts amounted to a public rejection of the Keynesian foundations of social democracy. In nearly two years since the spring of 1975 the government had undergone four rounds of savage reductions in public expenditure, they had increased taxation and considerably elevated monetary policy as an instrument of economic management. Benn's prediction, made in the spring of 1975, about the deflationary course the government had embarked upon appeared to have been vindicated. Notes by Crosland during 1976 capture a feeling of despondency: 'Now no sense of direction and priorities, only pragmatism, empiricism, safety first, £ supreme.'[122] Within a few months of the IMF deal Crosland died suddenly. His death further weakened the Revisionist case within Labour.[123]

Revisionism was based on the idea that a prosperous market economy and high public spending (to promote equality) were compatible. The UK's economic crisis and its culmination in the IMF crisis brought the relationship between economic well-being and public expenditure into doubt. Many Revisionists appeared to lose their faith in state spending. Roy Jenkins claimed in 1976, 'I do not think you can push public expenditure significantly above 60% and maintain the values of a plural society and adequate freedom of choice. We are close to the frontiers of social democracy.'[124] Crosland had coined the phrase 'the party is over'.[125] He also concluded, 'But there are limits – and in our present situation they are rigid limits – on how far such spending can go, for the simple reason that there are limits on the amount which we can raise in taxation.'[126] By 1975 he was arguably much more wary about the role of public spending in meeting social democratic objectives.[127]

After Crosland's death some Revisionists changed tack. The pamphlet *What We Must Do* from the rightwing Manifesto group of MPs emphasised the need for any government to promote successful accumulation by private firms in place of redistribution. Public expenditure should be kept under strict control and borrowing avoided: 'The creation of conditions for industrial prosperity must secure priority.'[128]

Nick Bosanquet suggested in a Fabian pamphlet that public spending could not rise without crowding out the private sector.[129] Such arguments and the trajectory followed by the Labour government might be interpreted as a fulfilment of the structural constraints model of social democracy. As Adam Przeworski's thesis suggests, the government seemed to have placed the requirements of the private economy before any welfare objectives. The highpoint of this rejection of Keynesian social democracy was James Callaghan's speech to the Labour party conference in 1976. He told delegates:

> We used to think you could spend your way out of recession, and increase unemployment by cutting taxes and boosting government spending. I tell you in all candour, that option no longer exists, and that in as far as it ever did exist, it worked on each occasion since the war by injecting a bigger dose of inflation into the economy, followed by a higher level of unemployment. . . . that is the history of the last twenty years.[130]

Even allowing for the need to provide a rhetorical statement of good intentions for financial markets, it was a direct rejection of the social democratic case.

The 1979 Election Manifesto

The dispute within Labour over economic strategy flared up over the drafting of the party's 1979 general election manifesto. Callaghan insisted that the draft considered was one produced by his research assistants. The sections on economic policy were extremely moderate. Tony Benn and Eric Heffer later claimed, 'Perhaps the most glaring omission in the manifesto, in terms of party policy, concerns the whole area of economic and industrial strategy.'[131] At the final meeting Benn attempted without success to include a large chunk about planning agreements directly from *Labour's Programme 1973*. Geoff Bish, the party's research secretary was especially bitter about the way his draft had been sidelined: 'What was also important was that the Labour government had publicly indicated its rejection of the party's "alternative" strategy (reflation, import controls, a much stronger NEB etc.).'[132]

A strong contrast can be drawn between the moderate domestic manifesto of 1979 and the European manifesto of later that summer. Callaghan had no control over the latter and privately he made little secret of his unhappiness with it. Benn wrote, at the launch, 'Under his breath, he [Callaghan] said "it is not my manifesto".'[133] Several contrasts can be noted. First, the domestic manifesto placed stress economically on the 'fight against rising prices' and on 'jobs and prosperity'. The European manifesto wanted 'democratic control of the economy'.[134] Second, Callaghan's introduction to the domestic document was extremely consensual. On industrial policy he argued, 'The government's industrial strategy is about how to create more wealth and more jobs through a constructive national partnership with unions and management.'[135] The European statement was, by contrast, aggressive towards industry, especially multinationals, and envisaged policy being developed with unions alone. Third, the European manifesto spoke of taking key firms into public ownership throughout the economy – a proposal which was central to the AES. The domestic manifesto saw public ownership only in terms of being in exchange for state aid (and a few other specific proposals such as the construction industry). Fourth, the European manifesto was much more specific about the need for import controls.

THE THIRD PHASE OF DEBATE: THE RETURN TO OPPOSITION

Labour's period in opposition between 1979 and 1983 was not marked by the same kind of arguments over policy that had occurred nearly ten years earlier. Rightwing Labour leaders did not endorse the party's economic strategy but they were even less effective in opposing the left than they had been between 1970–74. In the third phase of debate there was little positive consideration of policy as rightwingers rarely engaged with the left in discussions. The leftwing MP Joan Lestor complained that there was 'no other socialist party in Europe whose leaders have contributed less to the development of the party's thinking than ours'.[136] The absence of argument did not reflect an agreement within the party but illustrated the political and theoretical weaknesses of the right. After 1979, rightwingers' attention was focused on the struggles within Labour over its constitutional nature. Institutional change not only diverted attention from policy matters but encouraged some MPs to keep silent, fearing for their own position. Chris Mullin, the new editor of *Tribune* wrote, 'Although the right oppose just about all the main planks of party policy, they dare not say so publicly.'[137] Some rightwing MPs, tired of engaging in a struggle they felt was hopeless, abandoned Labour to form the Social Democratic Party. The split weakened the morale of remaining rightwingers.

Revisionism's alternative policy remained unclear. Many rightwingers were uncertain what form a social democratic economic strategy should take after the failures of the Keynesian-based approach. Ivor Crewe and Anthony King conclude bluntly that 'the right had run out of ideas'.[138] The commentator Peter Jenkins described the Revisionists as 'generals without a strategy'.[139] They had been able in 1970 to claim that Revisionism remained valid provided policy errors were corrected. In 1979 this option was not open. Labour's policy had not proved a success and there was no obvious remedy they could adopt. Crosland's death in 1977 created a vacuum in Revisionist politics. There was no comparable individual within Labour's right able to articulate original ideas. Leading rightwingers such as James Callaghan and Denis Healey, were not theoretically minded. Others who might conceivably have filled Crosland's mantle such as Roy Jenkins, Shirley Williams and David Owen left the Labour party to found the SDP in 1981. After 1979 rightwingers were undecided and extremely cautious about economic policy. At internal meetings rightwingers such as Denis Healey, Roy Hattersley and Peter Shore, were critical of Labour's strategy but their comments were largely negative and private. In part leftwingers were able to win arguments by default and Revisionism became a term little used.

Many leftwingers believed that the leadership remained committed to the kind of moderate policies they had implemented in office. A constant refrain was that Labour leaders did not support party policy. In the summer of 1980 the ex-

MP Tom Litterick stated, 'The bleak fact is that the majority of the policy proposals in the NEC document [*Peace, Jobs and Freedom*] are not acceptable to the overwhelming majority of the leadership and would not be implemented by them if they came to office.'[140] The Labour Coordinating Committee lamented: 'The plain truth is that no amount of conference resolutions on defence, incomes policy, public spending or any other subject is going to make the slightest impression on our leader.'[141] Soon after the election Healey concluded that economic policy 'must rest on three pillars – demand management, monetary control and incomes policy'.[142] *Tribune* attacked these views as 'nothing more than the recipe which landed Labour in such a mess last May'.[143] The lack of debate should not be taken to imply that rightwingers accepted Labour policy.

The Right's Contribution Towards Policy

On occasion rightwingers did appear to support elements of party policy. With the publication of *Peace, Jobs and Freedom* in 1980, *The Sunday Times* reported that Callaghan accepted the need for planning agreements, public ownership, price controls and industrial democracy.[144] However one commentator argued 'that the document could be read in a number of ways' and leftwingers were suspicious of Callaghan's apparent endorsement of it.[145] Callaghan was not the only member of the PLP to make gestures towards the left in this period. At various times Denis Healey offered qualified support for elements of the AES such as ceilings on imports, industrial democracy and a national plan as well as reflation.[146] Some of his economic proposals appeared to be close to Labour policy (by contrast his arguments about defence were extremely vague). In 1981, perhaps reflecting the pressure of the ongoing deputy leadership contest, he told the Labour conference, 'There is no alternative to her policy [Mrs Thatcher's] except the alternative economic strategy offered by the Labour party and the TUC.' He continued, 'The key element in our new strategy, which was not, I admit, there last time, is a fully developed strategy for regenerating industry in which a greatly developed National Enterprise Board will play a leading role' – a remarkable statement given the role he had played in the Labour government.[147] He claimed to be a supporter of the AES but his interpretation of it was extremely moderate, based around demand management, incomes policy, free trade, and an ill-defined industrial strategy.[148] Michael Meacher concluded that any conversion was largely tactical: 'It is difficult to imagine Mr. Healey making any such declaration except in the heat of a very tight election contest.'[149] Meacher quoted David Watts, *The Times* commentator: 'The fact of the matter is that the existing shadow cabinet cannot be "trusted" to adopt the kind of leftwing policies that the Labour conference, or even the TUC are enjoining.'[150]

In less public situations Healey was less in accord with Labour party policy. At several Liaison Committee meetings he criticised import controls, arguing that retaliation would be likely and they would not work.[151] He described them as 'a confidence trick'.[152] He also argued that further nationalisation and planning agreements 'would not provide the answers to improving efficiency'.[153] One reason that Healey was moved to be foreign affairs spokesperson in 1980, according to Lewis Minkin, was that he 'made known his reservations about the target for unemployment, the trade policy and exchange controls'.[154] On occasion Healey harked back to older Revisionist analyses: he told one Liaison Committee meeting that 'the main problem is lack of demand'.[155] In discussions about industrial policy during 1980, Healey continued to stress the role of sector working parties (SWPs) – a largely indicative approach used by the Labour government to coordinate the future needs of the economy and subsequently rejected by the party.[156] On another occasion Healey distanced himself from the left's strategy with a barbed reference to Benn: 'You will not solve the problems of Britain in one week simply by abolishing the House of Lords and cutting Britain off from 40 per cent of her export markets'.[157]

Senior members of the PLP frequently made negative points about Labour's economic policy, especially protection and the industrial strategy (usually in private). For example, Roy Hattersley criticised import controls, opposed Labour's plans to leave the EEC and felt that the party's strategy was overoptimistic.[158] Discussing import controls, John Smith, the relevant frontbench spokesperson, claimed, 'The problem was that what would happen would be the substitution of raw materials for the present level of manufactured goods. Although Brazil, therefore, might benefit, West Germany would clearly have a case for retaliation.'[159] Peter Shore concluded: 'One of the crucial parts of any alternative is, indeed a planned strategy for our trade, but we have got to do it this time in a way that does not lead to beggar-my-neighbour policies.'[160] The MP Gerald Kaufman criticised planning agreements and state intervention in industry.[161] David Owen, shortly to leave Labour, laid out a very moderate strategy in his volume, *Face the Future*. He accused the AES of being centralist and failing to come to terms with the private sector. He rejected public ownership, compulsory planning agreements and import controls.[162] Even the leftwinger Stan Orme indicated concern about the emphasis on planning agreements.[163] Labour's leader after 1980, Michael Foot, took little part in the debates over economic and industrial policy – his overriding objective was to try and unite the party. He was, however, a supporter of leftwing objectives and a strong advocate of full employment.

Rightwingers were often hesitant in supporting Labour Party policy documents. *The Times* reported that Labour leaders disowned the draft manifesto published in 1980, saying that Callaghan did not accept its stance on either public ownership or import controls.[164] When the PLP discussed the AES in 1982 it was criticised as being: over-complex; too reliant on import controls; anti-EEC; unclear; and lacking a policy on inflation.[165] Similar points were made in discussions about Labour's campaign document, the basis for the 1983 manifesto.[166] Roy Hattersley was scathing about Benn: 'The alternative that Tony offers is not a policy at all – it's half a dozen slogans which nobody has yet tried.'[167] In 1981 the academic Nick Bosanquet argued that Labour needed a 'real alternative to Thatcherism. It is a million miles away from this at the moment.'[168] The strongest restatement of the Revisionist case between 1979 and 1983 came from Hattersley, the shadow home secretary, who remained close to Crosland's central thesis that socialism was about equality.[169] He continued to emphasise demand management as the basis for economic strategy, claiming, 'The basis of an expansionist policy is a return to a genuine Keynesian economics.'[170]

It would be wrong to suggest that no member of the shadow cabinet supported the AES or advocated radical measures.[171] Stan Orme advocated price control as the 'the key to control of the private sector'.[172] John Silkin, Labour's industry spokesman during 1979–80 was a strong supporter of import controls and a well-known critic of the EEC. These measures, coupled with calls for reflation, marked many of Silkin's speeches. But many leading figures in the PLP were half-hearted at best in their public advocacy of the AES. The shadow cabinet's 1983 book *Renewal* revealed a moderate and unenthusiastic interpretation of the AES. The 'overlord' for Labour's industrial and economic policy, Merlyn Rees, stressed the National Investment Bank as 'the most novel of these [new institutions] and one of the most important'.[173] It is hard to imagine a leftwing advocate of the AES choosing such an emphasis. Rees went on to stress the uncertainty of planning and the need for a flexible approach to public ownership. He did not refer to the need for profitable public ownership or the extent of nationalisation required. In contrast to the rather guarded views of many of the shadow cabinet were the exuberant arguments made by leftwingers.

Peter Shore's Programme for Recovery

The exception to the relative inactivity over economic matters amongst the shadow cabinet was Peter Shore. As shadow chancellor between 1980 and 1983, Shore laid out an economic strategy which emphasised reflation and a competitive devaluation of sterling. He did not reject out of hand the party's industrial strategy: his proposals were 'only a start of the programme of measures that we need to implement'.[174] The shadow treasury frontbench did on occasion use the phrase Alternative Economic Strategy but Shore gave few details on industrial matters and his approach seemed more consensual and corporatist than that of the AES. At times he implied that his policies of reflation would stand up on their own.

In November 1982, Shore and the Labour treasury team,

produced a 70-page document entitled *Programme for Recovery* (drafted largely by Jack Straw, one of the shadow treasury ministers and Henry Neuburger, an ex-civil servant who advised both Foot and Shore).[175] At the heart of its proposals was a planned devaluation of sterling by 30 per cent over 2 years.[176] Shore accepted that the difficulties of securing full employment were 'formidable'. It would require 2.5 million new jobs. Nevertheless, with 4 per cent growth per year, unemployment could be reduced to under a million. Reflation would come before intervention because it would take time to get any industrial measures up and running. Shore accepted that eventually planning agreements with companies would be needed but he did not share the antipathetic attitude to industry of leftwingers. Unlike supporters of the AES, he did not conceive of them as mechanisms that would allow the government to impose its will on firms. Reversing the argument made for them, he claimed that planning agreements would help a government identify and meet the needs of the economy and individual companies.

Low real wage growth was an implicit assumption of the *Programme for Recovery* package. Shore did not spell out how the assumed restraint would be achieved. It was reported that the union leader David Basnett had insisted that Shore remove references to pay norms from an earlier draft.[177] The implication was that the National Economic Assessment would provide the basis for a voluntary and corporatist incomes policy. Successful wage restraint was built into the model tests contained in the document and where the assumptions were altered to allow for free collective bargaining, the results indicated that inflation would rise and the strategy would be unsustainable. *Programme for Recovery* came as close as any other document to calling for an incomes policy. Shore, like many other Labour leaders, regarded one as indispensable and apparently saw *Programme for Recovery* as one way of by-passing the party's policy-making machinery to raise the issue.[178]

Shore's proposals attracted critical comment: David Lipsey argued that Shore had been forced to promise far more than he could deliver, and 'has so far extracted from the unions less than he needs, if he is to have any prospect of success'.[179] Even some supporters, such as Wynne Godley of the Cambridge Economic Policy Group, felt that Shore was too optimistic about devaluation and the possibility of reducing unemployment.[180] The journalist, Peter Riddell wrote, 'It is likely to be argued that the favourable results shown by the simulation depend on arbitrary and implausible assumptions.'[181] Leftwingers disliked the emphasis placed on devaluation. In an interview with *The Financial Times*, Benn stated: 'I didn't think it was the answer and it would make it impossible for Peter to be Chancellor with that sort of pledge [for devaluation] hung around his neck.'[182]

The stress on a combination of devaluation, reflation and (apparently) incomes policy proposed by the parliamentary leadership suggested that they might be distancing themselves from the more extreme commitments that the AES involved.[183] *Programme for Recovery* was not endorsed by the NEC, although certain individuals, such as Labour Party researchers, Geoff Bish and Adam Sharples, as well as David Basnett and David Lea of the TUC, were consulted.[184] Its status within the party was uncertain – some saw it as a personal statement (by Shore) alone. Bish later stated, 'No one on the NEC had been properly involved in preparing the document.'[185] One Labour party official, Roy Green, criticised Shore's proposals as a retreat from planning and the AES.[186] The Labour MP Austin Mitchell noted that the shadow chancellor's strategy 'was different, using expansionary Keynesianism and the dynamics of the market through devaluation as a stimulus to growth where the Alternative Economic Strategy was *dirigiste*, centring on controls, managed trade and the use of the power of the state'.[187] *The Guardian* commented, 'The main baggage of the Alternative Economic Strategy – nationalisation, planning agreements, and import controls – loom rather small in Mr Shore's scheme of things.'[188]

Like the NEA, *Programme for Recovery* was open to interpretation and individuals were able to draw their own conclusions about the relationship between reflation and planning. It was never officially published by Labour. Benn had claimed earlier in the summer of 1982 that the shadow cabinet was downplaying their commitment to *Labour's Programme 1982* and that they wanted a free hand over policy. He declared, 'If the shadow cabinet gets its way Labour will go into the next election without any firm commitments decided by conference.'[189] During the drafting of *Labour's Programme 1982*, Benn claimed that Peter Shore and the shadow cabinet were 'fighting a tremendous rearguard action against anything radical'.[190] In the event when Labour's general election manifesto was drafted on 11 May 1983, Peter Shore presented the only dissenting voice. Most shadow ministers did not seem bothered to put up a fight for what, the opinion polls suggested, was a hopeless attempt to win the election. (They had earlier called for a shorter version.[191]) Shore criticised both the pedestrian language and the content of the draft without any success.[192] Benn and other leftwingers were pleased with the result, although they doubted the commitment of the PLP to the document: 'It certainly was the product of an awful lot of campaigning we had done over an awfully long period and although I know the shadow cabinet wouldn't do it if they were elected, at least we have got that as our commitment to the British people.'[193]

The Necessity of an Incomes Policy

Many members of the PLP were convinced that an incomes policy was needed to control inflation. One adviser said, 'Figures in the PLP did support an incomes policy. Whatever it was called and whatever form it took, there was an assumption that there would be an agreement on incomes.'[194] However, in the immediate aftermath of the collapse of Labour's pay policy in 1978–79, and the Winter of Discontent, calls for wage restraint were often elliptical. Privately many rightwingers were more direct.[195] For example, Roy Hattersley said at a Liaison Committee meeting that without an incomes policy 'we lack credibility'.[196] Later Hattersley argued that an incomes policy should be 'a permanent part of both our economic and social strategy'.[197] Such explicit measures of wage restraint were unacceptable to the Labour left and many trade unionists. On one occasion Healey stated that this absence was a major gap in Labour's strategy – a point often echoed, albeit in a different fashion, by the research department.[198] Likewise James Callaghan stated, 'The major weakness in the TUC's position was the lack of an alternative policy on inflation.'[199] At meetings of the joint PLP–NEC Policy Coordinating Committee Labour MPs attempted, without success, to get some commitment to an incomes policy adopted by the party.[200]

Formally Labour remained opposed to an incomes policy. The best the shadow cabinet could achieve was the loose framework of the National Economic Assessment and the kind of implicit assumption that Shore made in *Programme for Recovery*. The exact nature of the National Economic Assessment remained unclear. One adviser remembered, 'With the NEA everyone said the same thing and meant different things.'[201] *The Times* noted: 'This [the NEA] either means a pay policy or it means nothing. If it means nothing the party's claim to have a cure for full employment without inflation falls to the ground.'[202] The MP Jeremy Bray wondered whether the NEA was 'an incomes policy in disguise'.[203] Benn claimed that the right saw the NEA as a way 'really to get back to a pay policy'.[204] At policy regional conferences in 1982, delegates were concerned that the NEA was 'simply another form of incomes policy'.[205] One union leader, David Basnett, appeared to accept that the NEA might involve wage restraint, but he went on to see it as the means for greater union involvement in economic decision-making.[206] The proposal came to nothing.

The Liaison Committee agreed that the NEA required clearer explanation. But many members were adamant that there could be no pay norms and no constraints on wage settlements. During the drafting of *Partners in Rebuilding Britain* in 1983, it was agreed that the statement should make clear that the National Economic Assessment was 'not a policy imposing norms or fixed limits on pay'.[207] Many unions remained opposed to any interpretation of the NEA as a form of pay policy.[208]

By early 1983 some Labour politicians were fairly blunt about the need for an incomes policy. Peter Shore commented: 'I'm not a magician. I cannot deliver what can only be collectively and nationally delivered.'[209] Healey said that a Labour government would conclude some sort of deal on pay: 'The agreement must include social policy, housing policy and price policy. If you have these then they [unions] are prepared to accept discussion on pay as well.'[210] Shore and

Foot used the phrase 'planned collective bargaining' to describe the policy Labour proposed.[211] But the endeavours of rightwingers to promote incomes policy had no positive impact on party policy and leftwingers successfully resisted the addition of wage restraint to the AES.

CONCLUSIONS: AN ASSESSMENT OF THE POLICY DEBATE

Labour's leading rightwingers never reconciled themselves to the Alternative Economic Strategy in the period it dominated Labour party policy between 1973 and 1983. Many members of the PLP remained committed to Revisionism after 1970. Led by Crosland, they opposed the shift to the left in party policy. He continued to advocate Revisionism, although he was more cautious than he had been. Crosland's objective remained equality and he did not endorse the far-reaching goals of the AES.

After 1974, with Labour in government, this debate continued as rightwingers were able to reject the Alternative Economic Strategy. In this phase, Benn lobbied from within the cabinet for Labour to implement the policies that the party had adopted in opposition. He made little headway in persuading his rightwing cabinet colleagues and became a rather isolated figure. During the 1974–79 Labour government, some rightwingers accepted that Revisionism faced major problems but they did not endorse the AES. Instead, they adopted an even more limited and moderate social democracy which stressed the need to promote profitability. Labour's right had reluctantly come to advocate a social democracy whose nature is best represented by the work of Adam Przeworski.

The period after 1979 was marked not by debate so much as acquiescence on the part of the PLP leadership. There seems little doubt that Labour leaders were presented with an economic strategy they disliked during 1979–83. They tackled it, not with debate, but, for the most part, silence. When they did defend Labour policies, their arguments were often half-hearted. A research department note in the autumn of 1982 stated forlornly, 'There is a real need for party spokesmen, at all levels, to have confidence in the policies they are trying to support.'[212] *Tribune* attacked the attitude of the leadership during the 1983 election campaign as defeatist, alleging: 'When they have not been swiping at their own troops, many of Labour's leaders have appeared to be apologising for, rather than advocating, the policy of their party.'[213] Ron Hayward, Labour's general secretary, noted in March 1981, 'It appears to the active party member and to the electorate that the NEC and the shadow cabinet are at complete loggerheads.'[214] As in 1974, different interpretations could be made of official party strategy after 1979. When required to articulate policy publicly, the rightwingers could provide a bland rendition of Labour's proposals.

One other development occurred in the policy debate after 1979. Until that date leftwingers were relatively united amongst themselves, though there were some disagreements during the 1974–79 government. After the election defeat more serious disputes emerged. In 1980 the NEC dropped the commitment to the immediate restoration of full employment in the draft of *Peace, Jobs and Freedom*.[215] Some leftwingers, including Neil Kinnock, Judith Hart, and Joan Lestor, opposed the objective as being unrealistic. Later Labour documents restored the commitment to full employment but the argument presaged more serious splits within the Labour left. These were not, as Chapter 7 indicates, wholly connected with policy matters. In 1981 several Tribune group members, including Kinnock, Hart and Lestor, opposed Benn's candidacy for Labour's deputy leadership. Kinnock regarded Benn's economic proposals, at a time of recession, as unrealistic, reckless and so damaging to the party's prospects of office.[216] By the early 1980s some leftwingers had doubts about the way that Benn presented Labour's economic strategy. However, it is not apparent how great policy differences were in encouraging the split within the Labour left. Despite Kinnock's charges, other leftwingers opposed Benn precisely because he was jeopardising Labour's commitment to socialist measures, including the AES, by linking them with his apparently doomed candidacy for the deputy leadership.

One central theme emerges from this consideration of the debate over economic policy within the Labour party during the period 1970–83. It concerns the degree to which leading rightwingers within Labour remained opposed to what was official party policy. Although there was a strong degree of continuity in the AES advocated by the Labour party, many leaders never reconciled themselves to the proposals. The intellectual debate within Labour was marked by an endemic disunity. A policy report in 1981 concluded, 'It seemed to many in the party that there were two quite separate Labour parties each going their own sweet way on policy action and on policy development.'[217] The result was a remarkable divergence. It would be mistaken to characterise the whole party as taking sides in this debate. Many elements of it, especially trade unionists, did not get involved in such disputes. It would also be wrong to depict left and right as monolithic blocks. Nevertheless the intellectual debate reveals a struggle, of differing intensity over the period, between two very different strategic packages based on contrasting conceptions of social democracy. The Alternative Economic Strategy was never endorsed throughout the party and the conflict within Labour over policy was never resolved. The next three chapters will consider how such a split had developed within Labour by analysing the party's policy-making process.

5 The Adoption of the Alternative Economic Strategy

INTRODUCTION

After leading in the opinion polls during the campaign, Labour's defeat in the 1970 general election came as a surprise. One consequence of the result was that the opportunity existed for the party to re-think its economic policy. Many within Labour – not just leftwingers – felt that, given the government's performance in office, it was essential for such a reappraisal to take place. Immediately after the election, Richard Clements, the editor of *Tribune*, attacked Labour's economic record as a central cause of defeat.[1] Michael Foot talked of the administration's 'paralysing financial orthodoxy'.[2] The MP Norman Atkinson stated, 'The one alternative which remains untried is the socialist alternative.'[3]

Over the next four years leftwingers dominated Labour's economic policy-making. The culmination of this ascendancy came with the adoption by the party of *Labour's Programme 1973*, the first version of the Alternative Economic Strategy. Most Labour leaders were, as the last chapter indicated, hostile to the radical proposals contained in this document. The success of leftwingers in getting such policies adopted was not, therefore, determined by the inherent strength and coherence of their ideas. The left won few converts from Revisionism. In this chapter, I consider how the split between the policy desires of Labour's leadership and the party's formal stance developed. I analyse the nature of policy-making in the Labour party between 1970 and 1974 and I chart the evolution of the division over economic policy. First, I examine the increased strength of the left within the Labour party after 1970.

THE RISE OF THE LABOUR LEFT

Labour's leftwingers greatly increased their strength and influence within the party after the 1970 election, helped by a number of factors. These included the policy failures of the Wilson government, the emergence of a new alignment of trade union leaders, structural changes to the economy and labour movement, the organisational determination and abilities of leftwingers, and the failure of Revisionists to respond to their initiative. The left had appeared weak during the 1960s. Although the NEC was defeated and the policies of the PLP rejected by the party conference, such votes had little impact on the Labour government. The result was a general deterioration in relationships within the party, as the leadership appeared both arrogant and ascendant until 1970. After the election, however, leftwingers were in a strong position to assert themselves and to shape any policy reappraisal. Labour's economic failure acted as a stimulus to those who argued that more radical strategies were needed. The increased strength of the left was reflected in a number of areas. Within parliament, the main forum for leftwing MPs, the Tribune group, though still small, had grown in size.[4]

Discontent with the leadership was not confined to rebel MPs. Leftwingers were joined by others, including many trade union leaders, who wanted to register their dissatisfaction at the government's performance. Widespread discontent was evident in speeches at Labour's conference in 1970 in the aftermath of defeat.[5] Relations between senior trade unionists and PLP leaders were very poor as a new alignment of union leaders became apparent. In the mid-1950s with few exceptions union leaders were content to support the Labour leadership. By the early 1970s three of the most important union leaders were frequently identified as leftwingers, while another was close to the party's centre. Jack Jones, Hugh Scanlon and Lawrence Daly were all associated with the left while David Basnett was seen as something of a centrist. Representatives of the right, including Joe Gormley and Frank Chapple were still important but the two largest unions were now in the hands of the left (at a time when they had become more important). Jones and

Scanlon, elected in 1968 and 1967 respectively, had a strong influence on Labour party politics and shared a similar outlook.[6] Other figures aligned with the left, such as Clive Jenkins of ASTMS and Alan Fisher of NUPE, also became influential. The result was that trade union leaders represented a greater diversity of political opinion than they had since the war. Union representatives on Labour's NEC were more assertive and prepared to support radical proposals. For example, in 1970 Alex Kitson and Bill Simpson, union representatives on the NEC, separately pushed the NEC (without success) to take a more radical line in response to economic policy resolutions at the Labour conference.[7]

Leftwing unions had increased weight within the Labour party by 1970. In the late 1960s and early 1970s the Transport and General Workers and the Engineers continued to grow in size and became even more dominant.[8] By 1974 the top two unions controlled 31 per cent of the total conference vote compared to 24 per cent in 1953. Also increasing in size were unions such as NUPE and ASTMS. These unions were more closely aligned to Labour's left than in the past.[9] It would be inaccurate to conceive of a leftwing union block voting rigidly on all issues but after 1970 some unions were much more supportive of radical proposals as the successful votes for such motions at conference indicate.

The TUC had also become more radical, albeit gradually, since the late 1960s.[10] Historically the TUC had shown little interest in the detail of economic policies and produced few documents on the subject. In 1968 in a new departure the TUC produced an *Economic Review*, the first of what became an annual publication. The spur to this development was the Labour government's incomes policy and deflation. The first few *Economic Reviews* were relatively orthodox but by the early 1970s they came to advocate more interventionist measures. Some leftwingers claimed that the early 1970s was marked by the development of a new radical trade unionism, typified by work-ins and a growing socialist consciousness.[11]

From the mid-1960s onwards there was a general shift leftwards in the membership of Labour's NEC. By 1970 Denis Healey was the only moderate member of the constituencies' section. Leftwingers also dominated the women's section and made gains in the union section. Only three rightwing members of the shadow cabinet, James Callaghan, the party treasurer, Denis Healey and Shirley Williams were able to get elected to the NEC after 1970. Accurately estimating the balance of the left and the right on the NEC in this period is difficult. Some members, especially trade union representatives, were unaligned and changed their stance from issue to issue as well as over time. Samuel Finer's estimate is that by 1974 the left had a majority on the NEC of 15 to 14.[12] It seems likely that by 1973 the right and the left occupied similar sized groupings on the NEC, the left fractionally bigger.

Leftwingers were much more active in using the NEC as a base for developing radical policies. According to Ian Mikardo, after 1970, 'The National Executive Committee realised that we had to write a fresh political prospectus getting us back to the party's purposes which the government had partially abandoned.'[13] Leftwing MPs such as Tony Benn, Ian Mikardo, and Judith Hart used the NEC as a platform from which to lobby for a new strategy. It was around such figures that an organised, theoretically motivated and determined leftwing emerged in the policy-making process of the party. Benn was especially important.[14] He had not been noted as a leftwinger before 1970 but responded to the government's failure by moving sharply leftwards. A skilled and persuasive orator, he frequently topped the poll for the constituencies' section of the NEC and was chairperson of the party during 1971–72 and of the influential Home Policy Committee between 1975 and 1982. Labour's shift leftwards was also manifested by a new assertiveness on the part of the party conference. From the late 1960s it reacted against the government's policies and was less prepared to accept the bland reassurances of the party leadership. The NEC was defeated on eight votes, six concerning economic issues, between 1970 and 1973. In 1970 the conference passed a motion which deplored the refusal of the PLP to act on conference decisions.[15]

The Revisionist's disappointing experience in office diminished their authority and left them exhausted, even bewildered. Wilson did not appear to be an effective leader, indeed he devoted much time to writing his memoirs after 1970. The UK's membership of the EEC presented the right with a major problem in the early 1970s.[16] Many Revisionists were passionate supporters of it, but official party policy was to oppose the initiative of the Conservative Prime Minister, Edward Heath, to take the UK into Europe. In October 1971, 69 Labour MPs defied their whip and voted in favour of joining the EEC: given Conservative defectors going in the opposite direction, their decision determined the result. The issue isolated and divided the Revisionists as some, including Tony Crosland, did not vote in favour of entry. It would be wrong, however, to underestimate the influence of Revisionism within Labour. Most of the PLP leadership was associated with either the right or centre of the party. Only five leftwing MPs were elected to the shadow cabinet between 1970 and 1974: Tony Benn, Barbara Castle, Michael Foot, Peter Shore and John Silkin. Around 80 per cent of the places went to non-leftwingers. In such circumstances it was by no means certain who would dominate policy-making within the party in the aftermath of defeat.

THE EMERGENCE OF THE LEFT'S ALTERNATIVE ECONOMIC STRATEGY

The review of Labour's policy was launched officially after the party conference in October 1970. At the conference the NEC accepted a motion moved by NUPE calling for a new socialist programme. To formulate it, the NEC decided to upgrade the status of the party's policy-making sub-committees.[17] Rather than being advisory, these sub-committees became a direct part of the policy process of the Labour party. Six were set up to report to the Home Policy Committee which was in charge of the development of domestic policies (and in turn reported to the NEC).[18] Two of these were concerned with economic matters: the Financial and Economic Affairs Sub-Committee and the Industrial Policy Sub-Committee. Figure 5.1 below indicates the structure of policy-making during the period 1970–74.

From their formation, leftwingers put a great deal of time and effort into these committees. The influence that they were able to exert was important in determining the proposals that Labour eventually adopted. The new commit-

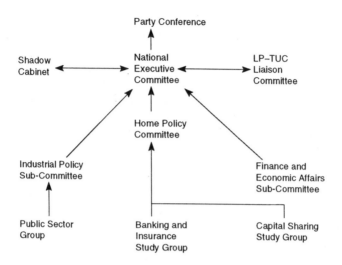

Figure 5.1 Policy-Making in the Labour Party 1970–74

tees were chaired by members of the NEC and not from the shadow cabinet. PLP members served on the committees but they had no special influence or status. It was intended that there should be more PLP members (4–6) than NEC representatives (3–4) on them.[19] In practice, however, there were usually more NEC members than cooptees from the PLP. Leftwingers also ensured that many of the outsiders drafted onto the committees to help policy development were sympathetic to their objectives and shared similar political values. One of these outsiders, Stuart Holland, an economist at Sussex University, was the major architect of the left's proposals for planning and public ownership.

The committees were serviced by the party's increasingly leftwing research staff. In July 1970 the research department called for 'a radical recasting' of policy.[20] Staff had more time to develop research proposals because they did not have to service the more mundane requirements of ministers. One memo noted that in office 'much time has been wasted in "consultations with ministers" often to the detriment of our concentration on future policy matters'.[21] Labour's research secretary, Terry Pitt, was sympathetic to the left and was able to influence the membership of the new committees and their remits. Also important was another leftwinger Geoff Bish who served as secretary to several of the economic policy-making committees and eventually took over from Pitt as research secretary.

The prime success of leftwingers in the policy-making process was in the domination of the Industrial Policy Sub-Committee. This committee captured the policy-making initiative when it undertook a consideration of employment policy. Terry Pitt had already given the committee a wide remit but it went on to decide that it could not look at employment aside from more general questions about the overall nature of economic strategy.[22] In contrast to this quick start, the largely Revisionist-orientated Finance and Economic Affairs Sub-Committee was slow to get going. Ian Mikardo as party chair was a member of both groups and knew that the opportunity existed for the Industrial Policy Sub-Committee to dominate Labour's policy development. Having taken control of the policy process, this committee, supported by various academics and research staff, became the focus for the elaboration of the new proposals. Michael Meacher, one participant, later called it 'the engine of change'.[23] Peter Shore wrote that it 'was to make the running in policy-formation for the whole of that parliament'.[24]

The Finance and Economic Affairs Sub-Committee had a narrow remit and much less impact. It failed to produce any discussion papers before the preliminary draft of Labour's 1972 policy document was put together.[25] Its draft for that publication was negative in orientation, comprising an attack on the Conservative government. It held only four meetings in the first year and focused on taxation issues rather than general economic policy.[26] After the 1971 party conference the Industrial Policy Sub-Committee decided to set up another policy-making body, the Public Sector Group, to study public ownership.[27] Judith Hart, the chair of this group, argued for and achieved a small homogeneous committee rather than one with more broadly based membership. The core members of this group were Judith Hart, Richard Pryke, an economist at Liverpool University who was a strong supporter of the nationalised industries, and (later) Stuart Holland.[28] The homogeneity of the group allowed it to focus in more depth on particular proposals. It was responsible for the core of the new strategy regarding public ownership and for the plan to establish the National Enterprise Board.

Both the Industrial Policy Sub-Committee and the Public Sector Group spent a considerable amount of time developing detailed policies during the winter of 1971–72. A central participant in the discussions within both committees was Stuart Holland. Earlier he had worked with some Revisionists, including Roy Jenkins, over proposals for a state holding company but his ideas were more radical than Jenkins could countenance. In January 1972 Holland joined the Public Sector Group and, with Richard Pryke, drafted proposals for a holding company which became the basis for the National Enterprise Board.[29] In March 1972 Geoff Bish, as secretary, suggested that the Industrial Policy Sub-Committee look at a paper on planning by Holland.[30] Soon after, Holland was coopted onto the committee and he produced a steady stream of papers.[31] The first 'Planning and Policy Coordination' made the case for planning agreements or 'Programme Contracts' as they were then called. It drew extensively from the French experience and was not as radical as his later papers. By the stage Holland introduced his theoretical argument about the nature of monopolisation in the autumn of 1972 the proposal for planning agreements was firmly rooted within Labour's policy-making process.

The NEC published a provisional policy document, *Labour's Programme for Britain* in July 1972.[32] The Industrial Policy Sub-Committee was largely responsible for the economic policy sections of it.[33] The draft proposed the introduction of Programme Contracts, and the extension of public ownership in each sector of the economy. But these policies were not developed in any detail and there was no theoretical underpinning at this stage. The Industrial Policy Sub-Committee had only recently turned to such matters as Programme Contracts. The reference to the holding company was toned down because such work was still ongoing in the Public Sector Group.[34] When published, *Labour's Programme for Britain* was more moderate and was presented as an interim document. The state holding company was still seen largely as a means of regional regeneration. The published programme included neither planning agreements nor the full proposals for the

NEB though the policy committees were by now working on such areas. It may be that leftwingers had been careful to tone down some of the radical language in order to avoid conflict.[35] Their reasoning was that the ideas in the document would be passed in principle at the 1972 conference and could then be tightened up before the final draft was produced in 1973.

The Attitude of the Revisionists

Many Revisionists wanted only a limited policy rethink after 1970. Roy Jenkins was worried by the inconsistency that a shift in policy would imply. He claimed that the party 'must strike the right balance between continuity and new thought. If the country believed we are saying different things just because we are freed from the responsibilities of government, they wouldn't think much of that.'[36] Harold Wilson and Tony Crosland expressed similar views.[37] Some Revisionists were slow to engage in policy-making and did not appear to take the formal processes of the party seriously. Much of Crosland's time was taken up with his frontbench responsibilities. Many of his speeches and his amendments to the draft of *Labour's Programme 1973* were about housing matters.[38] Moreover Crosland was never a member of Labour's NEC and was therefore excluded from its policy discussions. He was coopted onto the Industrial Policy Sub-Committee in 1971 but he, and others, appeared rather aloof and detached. In September 1971 Crosland told a Fabian meeting, 'No one can say the Party is in sight of formulating a better set of policies than we had in June 1970.'[39] He was a poor attendee and less of a driving force than might have been expected: in two years he made under half the meetings of the Industrial Policy Sub-Committee.[40]

Roy Jenkins was also hesitant in getting involved in policy-making. He attended only three meetings of the Finance and Economic Affairs Sub-Committee.[41] In April 1972, unable to accept Labour's advocacy of a referendum over EEC membership, he resigned as the party's deputy leader and also as chair of the Finance and Economic Affairs Sub-Committee.[42] Other rightwingers resigned as well so lessening their impact on policy-making. The issue divided the Revisionists as not all gave up their party positions.[43] Unsurprisingly the split caused some ill-feeling between former allies. Jenkins's replacement as shadow chancellor and as chair of the Finance and Economics Affairs Sub-Committee, Denis Healey, was a defence and foreign affairs specialist. By his own admission he knew little about economics and the committee continued to make slow progress.[44]

Many leading Revisionists, such as Crosland, preferred making policy through public speeches rather than the time-consuming procedures of policy-making committees.[45] David Lipsey said that the Industrial Policy Sub-Committee 'probably drove him mad. He held a degree of contempt for those making economic policy.'[46] He regarded many of the NEC groups as unrepresentative. Jenkins liked to work with a small team of his own advisers drafting major speeches which could then be picked up by the media. Crosland proposed that policy-making be based on smaller bodies drawn from the membership of the shadow cabinet and the NEC alone.[47] He criticised the split between the NEC and the PLP: 'It inhibits, rather than assists, the development of long term policy.'[48] In 1971 the Policy Coordinating Committee, made up of representatives from the PLP and the NEC, was set up.[49] Few meetings were held and little came out of them.

For several reasons rightwingers did not worry unduly about the first moves towards a commitment to public ownership from within the Industrial Policy Sub-Committee. First, the proposals, as indicated in Chapter 4, especially for the state holding company, were open to interpretation.[50] Revisionists were not at first opposed to this proposal: Jenkins floated the idea, although in a different and more limited form. Second, it may well be that the right did not study the proposals in any depth. Edmund Dell argued that rightwingers were not that interested in industrial politics because of its limited possibilities: it represented 'boredom for the right and excitement for the left'.[51] Third, for Revisionists, UK entry into the EEC was the central issue and they concentrated their energies on securing it. Fourth, it may be that Revisionists knew how weak they were within the party. Fifth, it was of little surprise that the party should move leftwards in opposition: activists had the chance to assert themselves. It appears to have been a feature of Wilson's leadership to let the party make policy as it wished, safe in the knowledge that the policy proposals could be ignored in office. The result of the Revisionists' weakness and the time it took for the details of the left's proposals to emerge was that there was relative unanimity over economic policy in the first years of opposition. The leadership did not pay a great deal of attention to economic policy, but, in as much as they did, they could stomach the measures proposed and put their own interpretation on them.

The Formation of the New Proposals

In October and November 1972 a radical and complete version of the left's strategy for planning was presented at meetings of the Industrial Policy Sub-Committee. In October the committee agreed 'that Labour's existing policies were unlikely to be enough'.[52] The new proposals, drafted largely by Holland, went beyond those in *Labour's Programme for Britain*.[53] The centrepiece was the introduction of planning agreements through which the state would put pressure on companies to adopt various economic targets. Holland's papers contained a detailed theoretical argument about the trend to monopolisation in the economy and its consequences. He also made the case for increased public ownership of profitable firms. By November, the radical extent of the proposals was apparent and Crosland was alarmed, asking, 'why the tasks [of planning] could not be done with the existing machinery, and the existing public enterprises, given a firm government approach'.[54] Other questions were raised about the likely effectiveness of the plans but Holland's arguments for planning agreements were adopted by the committee. Crosland now became a regular attendee at the Industrial Policy Sub-Committee, together with another Revisionist Edmund Dell, in an attempt to modify policy. They put forward a series of objections: 'In theoretical terms Holland was the enemy.'[55] Dell later remembered that 'the two of us were isolated'.[56]

In the spring of 1973, the Public Sector Group produced a draft document outlining the proposal for the National Enterprise Board.[57] The conception of the NEB, developed by Holland and Pryke, was different to that in earlier Labour documents. Rather than regional regeneration, the NEB was to be the basis for control across the economy through the public ownership of 25 of the top 100 companies. They argued that competitive public enterprise was the most effective means of countering monopolistic private firms. Again, Crosland tried to moderate these proposals. But such last minute resistance was ineffective and, despite Crosland's misgivings, Labour's proposals for the state holding company were passed by the Industrial Policy Sub-Committee.[58] These measures were then published as a Labour Party Green Paper entitled *The National Enterprise Board* in April 1973. Its publication provoked a furore because it contained the explicit commitment that Labour should takeover 25 top companies through the NEB.

On 16 May 1973 the draft of *Labour's Programme 1973* was considered by a joint meeting of the shadow cabinet and the NEC.[59] The draft had been toned down by the NEC but Judith Hart suggested afterwards that she and her leftwing colleagues had played up the rhetoric of the document before the NEC saw it so that token changes could be agreed without altering the substance of the proposals.[60] Despite this modification, there was considerable opposition from the shadow cabinet. At an earlier meeting on 13 May its members had raised a series of points which were amplified at the session with the NEC. Along with Harold Lever, Shirley Williams and others, Tony Crosland argued that the policies were economically unrealistic and electoral suicide.[61] Virtually the entire meeting on 16 May was spent on Labour's economic and industrial strategy. Nearly every member of the shadow cabinet present spoke against the proposal to nationalise 25 firms and many other aspects of the programme came under criticism. Even the normally nonchalant Wilson registered concerns over the detail of the left's plans including the proposal for an Official Trustee to run some companies.

Members of the shadow cabinet felt from the drift of the debate at the joint meeting that the NEC would remove the proposal for the 25 and modify the outline for the NEB as the document was finalised.[62] In summing up Wilson said that the final version could be left to the NEC.[63] But at the last NEC meeting prior to publication there was another huge row over public ownership.[64] Wilson led the opposition saying that the manifesto committee would in any case have the right of veto. He was joined by Callaghan and Healey while Benn and Hart defended the left's suggestion for the 25 companies. The meeting lasted eleven hours and six NEC members had to leave. Denis Healey decided eventually that the issue should be put to a vote (which the moderates should win) and he proposed to delete the offending passage. In fact he had miscalculated and his amendment was lost, by seven votes to six.[65]

Three present abstained and thirteen members of the NEC were absent. John Cartwright, nominally a rightwinger, had voted with the left. Apparently he was annoyed at a comment of Healey's about the Cooperative movement (of which he was a member) and in a fit of pique decided to vote in favour of the 25 being taken over. As unexpected as Cartwright's vote, was the abstention of Wilson on the grounds that the leader should not vote on such matters. Given that Wilson said that he and the shadow cabinet would veto the policy, he might have been expected to use what powers he had to seal its fate. John Chalmers, nominally a rightwinger, had also abstained. He had been chair of the Industrial Policy Sub-Committee and was much influenced by the arguments from it. The abstentions and John Cartwright's bizarre behaviour assured victory for the left and on 7th June 1973 *Labour's Programme 1973* was published including the commitment to nationalise 25 companies.

Wilson issued a strongly worded statement saying that he and the shadow cabinet would not be bound by the promise. It was, he claimed, 'inconceivable' that Labour would implement such a policy of nationalisation.[66] Tony Benn described Wilson in his diary as 'the man who has been trying to stop the industrial policy all summer'.[67] Peter Shore wrote later that Wilson and 'virtually the whole shadow cabinet' felt the commitment to be 'madness'.[68] Crosland described the nationalisation as 'a half-baked proposal'.[69] His former assistant, Wilfred Beckerman, attacked it and the whole industrial strategy: 'The proposal to nationalise 25 companies is only one of the more lunatic proposals. But the rest are not much better.'[70] Harold Lever later called it a 'a naive dream'.[71] Jenkins, Hattersley, and Healey all made speeches within a few days distancing themselves from the proposal.[72]

For a time it looked as though Labour was heading for a major crisis over the issue. Many leftwingers and some senior officials were incensed at the leader's response to what they regarded as the party's approved policy. However, Wilson was able to head off a clash. He came down in favour of substantial public ownership at NEC meetings and at the party conference.[73] He was helped by leftwinger Michael Foot who opposed the commitment to the 25 companies and by Jack Jones who apparently assured Wilson that the TGWU would not vote against the Labour leadership on this matter.[74] More importantly as the result of a procedural device, Wilson was able to get the conference to vote against the proposal for the 25. The composite motion, put together by the Conference Arrangements Committee, which called for the public ownership of the 25 went on to demand that Labour should go on to take over the top 250 major monopolies. Unsurprisingly, the NEC joined Wilson in opposing the composite and the conference overwhelmingly rejected it, thus ditching the plan for the 25. Ironically Benn spoke for the NEC against the motion. The 1973 Conference did not actually vote on *Labour's Programme 1973*, something that Lewis Minkin discovered, in his extensive interviews, few had realised.[75] *The Times* noted the significance of this decision and called Wilson 'characteristically tactical'.[76] The result was that the proposal for the 25 was dropped as party policy, though Labour remained committed to a substantial extension of public ownership of profitable firms.

THE TUC–LABOUR PARTY LIAISON COMMITTEE

The Industrial Policy Sub-Committee and the Public Sector Group were not the only important economic policy-making bodies within the Labour party after 1970. Another policy-making forum developed between Labour and the trade unions, which proved to be of considerable importance, especially over the development of the party's anti-inflation policy. As already noted, Labour had left office with its relations with the trade unions in a parlous state. The unions felt that they had been made scapegoats for the government's own failures. But, as the policy of the Heath government (considered below) antagonised the unions, so they came to accept the potential value of improving relations with the party.[77] In 1971 several liaison meetings were held between Labour and the TUC as to how to oppose the industrial relations legislation of the Conservative government. These meetings went well and as a result a formal body, the TUC–Labour Party Liaison Committee, was set up in January 1972 as the basis for policy discussions with six (later seven) representatives each from the shadow cabinet, the NEC, and the TUC.[78]

There was a hesitant start as some trade unionists remained suspicious of the PLP leadership. They were still concerned that Labour would attempt to impose some form of wages policy on them.[79] The focus at first was entirely on industrial relations.[80] Gradually the meetings helped, along with the influence of Jack Jones, to restore a degree of harmony to party/union relations. By late 1972 the Liaison Committee had turned from industrial relations to broader matters and with the document *Economic Policy and the Cost of Living*, Labour and the unions reached an agreement over how inflation might be controlled.[81] The Social Contract proposed that the government offer price controls and reflation in exchange for an ill-defined form of voluntary restraint on the part of the unions. The agreement was vague and leftwingers, trade unionists and Labour's leaders all drew different conclusions about it. Leftwingers saw it as an integral part of their industrial strategy. For the most part, trade union leaders saw it as a commitment to free collective bargaining and reflation.[82] Labour's leadership hoped that it was the potential basis for an agreement on wages.[83] Barbara Castle later wrote that 'it was the nearest they could get to voluntary incomes policy'.[84]

Despite their differences of emphasis, there appeared to be some agreement between the unions and leftwingers. NEC members and union representatives were united against the policies of the last Labour government. The central concern of the union leaders was to ensure that there would be no incomes policy under a future Labour administration.[85] The left's industrial and economic strategy envisaged inflation being tackled mainly through price controls and planning agreements. The unions responded positively to this plan, if only because it rejected wage restraint. Thus the demands of the unions that incomes policy be rejected led them broadly to endorse, with the Liaison Committee's Social Contract, the industrial strategy developed by the NEC. Those sections of *Economic Policy and the Cost of Living* dealing with the wider aspects of strategy were imprecise but it approved public ownership and industrial democracy as well as price controls.[86] One TUC official later described it as being 'of necessity very broad brush stuff'.[87] Wilson's biographer, Ben Pimlott, concluded that the document indicated 'the advances made by the left'.[88]

Whether or not many trade union leaders had a substantive commitment to the industrial strategy is another matter. Individual union leaders such as Hugh Scanlon, Alan Fisher and Jack Jones frequently advocated the kind of policies being developed by Labour. But their central concerns included the repeal of the Industrial Relations Act, reflation, and manpower policies.[89] In comparison Labour's industrial plans were a low priority. From interviews, Stephen Bornstein and Peter Gourevitch concluded: 'Those [unionists] who endorsed the NEB planning and intervention proposals did so, we suggest, for essentially tactical reasons, seeing in them a handy form of political cement for solidifying a pro-union coalition in the party.'[90] Meacher admitted later that union leaders 'didn't get involved in policy-making, even in industrial policy other than superficially'.[91]

The PLP leadership were unhappy about the left's industrial strategy but they went along with the Social Contract because they wanted to maintain a united front with the unions.[92] Labour also needed union support because it was an important part of their electoral strategy: that the party could replace Heath's confrontation with conciliation. They could put their own interpretation on exactly what the Social Contract meant. The PLP tried without success to get a firmer commitment to wage restraint in Labour's 1974 manifesto. The TUC remained hostile to the use of the phrase 'incomes policy'.[93] David Lipsey remembered that the Social Contract was the best deal that could be negotiated: 'It was fig leaf. Some people deluded themselves that it had a content. Crosland's hope was to build on it. But the attempt to do that came too late.'[94]

Developments within the TUC over economic policy generally mirrored those within the Labour party after 1970, as its economic proposals gradually became more radical. Support for the party's new policies was expressed at the 1973 congress and a motion advocating Labour's new plans for public ownership was passed.[95] Individual unions such as the TGWU also endorsed Labour's industrial strategy.[96] Between 1970 and 1974 the annual TUC *Economic Review* was usually a pragmatic document, partly because it was aimed at the Conservative government. By 1972 it endorsed a moderate version of the left's proposals but without any detail or theoretical base. In 1972 a Labour research paper, in comparing the party's policies with those of the TUC, concluded: 'The remarkable thing that emerges from this analysis is that – at this stage at least – there are no policies which can be confidently placed in the category "genuine disagreement" on policy concepts.'[97] One official commented, 'There was a great similarity between congress motions and Labour party conference resolutions.'[98]

THE HEATH GOVERNMENT

Labour's policy-making during 1970–74 took place in an environment shaped decisively by the Conservative government under Edward Heath.[99] Heath had been elected on a distinctive programme which was at odds with the prevailing postwar consensus and his initial policies were based on laissez-faire approach incorporating tax cuts, selective rather than universal social policy, a rejection of incomes policy, the abandonment of industrial intervention and reform of the trade unions. This course did not last and the government embarked on a series of U-turns including reflation, the imposition of an incomes policy, and the introduction of a new Industry Act which gave it sweeping powers.

The Conservative government affected Labour policy-making in important ways. Heath, quite possibly more than any Labour politician or union leader, was responsible for the rapprochement between Labour and the unions. The Industrial Relations Act of 1971 created a new framework for trade unions – one which virtually all unions rejected and with which they refused to cooperate. Such a measure demonstrated to unions the value of rebuilding their relations with the Labour party. Without the Industrial Relations Act, the unions and the Labour party might well have remained at a distance. Moreover Heath's economic policy served to legitimate the radical measures proposed by Labour leftwingers. His initial policy package served to indicate that the consensus between the parties was at best fragile. Later, in his interventionist U-turns, Heath further legitimatized the policies advocated by the left by conceding much of their argument. Labour party internal memoranda after 1972 contained references to the way that Heath's interventionism was preparing the ground for the party's own policies.[100] In a memorable phrase, Benn spoke of 'Heath's spadework for socialism'.[101]

CONCLUSIONS

The publication of *Labour's Programme 1973* was a remarkable triumph for the party's leftwingers. How had they succeeded in getting it to adopt formally their policy? The development of the strategy reflected and was linked to Labour's general shift leftwards after 1970. The content of the new policy can also be attributed to more specific factors. Rightwingers had not engaged actively in the policy process. They did not enjoy policy-making and possibly thought it irrelevant. Some appeared complacent and lazy concerning their commitment to committee work. It may also be that shadow cabinet members felt they had much more legitimacy than activists by virtue of their position as MPs and concluded that they could ignore aspects of party policy that they disliked. Overall, the Revisionist right was weak both in terms of organisation and ideas after 1970.

Leftwingers, by contrast, dominated the most important policy-making committees. They had taken the policy process seriously and developed proposals carefully and with a strong theoretical backing. The Industrial Policy Sub-Committee had met frequently and covered a great deal of ground. By contrast, the Finance and Economic Affairs Sub-Committee had met less often and had focused on narrow subject matter.

The homogeneous Public Sector Group had developed radical proposals while the more diverse Banking and Insurance Group had been bogged down in argument and failed to reach agreement.[102] While some committees were poorly attended by Revisionist members of the PLP, certain leftwingers were assiduous in their regular presence. This commitment meant that leftwingers, even those who were coopted onto committees, had been able to exercise substantial influence. Some Public Sector Group meetings were attended by as few as two coopted members together with the group research secretary.[103] These individuals, such as Stuart Holland, had been able to have considerable impact in shaping the policies which had been developed and then passed through the Industrial Policy Sub-Committee, the Home Policy Committee and the NEC before being published. Leftwing policy-makers had received considerable backing from Labour's research staff. Eric Heffer noted that research staff had been 'very influential indeed'.[104] Dell remembered, 'Geoff Bish was not a pragmatist. The research department strongly supported the shift to the left.'[105]

The left had secured strong support from the NEC, the party conference and affiliated trade unions. However, it would be wrong to exaggerate the role of these elements of the party. The NEC promoted the policy review and it discussed and amended the proposals which came before it. But by that stage the strategy had already taken shape and no substantive changes were made to the economic measures the left had designed. Moreover, the NEC should not be treated as a monolithic body. Many on it were unhappy with the new proposals, while others did not want to take sides. The vote over the proposal to nationalise twenty-five companies in 1973 indicated the bitter divisions within the NEC.

The conference was an important forum for discussion and there was considerable pressure within it after 1970 for radical policies. In 1972 Alan Fisher, leader of NUPE, told the conference that *Labour's Programme for Britain* was too moderate.[106] However, the proposals that made up the left's strategy did not originate from the party conference but from its policy-making committees. Although Labour had moved leftwards, there was little concern from ordinary party members about the detail of the new policies. Conference was important in legitimating the left's proposals but it initiated few policy developments. Even when it did vote directly for a new measure, such as its proposal in 1971 to nationalise the banking sector, it did not lead to the policy going into party documents.[107]

Trade unionists proved to be important backers of the left's proposals, both on the NEC and TUC–Labour Party Liaison Committee. Like the conference, they were less important in launching original proposals. A partisan commentary on the period concluded, 'The trade unions have tended to *react* to political ideas coming from within the Labour party... [the unions] supported these party policies fairly automatically but did not discuss them deeply.'[108] Individual unions voted at their own conferences and the TUC endorsed proposals similar to those developed by Labour but in doing so they followed the party's lead. Bornstein and Gourevitch concluded that, in its economic proposals, 'the TUC was drawing on the findings of policy groups established within the Labour party'.[109] Moreover union support was limited and vague. It may have owed more to tactical considerations than principled support.[110] It is not apparent that there was sustained grassroots interest in the left's strategy, let alone pressure for it from trade unionists. While the TUC passed motions supporting aspects of the left's policies, they were not presented in detail as an economic package. Economic strategy was not a central concern for the TUC and other issues were perceived as more important.

Labour's leftwingers could claim that they had developed a coherent and theoretically sophisticated set of measures in the aftermath of 1964–70. Those measures had emerged, above all, from the policy-making committees of the party and the work of theorists such as Stuart Holland. It was in these committees that the new proposals had been discussed and the new policies hammered out. The open structure of Labour's policy-making process was important in determining this outcome. Alan Budd wrote that '*The Socialist Challenge* [Holland's book] had thus become the basis of a radical programme which once again put ownership and planning at the centre of the Party's programme'.[111] One political commentator stated: 'Stuart Holland had virtually single handedly committed a great party to his particular view in the vital industrial policy field.'[112] This quote may over-emphasise Holland's contribution but the lead in policy-making within the Labour party was taken by the network of committees reporting to the NEC. Lipsey remembered, 'Party policy was drawn up by a dozen enthusiastic leftwing people, the research department and a few intellectuals. Trade unionists went along with anything which wasn't going to cause them problems with their own organisations.'[113] Like-wise academic George Jones claimed, 'A small group had captured key policy-making institutions at transport house and foisted doctrinal policies upon the party.'[114]

Labour's Programme 1973 neither reflected a consensus within the party over policy nor owed its triumph to its content and coherence. Labour's policy was determined neither by the support for it within the wider party nor by the theo-retical characteristics of its ideas. The successful adoption of the AES was not the result of lobbying and pressure throughout the party, though the conference voted for the measures. The support that leftwingers had garnered for their strategy should not be over-emphasised. *Labour's Programme 1973* was their creation. But many in the party were not involved in the arguments between the Revision-ists and the left over economic strategy. The extent and depth of support for the new strategy within the party was open to question. The crucial determinant of Labour's policy-making process was the institutional structure of the party which allowed leftwingers to exert so much influence on policy drafts which in turn were subsequently endorsed by the NEC and the conference. The organisation of the party's policy-making process is a central aspect of any explanation as to how leftwingers had been able to get Labour to adopt a radical strategy.

6 Labour in Office, 1974–79

INTRODUCTION

Labour returned to office in March 1974 and policy-making within the party received less attention than it had during the preceding years. The paucity of consideration given to internal policy matters was not surprising because Labour had adopted a new programme and now had the opportunity to implement it. Five years later when Labour lost power in May 1979, supporters of its industrial strategy were bitterly disappointed: they claimed that the government had not carried out the plans contained in *Labour's Programme 1973*. In this chapter I examine the attempt to realize the Alternative Economic Strategy – as the left's strategy was termed by 1975 – while Labour was in government. I outline the development of the legislative proposals produced by Tony Benn and others at the Department of Industry after March 1974. I look at the impact of these industrial policies in practice and I consider to what extent the party's strategy was shaped by the difficult economic circumstances that the government encountered. I also examine the developing relationships between the Labour government and the wider party. My central aim is to explain why Labour failed to introduce the measures which were contained in its election manifesto.

THE IMPLEMENTATION OF LABOUR'S INDUSTRIAL STRATEGY

As Secretary of State for Industry, Tony Benn was responsible together with his ministers, Eric Heffer and Michael Meacher, for the development of legislative proposals for Labour's industrial strategy.[1] Labour's February election manifesto, *Let Us Work Together – Labour's Way Out of the Crisis*, was more moderate than *Labour's Programme 1973*. It did not spell out what powers the new industry act would involve. No details were given about planning agreements and the explicit commitment to take over the 25 firms was dropped. But the manifesto maintained sweeping intentions for profitable public ownership and it stated explicitly that the NEB would be created in accordance with Labour's earlier proposals.[2] In May 1974, Benn laid out his radical legislative intentions at the Liaison Committee including a proposal for the introduction of 100 planning agreements as soon as possible through which all financial aid from the state should be channelled.[3]

The White Paper *The Regeneration of British Industry*, published in August 1974, contained a very different set of proposals.[4] The terms in which planning agreements and the NEB were conceived had changed dramatically. Planning agreements were presented as the basis for harmonious relationships in industry and were not designed to change the behaviour of private firms. They represented a much weaker arrangement as there would be no statutory requirement on a firm to conclude one. Where an agreement was made it would not be legally enforceable. State aid would still be available for firms that did not engage in the system. The White Paper noted that firms must have freedom to respond to market changes and that rapid adjustment might be needed to any agreement. The target of 100 agreements in the near future was dropped – a decision described by the Tribune group as a 'big climb down'.[5] Some elements of the left's original proposals remained. Unions would be involved in discussions but they would not be a formal party to the agreement. They would be entitled to the information that firms disclosed except in cases of commercial or national interest. The White Paper indicated that firms would be asked to disclose information even if ultimately they did not reach agreement with the government.

The National Enterprise Board was explicitly presented as a reincarnation of the Industrial Reorganisation Corporation with some additional functions. It was to be a new source of investment capital for manufacturing firms. It would normally take a stake in the companies to which it provided finance. The NEB would help firms in difficulties and promote economic reorganisation. It would be guided by commercial criteria and make a profitable return on its activities. Acquisitions by the NEB should be by agreement and any new public enterprise appeared to require the support of the relevant private firm. Any acquisition over £5 million would require the support of the government. The proposal for an Official Trustee was retained but only tentatively and specifically to keep a private firm running which would otherwise close. The White Paper suggested that the number of full nationalisations of companies would be limited and would only occur either to prevent a foreign takeover or to stimulate a sector where competition was weak. The document went on to state that these proposals (plus some earlier mentioned specific cases) represented the limits of Labour's nationalisation intentions.

The White Paper was written in a different language to earlier documents. The extreme hostility to private industry stood out in Benn's Liaison Committee memo. Industry was to blame for the UK's economic problems. Benn talked of 'securing the compliance' of firms, of 'empowering a tougher bargaining stance for government' and of reducing monopoly power. The first paragraph of the White Paper stated Labour's support for private industry and the whole tone of the document was far removed from the aggressive wording used earlier. It was much more consensual and spoke of the need for government and industry to be 'partners' working in a 'closer, clearer and more positive relationship'.[6] Labour's October manifesto retained the commitment to planning agreements and the NEB but they were couched in the terms of the August White Paper and not the party's earlier policy documents.[7] In November Healey's budget gave financial aid to private firms – a move many leftwingers interpreted as being at odds with Benn's industrial strategy.[8]

At the end of January 1975 the government's Industry Bill, made up of four sections, was published.[9] The first section outlined the proposals for the NEB. There was a limit of £700 million made available for it and, if it was to acquire more than 30 per cent of shares in a firm or invest more than £10 million, it would require the consent of the Secretary of State for Industry. The second section gave the government powers to prevent foreign acquisition of companies, possibly through public ownership. The third section outlined the planning agreements system. The fourth section concerned provisions for the disclosure of information. The Secretary of State would have the power to ask certain companies to release specified information. After certain safeguards had been observed this information could be passed to trade unions.

The Industry Bill remained close to the proposals of the White Paper and in some areas continued the dilution of Labour's original intentions. The proposal for the Official Trustee was now dropped altogether. Disclosure of information was no longer linked to planning agreements but to a much more general process. Labour's research department was concerned that the level of funding for the NEB would provide inadequate leverage on the economy.[10] It was also noted that the Bill offered little inducement for firms to enter into planning agreements and that the powers of the NEB appeared unclear. The Bill did not state that the NEB would require a company's consent before it invested in that firm, though the Prime Minister apparently told the CBI that this would be the case.[11]

When the Industry Act finally received assent in November 1975 further changes had occurred. The government made 83 amendments to the legislation at the report stage.[12] Most of the Act was concerned with the establishment of the NEB. It had limited funds and limited autonomy. Planning agreements, now termed a 'voluntary agreement', were dealt with briefly – in only one clause.[13] When the Industry Department published a discussion document on the contents of agreements in August 1975, the stress was on the help such arrangements might be in allowing the government, rather than private firms, to adjust: 'One of the principal benefits of Planning Agreements is likely to lie in the opportunity they will provide the government across the whole field of its activities to attune its policies to the needs and plans of industry.'[14] The original argument had been reversed: the planning agreement would help the government meet the needs of firms and channel assistance to them.[15] The powers to obtain information were limited and subject to a complex process. Without the cooperation of firms, unions could only receive information through the Secretary of State for Industry (who was no longer obliged to pass it on). There were extremely limited penalties for those firms which did not meet the requirements over disclosure.

By the time the Bill completed its passage in Parliament, Tony Benn had been replaced at the Department of Industry by Eric Varley and a new industrial strategy had emerged from within the government. A new White Paper was issued following a meeting of the NEDC at Chequers on 5th November 1975. Ministers called this the launch of the government's industrial strategy – in contrast to their earlier efforts.[16] The ideas outlined in *An Approach to Industrial Strategy* were very different to those Labour had been elected on and amounted to a return to tripartite discussions. The document, drafted by Eric Varley and Denis Healey, called for a flexible and realistic approach and stressed the need for cooperation between management and unions.[17] The new White Paper retained references to planning agreements in the form of voluntary arrangements, although it was unclear what the substance of any would be. Eric Varley called them 'planning discussions'.[18] The new approach placed considerable stress on the role of the private sector and emphasised the need for sufficient profits to be made to finance investment. The government proposed a new voluntaristic framework based on a separate analysis of each industrial sector to see what was needed to improve its economic performance. Sector Working Parties, often based on Economic Development Councils were set up to examine many areas of manufacturing production. Wilson, with characteristic rhetoric, called the White Paper 'a major breakthrough on the problem that has dogged the British economy ever since the war'.[19]

In practice, the NEB, far from becoming the promoter of structural change in the profitable areas of the economy, came to focus on propping up 'lame ducks', firms in financial trouble, something it had been devised explicitly not to do.[20] It had a limited impact: between 1975 and 1978 the Government gave around £15 billion to industry, less than £1 billion (or about 8%) went through the NEB.[21] By 1979 the NEB had received £777 million of which well over half, £569 million, had gone on British Leyland.[22] In all 95% of its funds went on lame ducks. Even Harold Wilson admitted subsequently that 'its preoccupation with British Leyland. . . . has crippled its finances'.[23] The first chair of the NEB, Sir Donald Ryder said that he saw its main function as 'the provision of equity funds for private companies which could not obtain enough funds from private sources'.[24] The statement of aims produced by the NEB in March 1976, unlike the Industry Act, made no mention of public ownership, profitable or otherwise.[25] The NEB's 1977 guidelines made it explicit that it had no powers of compulsory purchase.[26] It could only purchase more than 10 per cent of a company's shares against the wishes of its directors, if the Secretary of State for Industry agreed. In the event the NEB never bought against the wishes of a company.[27]

Planning agreements were even less impressive in practice.[28] Few were considered and only two ever agreed. Only one of these was with a private sector firm, the Chrysler car company which signed a deal in March 1977. The agreement was part of a massive injection of government funds to save the company from collapse. It is unclear how much impact it had on company policy, although arguably industrial relations improved. In 1978 Chrysler broke the agreement when they sold out to the French company Peugeot Citroen. The provision for the disclosure of information was equally ineffective. In 1977 trade unionists noted: 'The procedure for obtaining information under these sections [of the Industry Act] is extremely cumbersome and to the TUC's knowledge no use has been made of it to date.'[29]

Public ownership and planning were not the only aspects of the AES that the Labour government moderated in practice. During 1974 it maintained the level of aggregate demand in the economy. But in 1975 the government made the first in what became a series of dramatic cuts in public spending. Although some reflation did take place later in the Labour government, it was nowhere near the level advocated by leftwingers. Likewise the administration made little progress over industrial democracy. The government prevaricated before setting up in 1975 a committee under Sir Alan Bullock which failed to reach agreement. In January 1977 the majority report of the committee proposed that companies with over 2000 employees should be compelled to accept equal numbers of worker representatives onto their

boards.[30] The employer representatives on the Bullock Committee were utterly hostile to these proposals.[31] The government proposed legislation based on a moderated version
but, in the face of further opposition from the CBI, it was
postponed. A White Paper was produced in May 1978 but
no legislation followed.

The attempt to promote worker cooperatives was also
unsuccessful as the firms which received funds ran into difficulties. In 1974 Benn authorised aid to the Meriden motor-
bike factory, the KME factory, and the Scottish Daily News.
There was strong opposition to such endeavours from
rightwing ministers and civil servants.[32] Ultimately all failed.
Labour used price controls in its attempt to control inflation but they were based on those inherited from the Conservative government.[33] *The Economist* described them as
ineffective after their relaxation in the November 1974
budget.[34] The Prices Secretary, Shirley Williams claimed that
price controls had to be adjusted to help investment.[35] Between 1975 and 1978 the basis of Labour's anti-inflation policy
was a formal incomes policy. The resulting mix of controls
on wages and prices was far removed from the policies for
which Labour's left had lobbied. During 1975 the Labour
party adopted import controls, but the government rejected
their use. Overall little progress was made in the implementation of the kind of policies that Labour had come up with
in opposition.

The Left's Isolation within the Government

Throughout 1974–75 there was considerable disagreement
and personal animosity, especially in private, between the
Prime Minister, Harold Wilson and the Secretary of State
for Industry, Tony Benn. From the start Wilson appears to
have been determined to moderate Benn's plans.[36] He did
not stop Benn going to Industry but he did cut down the
responsibilities of the department by hiving off trade and
consumer affairs matters. The Prime Minister carefully moni-
tored work within the Department of Industry: a member
of his policy unit, Richard Graham, was appointed as a special
adviser on industrial matters – a 'Benn watcher'.[38] Wilson
was not alone in his opposition to Benn's proposals – Treasury

ministers were unanimously hostile. Denis Healey said that
the recovery of the private sector should be the government's
priority.[38] Joel Barnett, Harold Lever and Edmund Dell were
also frequent critics of Benn's plans. His interventionist memo
at the Liaison Committee in May 1974 received considerable adverse comment. Benn later remembered, 'The majority of the cabinet did not understand or support the policies
on which we were elected.'[39]

It was during the drafting of the White Paper, *The Regeneration of British Industry*, that the depth of opposition to
the left's industrial strategy became apparent.[40] The government's original intention was to produce a Green Paper laying
out its proposals. Given that Labour was a minority government and there would shortly be another election, Wilson
was concerned that the radical extent of Benn's plans would
result in poor publicity and scare voters. He decided that
the industrial strategy should be the subject of a White Paper,
rather than the more general Green Paper: 'It was vital that
no vague statements or half-veiled threats should be left
around for use as a scare by the opposition.'[41]

The draft was written by a committee under the leftwing
Minister of State for Industry, Eric Heffer. Benn decided
that Heffer's draft was too mild and toned it up. Heffer had
deliberately played down the language in an attempt to
anticipate criticisms of it. As he feared, the spiced up draft
came under heavy criticism when discussed at the government's Industrial Development Committee in June 1974.[42]
Healey attacked the effect that Benn's plans would have on
the confidence of private industry. He claimed that the NEB
would not be profitable and he opposed any measures to
promote industrial democracy. James Callaghan, Shirley
Williams, and Harold Lever made similar points. Wilson was
concerned by the lack of accountability and powers of the
NEB. Crosland said Labour had to promote profits. *The
Economist* stated that ministers were horrified by the draft.[43]
Only two ministers spoke in Benn's defence, Peter Shore,
the Trade Secretary, and Willie Ross, the taciturn Scottish
Secretary.

Wilson called Benn's draft 'a sloppy and half-baked document, polemical, indeed menacing in tone'.[44] His press secretary, Joe Haines remembered that 'Harold read it briefly,

quite angry, said it was woolly rubbish and that he would have to do it himself'.[45] Bernard Donoughue, the head of the policy unit, wrote later that it was written in a 'very aggressively interventionist language'.[46] Publicly Wilson did little to hide his antipathy for Benn. His irritation over his Industry Secretary was clear in an interview with Robin Day. Wilson said, 'I have taken charge of the whole operation, when I thought the thing was getting out of hand in too much public debate.'[47] Michael Meacher felt that Wilson had initially been caught off-guard by Benn's designs for the NEB: 'I'm sure that Wilson did not expect Benn to go as far as he did. I expect he thought we'd have something like the state merchant bank that Wilson favoured in the 60s.'[48] Richard Graham remembered, 'Wilson went around telling everyone that the NEB was going to be the IRC again. . . . and of course the planning agreements were to be made voluntary. And the moment that Benn accepted that they should be voluntary, the policy had lost its teeth.'[49]

The Prime Minister produced a new draft, considerably altered in scope and intention.[50] Benn called the Wilson document 'absolutely crazy', claiming the party's policy had been 'thrown away'.[51] He quoted Wilson's apparently radical speech to the 1973 party conference in support of public ownership as relations between the two deteriorated further. Wilson disowned his own words, saying 'that was part of a longer sentence'.[52] The Prime Minister's draft was endorsed by the cabinet. Barbara Castle wrote of Benn, 'One after another his colleagues turned on him.'[53] *The Regeneration of British Industry*, was a 'pale shadow' of his original intentions.[54] Wilson wrote in the introduction that 'we need both efficient publicly owned industries, and a vigorous, alert, responsible and profitable private sector' – a phrase that both Healey and Jenkins had used in speeches. *The Guardian* headline read 'Benn's industry blueprint turns pale pink'.[55]

Before the October 1974 election a major shift had taken place in Labour's industrial strategy. Benn later remembered, 'Wilson, in the manifesto for October 1974, transformed its contents from being based on the policy of the conference to being based on the decisions of the government in the previous six months. He was able to weaken it substantially.'[56]

Given his poor relations with Wilson, Benn was relieved to be re-appointed to the Department of Industry after the October election. Robert Jenkins records an anecdote which illustrates the direction of government policy by October. When he got back to the Department, Benn found three briefs prepared by civil servants: one for the Tory party, one for the Labour party and one specially for Benn should he be re-appointed![57]

The Industry Bill, published in January 1975, owed much to Wilson's redrafted White Paper. Further amendments took place. Ian Mikardo remembered, 'The Prime Minister's intentions were clear in the drafting of a series of amendments to the Industry Bill in committee. It was clear-cut: the Bill was being emasculated.'[58] One MP on the Standing Committee said, 'Here was this Bill which was a watered down version of a White Paper which was a watered down version of a watered down manifesto commitment. And then the three ministers on top of this kept bringing what were really wrecking amendments.'[59] Ben Pimlott's conclusion was that Wilson 'had indicated from the outset his intention to kill off' the industrial strategy. After the October election he 'sought to bury it'.[60] Benn did not manage to see these limited measures come into operation as Secretary of State for Industry. In the June 1975 referendum the UK voted to stay in the EEC and Wilson took the opportunity to demote Benn by moving him to the Department of Energy. Benn hesitated about the switch, considered resignation and finally accepted the move. The reshuffle indicated the strength of Wilson and rightwingers within the government.

It was not just rightwingers within the Labour government who were opposed to Benn's plans. Throughout 1974–75 the Confederation of British Industry expressed significant hostility to planning agreements and the NEB. Considerable pressure was put by businesses on the government, directly in meetings and indirectly through a media campaign which ridiculed Benn and vilified his proposals. The CBI's President, Ralph Bateman said that they were 'certain to create further damage' to industry.[61] He suggested that firms would not cooperate with the government whilst Campbell Adamson hinted later that extra-legal action was considered.[62] Harold Wilson went to considerable efforts to placate the concerns of industry and many leftwingers felt that concerted lobbying of the CBI had a critical impact on policy development. Supporters of Benn felt that civil servants were equally antipathetic to Labour's industrial strategy and claimed that they deliberately sabotaged the development of legislation at the Department of Industry.

The Impact of Economic Circumstances on the Industrial Strategy

One assertion made by ministers was that deteriorating economic conditions during 1974–75 had rendered the left's strategy impractical. The proposals had been conceived in different conditions to those that the Labour government faced once in office. The period saw high inflation, a massive balance of payments deficit, and increasing unemployment. Firms reported falling profits and bankruptcies increased – there were persistent rumours about some major companies being in severe trouble including one of the big four banks.[63] Employers argued that low investment was a consequence of profits being squeezed by higher wages, price controls and taxation and that if the government wanted higher investment it would have to accept higher profits and ease taxation. It could not expect higher investment simply through planning agreements. As early as August 1974 *The Guardian* suggested economic difficulties would derail Labour's plans.[64] Throughout much of its time in office the government found itself reacting to extremely unfavourable economic circumstances.

In its original conception Stuart Holland had wanted the NEB to 'reinforce and promote success rather than simply to underwrite or subsidise failure'.[65] Leftwingers assumed that adequate profits existed and that the problem was the willingness of firms to invest. The economic crisis of 1974–75 suggested that profits were lower than leftwingers had presupposed. This situation raised difficult questions (some of which Revisionists had articulated earlier): what should the government do in such circumstances? Should it help companies in economic difficulties and under what criteria and conditions should help be given?

Rightwingers in the government claimed that the recession was evidence of non-buoyant profits. In June 1974 *The*

Economist claimed that profits had fallen below 10% of total domestic income for the first time.[66] *CBI Industrial Trends* reported collapsing business confidence in August 1974 caused by rising costs, liquidity problems, political and economic uncertainty and the threat of increased government intervention. *The Times* called it 'one of the gloomiest surveys ever'.[67] Healey acknowledged the squeeze on profits in the November 1974 budget.[68] He eased the Price Code and provided relief on stock appreciation to reduce corporation tax. His argument was that higher profitability – not planning agreements – was the key to higher investment. Wilson made similar points – as did the Governor of the Bank of England.[69]

Some leftwingers recognised these problems. Michael Foot, writing later, was blunt: 'The policies which the party had devised were insufficiently apt and immediately applicable.'[70] Peter Shore argued planning agreements were abandoned 'under the pressures of a virtual collapse of industrial investment'.[71] One party researcher concluded, 'Labour didn't have a strategy for managing weak capitalism. Planning agreements were based on a period of high profits. It was not clear what should be done when profits were falling so dramatically.'[72] Others retained their support for the left's strategy. They doubted the fall in profits that so many firms claimed.[73] Stuart Holland had long argued that firms underreported profit levels: 'There was considerable question whether there was a general profits crisis and collapse in 1974.'[74] Labour's research department took a similar position: 'We doubt whether the squeeze on companies' liquidity and profitability during 1974 was anything like as harsh as suggested in some quarters.'[75]

Furthermore leftwingers claimed that if the firms needed public aid then they should open up their books and be prepared for the state to take equity in them. It should be up to firms to demonstrate their economic difficulties and conclude a planning agreement in exchange for help.[76] Richard Clements argued, 'The government must not simply bend to pressure from business about liquidity problems; it must continue to insist that they open up their books and show us the true level of their problems.'[77] Meacher claimed the economic crisis strengthened the left's case because it was indicative of the failure of the market economy: 'The worse it became, the more policies like that were necessary.'[78] Holland remained optimistic about the prospects for industrial intervention. He felt that by using 'planning agreements to reactivate investment projects which companies had postponed, an increase in investment could be achieved in less time than was generally believed and at a lower cost in resource terms'.[79] Both Holland and Hughes claimed that the Labour government's help for companies had boosted profits.[80]

The dispute over profit levels during 1974–75 was unresolvable. Evidence supported the rightwingers' claim that profits were being squeezed.[81] Leftwingers such as Holland simply challenged the accuracy of the evidence. Benn suspected that Wilson had allowed the economic crisis to get worse in order to panic the government and unions into a more moderate strategy: 'The economic crisis following the referendum was, in my opinion, masterminded to create the atmosphere in which it was possible to get a pay policy and drop the industry policy.'[82]

Whether Wilson masterminded it or not, the economic crisis was an important factor in motivating unions to support the government in the summer of 1975. Soon after the EEC referendum, accelerating inflation and intense pressure on sterling led to a currency crisis. The level of wage and price increases indicated that the original voluntary Social Contract was ineffective in containing inflation. It was replaced by a formal incomes policy which consisted in its first year of a flat rate increase of £6 a week. Coming on top of public spending cuts in April, the introduction of an explicit and relatively rigid incomes policy amounted to a substantial modification of the government's original economic strategy. Trade union leaders, galvanised by Jack Jones, reluctantly accepted the new arrangement. In 1976 and 1977 the government was able to secure renewed support for restraint, albeit in a very informal manner in the latter year. The result was lower inflation and a gradual improvement in the economy's performance. However, in 1978 the government was unable to reach agreement over pay restraint with the unions and proceeded to go it alone with a tough 5 per cent norm for increases. The policy fell apart as a succession of private and public sector groups challenged it in the so-called Winter of Discontent. Labour had been elected to office partly on the basis of its ability to work with the unions: the Winter of Discontent left that cooperation in tatters and the government subsequently went down to election defeat in May 1979.

RELATIONS BETWEEN THE LABOUR GOVERNMENT AND THE LABOUR MOVEMENT

As the Labour government progressively watered-down and then abandoned the industrial plans developed in opposition there was little resistance from within the party. This lack of advocacy for the AES is somewhat surprising given the left's strength within Labour. Leftwingers dominated the NEC. In 1975 Denis Healey, the last moderate in the constituencies' section, lost his place. By 1978 the only moderate member of the cabinet elected to the NEC was Shirley Williams. Despite this, for much of the period, the NEC remained loyal to the Labour government and was, as a result, defeated twenty-two times at the five conferences between 1974 and 1978.[83] As the government moved further from the policy on which it was elected, so tensions developed between the cabinet and the NEC. By 1977 the NEC was much less supportive of the government and prepared to back resolutions which were openly critical of the cabinet.

Labour's left should not be considered as a monolithic block in this period (as in any other). A new political alignment emerged as some leftwing union leaders became especially supportive of the Labour leadership. Jack Jones and Hugh Scanlon extended considerable loyalty to the government. Jones was a pivotal figure: his support for the introduction of the flat rate £6 policy in 1975 was critical in its acceptance by the labour movement. Together with Michael Foot, Jones provided the basis for a leftwing position which was less doctrinaire than Benn's and more sympathetic to the government's difficulties (of which Foot was a senior member). For Jones and Foot sustaining the Labour government was a higher priority than ensuring the implementation of the industrial policy. The *Tribune* meeting at the

Labour conference in 1975 was symbolic of this shift in political alignment: Ian Mikardo launched into an attack on the government's pay policy and the role that Jack Jones had played in organising it. Foot sat in embarrassed silence while Jones responded by storming to the platform and making an angry off-the-cuff reply.[84]

Despite disagreements between leftwingers as to what was the appropriate course of action, Labour's policy documents continued to advocate the strategy developed in opposition. Policy-making bodies met infrequently and some were inactive altogether. In April 1975 the party's Home Policy Committee endorsed a paper by Benn, co-authored with his assistants Frances Morrell and Francis Cripps.[85] They argued that the left's strategy was 'the only alternative' to Tory policies.[86] Later in 1975 the Industrial Policy Sub-Committee was responsible for the draft of *Labour and Industry*, a statement passed at the party conference based on the Benn, Morrell and Cripps paper.[87] It was savaged by Healey in a rare appearance at the Home Policy Committee – ministers, given their official obligations and isolation from the party's policy trajectory, were poor attendees at the sub-committees.[88] In the summer of 1975 the Industrial Policy Sub-Committee proposed that Labour introduce import controls – a commitment which was also included in *Labour and Industry*.[89] The research department, now under Geoff Bish, also promoted the AES and frequently criticised the government's economic policy.

Between 1974 and 1976 the central policy task within the party was in drafting a new policy programme. The Home Policy Committee proposed that the conference should vote on the new document – unlike *Labour's Programme 1973*.[90] The new programme upheld the AES in strong and robust terms and Labour leaders were critical of it. Callaghan stated that he was not responsible for the content of the document, telling the NEC: 'He must make it clear that the government's overall economic and financial strategy remained as announced by himself and the Chancellor of the Exchequer.'[91] When the draft was agreed by the NEC in May 1976 Callaghan was absent.[92] The document's introduction noted with some understatement 'there are policies and priorities outlined in this document on which the government takes a different view'.[93] *The Times* stated that the document was a 'considerable embarrassment' to ministers with its 'breath-taking extension of state intervention right across the nation's business life'.[94] Peter Shore later described the new programme as 'an indirect, but unmistakable, critique of the current policies of the Labour government'.[95]

When party officials met ministers to discuss policy, Eric Heffer, now a backbencher, remarked, 'the two sides seemed to be talking completely different languages'.[96] A string of subsequent documents detailed the split.[97] One contrasted the 'completely voluntary' approach towards industry of the government with the 'bargaining plus selective sanctions' of the party.[98] When a joint NEC/Cabinet Working Party on Industrial Policy was set up – as part of the discussions over the next manifesto – it failed to reach agreement. Defiant ministers gave no ground either in discussions with Labour delegations or at PLP meetings. Bish complained that ministers treated the NEC as an ordinary pressure group.[99] The differences persisted as the Home Policy Committee and the NEC pushed, without success, for new policies from the government.[100]

Leftwing MPs articulated the AES, often in *Tribune* newspaper, but they had little impact upon the government's economic trajectory.[101] They were constrained by Labour's perilous situation in the House of Commons – by the spring of 1976 the government had lost its majority. They were well aware that a determined backbench rebellion could defeat the government at a time when the party's electoral prospects were extremely poor. Foot later wrote, 'We were not prepared, any of us, to risk the alternative; opening the gate to the Tory enemy, through resignations and the destruction of the government.'[102] Jack Jones remembered, 'Even though, try as we might, we could not change the government's outlook, we were not prepared to do anything that might threaten its existence'.[103] *The Times* summarised the impotence of the Tribunites: 'An important part of it [the PLP] is systematically opposed to the government's current economic policy. Yet the same members wish to sustain the government in office.'[104]

The party conference was equally limited in its impact on the government. At first the harsh economic situation allowed the government to deflect criticism and draw a residual loyalty from the party. By 1976 such support could no longer be sustained. This conference rejected the government's spending cuts and passed *Labour's Programme 1976* and *Banking and Finance*. The 1978 conference was a disaster for the Callaghan administration as relations between party and government plumbed new depths. A resolution attacking the government's incomes policy was passed, whilst one supporting its economic strategy was lost.

The TUC endorsed the components of the AES between 1974 and 1979 in a variety of motions at its annual congress. Its *Economic Review* backed a moderate but recognisable version of the AES, including the industrial strategy and protection. Whilst more sympathetic to the government than leftwingers, trade union leaders were critical of its post-1975 industrial strategy.[105] The 1977 *Economic Review* asserted, 'An industrial strategy based solely on the sectoral approach is doomed to failure.'[106] Many union leaders continued to support the left's strategy in various forms and hoped to bring about changes to the government's economic strategy.[107] But their endorsement was often implicit and limited and they also called, on occasion, for more moderate policies. Some leading trade unionists had doubts about elements of the detailed package of measures advocated by the left.[108] Moreover, these figures placed a high premium on loyalty to Labour ministers. Jones said, 'I felt just as strongly as the MPs about the cuts but keeping the government in office was still more important.'[109] The AES was not as great a priority for trade unionists as such matters as reform of industrial relations, the strengthening of workers' rights and the establishment of the conciliation service (ACAS) – all areas where progress was made. Union leaders could claim some success in influencing the government: 'Some policies [such as planning agreements] didn't come off. But some did; for example, the Employment Protection Act, child benefits and the increase in pensions.'[110] Bornstein and Gourevitch concluded that, given achievements elsewhere, many union leaders in 1975 'were satisfied to allow the industrial policy component of the Social Contract to be neglected, delayed or watered down'.[111]

The economic crisis of the summer of 1975 persuaded

some union leaders that more radical measures would have to wait until the situation had improved.[112] Benn claimed the unions were so frightened and so loyal to the government that they were not prepared to do anything.[113] Many unions did not engage directly in the debate over economic and industrial policy: only a few produced pamphlets advocating the AES.[114] The failure of union leaders to achieve amendments to the government's industrial strategy eventually led to a deterioration in government-TUC relations. Even Jack Jones acknowledged, 'The record of the government in industry fell far short of its promises.'[115] However, the government's persistence with an incomes policy and the impact of the public expenditure cuts carried out during 1975–76 were more important than industrial matters in this deterioration.

The most surprising quarter that gave support to the AES was the government itself. Having undermined the industrial strategy in practice, the government was party to a series of Liaison Committee documents which proposed the very measures it had abandoned. In 1976 the Liaison Committee described the introduction of planning agreements and greater accountability in industry as indispensable and urgent.[116] Similar proposals, including increased funds for the NEB were made in the next two years.[117] Liaison documents supported aspects of the government's economic strategy and some leftwingers were concerned that they might water down party commitments.[118] But the publications were unambiguous in emphasising the interventionist measures of the AES. It was remarkable that ministers were prepared to endorse these documents and it is hard to explain their reasons for doing so, other than in cynical terms as public relations exercises to promote unity and a price worth paying to get union support for the incomes policy.

CONCLUSIONS

Unsurprisingly leftwingers were bitterly disappointed by the results of Labour's industrial strategy. Many felt that the party's original strategy had been effectively derailed before it was passed through parliament. Stuart Holland claimed that developments to the Industry Bill amounted to 'a complete reversal of the strategy of the 1974 manifesto'.[119] Barbara Castle wrote later, 'The Act which finally emerged had no teeth.'[120] Labour's research department concluded: 'The government's approach is, however, now precisely that which was rejected by the party.'[121] Leftwingers were equally disappointed by the impact the new institutions had. One concluded that the NEB was 'a safety net for private capital' while Doug Hoyle described it as 'a toothless tabby cat'.[122] A research department document concluded, 'The NEB as it is now is a very different animal from that originally conceived in party policy.'[123] The Industrial Policy Sub-Committee expressed concerns over the aims of the NEB, its lack of finance and its preoccupation with lame ducks.[124] The magazine *Management Today* concluded: 'No British institution has ever diverged quite as sharply as the NEB from the track which its designers tried to lay down.'[125]

During 1975 Harold Wilson found it easy to isolate leftwingers, to modify their strategy and to weaken their influence on his government. In attempting to introduce radical legislation, Tony Benn received little support. He said later, 'There really was no top level trade union support for the industrial policy at the crucial moment when it was reversed.'[126] Michael Meacher claimed, 'None of the senior trade union leaders were champing at the bit to get the new industrial policy implemented.'[127] The dearth of support for the industrial strategy was true of the whole labour movement. Stuart Holland felt that what was lacking was 'very considerable pressure from the trade union movement, not only from the shop floor but especially from the trade union leadership'.[128] One trade union official remembered, 'Unions were unclear about how the industrial strategy would work out.'[129] The IWC had often tried, apparently with little success, to generate grassroots support for the AES – something many of its advocates felt was indispensable. Jack Jones admitted later, 'There was not enough understanding of planning agreements and the NEB.'[130] Such a lack of concerted support from the wider Labour movement was indicative of the way that the left's strategy had developed internally within the party's policy-making committees.

The economic and industrial strategy the Labour government

eventually implemented was far removed from the policy that the party had formally adopted in opposition. There are many potential explanations for Labour's abandonment of the policies on which it was elected, including the hostility of the CBI and civil servants to the strategy, the perilous economic situation the government encountered and the manifest animosity of so many of the party's leading figures to Benn's interventionist proposals. These causes are interrelated. Rightwingers within the government frequently claimed that the policies had to be jettisoned precisely because of the antipathy of industry and because they were unsuited to the existing economic environment: Labour's plans would do immense damage to business confidence if unaltered.

However, the role played by either employers or civil servants in the development of economic and industrial policy during 1974–79 should not be over-emphasised. Had the party been united in favour of implementing *Labour's Programme 1973*, the hostility of the CBI or bureaucrats might have been decisive or at the very least provoked intense conflict. But such conflict between a united Labour government and either employers or civil servants never erupted. The success of employers and bureaucrats in modifying the left's strategy stemmed from the already expressed hostility of ministers. Without the support of rightwingers the outcome might well have been different and would definitely have resulted from a different trajectory of choices. The limited support for the AES within the Labour government and the party was of greater importance to the fate of the left's strategy than the attitude of either the CBI or the civil service. Despite the economic crisis a modified leftwing strategy could have been initiated. Labour ministers did not attempt it because they did not support the arguments that the strategy was based upon.

Rightwingers opposed the AES for a number of reasons – they feared the electoral consequences of such policies, and because they regarded the measures as unnecessary, extremely bureaucratic and potentially very damaging. Many were antipathetic to the left's proposals from their original adoption during 1972–73.[131] Brian Sedgemore claimed that Wilson had 'systematically worked for its [the industrial strategy's] destruction'.[132] Barbara Castle noted in her diary, 'It is perfectly true that Harold Lever, Denis [Healey] and Eric [Varley] have succeeded in emasculating the party's industrial policy. . . . The Varleys and the Healeys don't even try to win consent for more radical policies.'[133] Labour's research department concluded that there was 'a very real divergence. . . . The government seems willing to see a return to the relatively high profits (and especially retained profits) in order to encourage investment. This seems to go very much against party thinking.'[134] Benn and Holland reached similar conclusions.[135]

The Labour party had little impact on the Labour government. One internal paper concluded later, 'The government displayed little serious interest in the policy making effort of the NEC and the party except, that is, on occasion to repudiate publicly certain of the proposals put forward.'[136] Ministers resolutely refused to accept the arguments developed in Labour documents – including those from the Liaison Committee to which they were a party. *Labour's Programme 1976* was endorsed by the conference in the same week that Callaghan made his famous speech attacking conventional reflation – an indication of the turmoil within the Labour party. The result was mounting frustration within the Labour party and towards the end of the Labour government relationships between ministers and the NEC deteriorated badly. The relative economic failure of the government added to this frustration. Not only was a Labour government once again ignoring the views of its party base, but it was failing to provide the economic results which might justify such an attitude. The cause of the split between party and government was not just the failure to implement the AES but also the government's persistence with its incomes policy. The overall result was that when Labour lost office in 1979, it was once again in a poor internal state and many activists felt acutely frustrated at the lack of progress that the government had made regarding its economic strategy.

7 Politics and Policy-Making in the Labour Party after 1979

INTRODUCTION

Labour's return to opposition in May 1979 did not result in a far-reaching assessment of the party's economic strategy, though debate about it continued. Instead the election defeat marked the beginning of a period of severe internal conflict within Labour which had profound and negative consequences for the party. Denis Healey later called it 'an exhausting struggle for the survival of the Labour party'.[1] Peter Shore termed it 'an orgy of venomous recrimination'.[2] The election result gave a huge stimulus to demands for constitutional change within Labour. The overriding reason for reform, leftwingers argued, was the need to render the party leadership accountable. What was wrong with Labour's performance in office was not the policies for which the left had fought so hard in the early 1970s, but the decisions and patronage of the leadership.[3] The government's rejection of the left's economic strategy (as well as other policies) led directly to the demands for constitutional change to the party structure and the bitter internal power struggle which marked the years after 1979. Chris Mullin claimed, 'The problem is that we have the policies but we don't have an accountable leadership prepared to make a serious effort at implementing such policies.'[4] Michael Meacher stated, 'There is little point in having a radical agenda in opposition, if later in office the substance of it is ignored.'[5]

Policy-making was not abandoned during this period. But for much of the time those in control of Labour's internal machinery were content to reassert already agreed proposals including the Alternative Economic Strategy. In this chapter I examine the relationship between political debate and policy-making in the party between 1979 and 1983. I analyse the nature of the demands made by leftwingers for constitutional reform and the explanation they gave for the necessity of such reforms. I go on to consider the policy-making that did take place. I also assess the contributions of rightwingers and of the trade unions to the formation of economic policy. First, I outline the relationship between left and right within the Labour party after 1979.

LEFT AND RIGHT IN THE LABOUR PARTY AFTER 1979

The left was already active and strong within Labour in 1979 and the shift into opposition served to increase its power.[6] With the party out of office leftwingers had greater freedom and Tribune MPs were prepared to use it, many taking part in criticism of the PLP leadership. Activists were disappointed at Labour's performance: their disillusion reinforced the shift leftwards and generated considerable hostility which was directed at the Labour leadership.[7] Leftwingers, partly through the work of the Campaign for Labour Party Democracy and other groups, were extremely well organised.[8]

The changes within the union movement which had strengthened the left ten years earlier continued at the end of the 1970s. The left-inclined Transport and General Workers Union, under its new leader, Moss Evans, affiliated 1.25 million members to Labour in 1979. The union represented 18 per cent of the whole conference vote – a slight increase on the figure of 1974. Another left-leaning union, NUPE had also grown and was now the fourth largest union affiliated to Labour. As after 1970, some senior trade union leaders, such as Moss Evans, Alan Fisher and Clive Jenkins were associated with the left. Leftwingers were not guaranteed control of Labour's conference but for a time they had a substantial degree of support from unions within the party.

Labour's left dominated the NEC between 1979 and 1981. In 1979 *The Times* estimated that there were 17 leftwingers on it.[9] No member of the shadow cabinet was elected to it, placing James Callaghan and Michael Foot as leader and deputy leader in an even more isolated position than usual. In 1981 a major rearrangement took place in the NEC's membership as five leftwingers were defeated.[10] As a result rightwingers had around 14 votes on the NEC with the remaining members being split into two camps. These reflected the fragmentation that had taken place within the left during 1981. The 'soft' or old left comprised six places while the 'hard' or new left held nine seats. The left could still outvote the right – but only if it was united. The shift on the NEC was confirmed in 1982, as rightwingers gained a majority of seats.[11] These developments reflected a major realignment within Labour and many trade unions.

The right within the PLP was not well organised in 1979 and could not account for the failure of the Labour government in the same appealing way that the left could. David Owen, a leading rightwinger, wrote later, 'There was no adequate response to the Labour left from the centre or right of the Labour party. Exhausted after years in government and intellectually demoralised, they were content to fight a defensive battle.'[12] Another rightwing Labour MP wrote later of the moderates that their economic policies 'had been discredited by the winter of discontent'.[13] A *Daily Telegraph* leader was scathing: 'It is not possible to underrate the courage and resolution of the demilitarised zone of politics, the Labour right.'[14] Rightwingers were increasingly divided amongst themselves as to what was the appropriate strategy to combat the left. Despite these weaknesses rightwingers dominated the shadow cabinet.

The Political Debate within the Labour Party

Before the 1979 election, the drafting of Labour's manifesto had demonstrated to leftwingers the imperative of reforming the party's constitutional structure.[15] For two years considerable effort by the research department, along with various working groups, had gone into producing a document combining a defence of the government's record with radical future proposals. In April 1979 the NEC proposed using the resulting package of papers as the basis for the final version.[16] At the last minute, however, these documents were abandoned and the final draft was prepared by two of Callaghan's research assistants, Tom McNally and David Lipsey. Leftwingers were scathing about the version with which they were presented. Geoff Bish wrote, 'It was appalling. Not only did it ignore entire chapters of party policy; it over-turned and ignored many of the agreements which had been laboriously hammered out in the NEC/cabinet working group.'[17] Callaghan claimed a leader's right of veto as to what went into the finished product.[18]

The drafting of the manifesto became very important for leftwingers as evidence of what was wrong with the party's structure.[19] It was seen as symbolic of a much wider malaise stemming from the power of the leader. Bish concluded, 'At the heart of the problem of agreeing the manifesto lay the unwillingness of the Labour government to concede to the party any real measure of joint determination or joint control in terms of policy or strategy.'[20] Eric Heffer described the final session as 'one of the most painful meetings I have ever attended'.[21] The moderate manifesto and Callaghan's attitude provided a huge stimulus to the campaign for reform. One of the major reforms that leftwingers demanded was the amendment of Clause V of the party constitution to give sole control of the manifesto to the NEC.[22]

Within a few days of the election defeat, an informal, intense and acrimonious debate was launched throughout the party about what had gone wrong. Much of the dispute focused on bitter personal accusations against the Labour leadership. Aside from such indictments, the theme of constitutional change was dominant. Tony Benn, increasingly the focal point of much leftwing discontent without Labour, made clear the link that he perceived between leftwing measures and accountability in the party when he called for both a reformed structure and radical policies.[23] He announced that he would not stand for election to the shadow cabinet so as to be free to speak his mind. In June 1979, with Eric Heffer, he produced an eight-point plan for reform to the party's constitution.[24] Other leftwingers made similar arguments. The MP Frank Allaun argued, 'We had a fine programme which was not carried out. Our job now is to find a way of so democratising the movement that the parliamentary leaders implement the decisions [made by the movement].'[25] Ian Mikardo asserted, 'Our problem isn't that we didn't have good policies – it is that our good policies . . . don't get implemented.'[26] Benn claimed, 'At present the main barrier to the realisation of that hope [for the implementation of radical policies] seems to be the use of the power of the leader.'[27]

Electoral defeat did not stimulate a policy reappraisal. Leftwingers were adamant that a successful socialist party would require more than the kind of policies which Labour had developed before 1974. It would need a structure to render the leadership accountable to the members.[28] The Campaign for Labour Party Democracy focused on three constitutional reforms to bring about such a structure. They were: mandatory reselection of MPs between each election; NEC control of the manifesto; and an electoral college to elect the leader.[29] In the summer of 1979 the left-dominated Organisation Sub-Committee of the NEC suggested that the leadership election system and the reselection of MPs should be considered by the party conference.[30] In July the NEC agreed to look at these issues and proposed that it alone should decide the manifesto's contents.[31] In contrast to these demands, policy matters seemed almost unimportant.[32] Labour's parliamentary leadership rejected the reforms. The shadow cabinet described the NEC's attitude and lack of consultation as 'deplorable'.[33]

At the 1979 conference the themes of accountability and reform of party structures were frequently raised. Frank Allaun repeated his charges against the party leadership, stating that reforms would 'ensure that our parliamentary leaders respond more closely to the wishes of the rank and file'.[34] He was not alone: the anger that had been bottled up by activists during the latter years of the government was now released. Many delegates accused the Labour government of ignoring party policies and of betraying the movement. The conference went so far as to pass a motion that the general election defeat 'was due largely to the failure of the Labour government to implement policies agreed by successive party conferences'.[35] Clutching policy documents Tom Litterick announced:

> It was these documents that your NEC sought to incorporate in our election manifesto this year. Then, one day in April of this year, Jim Callaghan turned up and that is what he did to your policies [Litterick dropped the documents].

The end result was that fatuous, vacuous document called 'the Labour party election manifesto of 1979'. Jim'll fix it, they said. Ay he fixed it. He fixed all of us. He fixed me in particular.[36]

Ron Hayward, the party's general secretary, asked rhetorically, 'Why was there a winter of discontent? The reason was that, for good or ill, the cabinet, supported by MPs, ignored congress and conference decisions.'[37] Leftwingers were successful in two out of three proposals for constitutional change: mandatory reselection of MPs was passed as was NEC control for the manifesto.[38]

A year later at Labour's conference in 1980, the left retained the upper hand as the party voted for a new electoral college (rather than MPs) to choose the party's leader.[39] In a rare success for rightwingers, however, the conference now voted against NEC control of the manifesto. Soon afterwards in October 1980 James Callaghan resigned as leader of the Labour party and was replaced by Michael Foot. Although long associated with the left, Foot was not close to Benn and had emerged from the Labour government closer to the centre of the party. Denis Healey, the right's candidate for the leadership, became Foot's deputy. Foot's election served only to exacerbate the disillusion of some rightwing MPs – though some of them, enough to deny Healey victory, had voted for Foot in order to ensure his election and so provide a greater justification for their subsequent decision to leave the party.[40] In March 1981 those rightwingers who felt that the struggle for the Labour party was lost, left it to found the Social Democratic Party.[41]

At 3.30 am on 2 April 1981 Benn announced he was a candidate for the party's deputy leadership against Healey. The reason for the odd timing was straightforward: a Tribune group letter was about to call on Benn not to stand and he wished to pre-empt it.[42] Benn claimed that the election would allow the party to discuss policy and he laid out the policies that he stood on – including 'the alternative economic strategy'.[43] More importantly leftwingers feared that Foot would not stand up to the right and felt there was little point in campaigning for the new structure of the party, if they were not then prepared to use that structure. Healey was seen as being at odds with the party's policy commitments and as a symbol of the right's dominance of the last Labour government. Benn wrote in his diary in the summer of 1981, 'I don't believe that policy work is all that relevant at the moment given that there is no prospect whatever of it being implemented by the present shadow cabinet.'[44]

The result of the contest was an extended period of disunity as the extremely rancorous campaign lasted from April until the election in September 1981. Benn and Foot became embroiled in a public and bitter dispute in which the former was scathing about the attitude of many members of the PLP leadership. Once again intra-party politics dominated Labour. Policy formation and analysis, let alone any criticisms of the Conservative government, received relatively little attention. Despite a serious illness, Benn campaigned vigorously and with much success in winning over unions. Ultimately, at the 1981 conference, he came very close to winning. After a third candidate, John Silkin, had been eliminated he received 49.574% with Healey getting 50.426%. Benn had lost by just 0.852%.[45]

The Fragmentation of the Left

The deputy leadership contest had far-reaching consequences for Labour's left. Many leftwingers had not wanted a contest. They feared, with some evidence, that the election would indicate to the electorate that Labour was an extremely disunited party whose own members did not appear to trust or respect each other. Judith Hart claimed in an open letter to Benn, 'The effects will be divisive and damaging.'[46] John Silkin entered the contest with the central aim of stopping Benn by dividing the left's vote. That few had been consulted over Benn's decision to stand added to the resentment felt.[47] At a Tribune group meeting the challenge was criticised as a unnecessary diversion from policy-making.[48] Many leftwingers were concerned by the near idolisation that Benn attracted. Hart suggested, 'If you stand and are defeated these policies are at risk. Yet they are not your property.'[49] Neil Kinnock pointed out in *Tribune* that policies had been 'obscured by the coverage of our disputes'.[50]

Joan Lestor claimed , 'We have spent so much time on constitutional issues within the Labour party that we are failing to get our message across.'[51] Some leftwingers disliked the simplicity of Benn's arguments. Kinnock claimed, 'Tony gives false hopes to those who believe that monumental changes can be brought by the device of reforming the party constitution.'[52] Kinnock had emerged as a figure, who while being on the left and supporting radical policies, was extremely suspicious of the sweeping promises Benn made.

The left's polarisation culminated when a section of the Tribune group led by Neil Kinnock chose not to vote for Benn on the second ballot after Silkin's elimination. Sixteen abstained and four voted for Healey.[53] Such was the tightness of the result that they denied Benn victory. It was an ironical outcome given that their argument was open to reversal: a Benn victory might have legitimated leftwing policies, in the same way that they claimed defeat would damage them. Their decision probably owed more to a straightforward desire to guarantee Benn did not become deputy than a concern over the election's impact on policy matters.

The disagreement within Labour's left hardened after the deputy leadership election, with a split into two camps – one 'hard' around Benn and one 'soft' closer to the centre of the party around Kinnock. The division did not immediately affect the substance of the AES. One member of the 'soft' left, Judith Hart, was as much associated with the left's industrial policy, as was Benn. Most critics from the soft left were agreed in objecting to the way that Benn and others used and articulated the proposals of the AES (and other measures) rather than in censuring the policies themselves. Kinnock felt, 'Tony has fostered antagonism within the party, he has undermined the credibility of credible policies by over-simplification.'[54] Both leftwing groups supported the AES, though the soft left was more cautious about what it might achieve and more careful about the terms in which it should be expressed.

The most important feature of the split into hard and soft camps was the degree to which it weakened the left within Labour. Coupled with the resurgence of the right in the NEC elections in 1981, it meant that leftwingers lost their dominance of the party. After the 1981 conference it was possible for Foot and the soft left to unite with rightwingers and outvote the hard left. After 1982 the right no longer had even to rely on the support of the soft left. The split between the soft and the hard left was formalised by the formation, in December 1982, by Benn and others of the Campaign group of Labour MPs.[55] The origins of the new group were the MPs who had actively backed Benn's deputy leadership campaign. Many of its members were not on good terms with the other leftwing body for MPs, the Tribune group.

Benn's near victory marked a highpoint for the left. Aside from the fragmentation of the left, Benn's own position received a serious setback soon after the contest. Earlier in 1981 Benn had returned to the shadow cabinet. In November he wound up a Commons debate on energy policy and repeated a conference commitment of renationalisation without compensation. Shadow cabinet colleagues distanced themselves from such a pledge and Foot accused Benn of being in breach of collective discipline.[56] After a series of protracted and bitter meetings, Foot told Labour MPs he could not support Benn in the next shadow cabinet elections.[57] Benn got only 66 votes and did not win a place. Given Foot's intervention, that Benn did so well was remarkable. He was unable subsequently to regain a place on Labour's frontbench.

After 1981 Labour was less focused on constitutional reforms and there was no further electoral challenge to the party leadership. There was a growing desire, especially from the party's non-aligned elements and many unions, to try and restore some semblance of unity. A conference of NEC members and union leaders in January 1982 mapped out an uneasy basis for a truce: Leftwingers agreed to desist from further reforms and leadership challenges while rightwingers agreed not to re-open constitutional questions. The right's concern after 1981 was not with Labour's structure or policy but with entryism. An increasing amount of time was taken up with this issue as the NEC sought to proscribe the main entryist organisation, Militant and expel its leading members.[58] Once again, policy concerns took a back seat.

LABOUR'S POLICY-MAKING PROCESS 1979–83

Economic policy-making was not neglected altogether after 1979. The Home Policy Committee, with Tony Benn as its chair until 1982, was responsible for the production of various documents which restated the case for the AES including *Labour's Programme 1982*.[59] It co-ordinated the party's policy-making machinery, set up working groups and directed others into specific areas. Figure 7.1 indicates the policy-making process in this period. The Industrial Policy Sub-Committee remained the crux for work on industrial regeneration with a wide remit of inquiry. It was responsible for industrial policy, existing nationalised industries, new public enterprise and planning.[60] The committee coordinated the drafting of the sections on industrial planning, new technology, workers' cooperatives and common ownership for *Labour's Programme 1982*.[61] A trade policy working group was set up in December 1979 on the premise that 'a return to full employment, which was not associated with a serious balance of payments difficulties, would not be possible without direct intervention to control the **rate of growth** of manufactured imports'.[62] This group studied the form that import controls should take and was responsible for the proposals in *Labour's Programme 1982*. The Finance and Economic Affairs Sub-Committee met frequently after 1979. It focused on taxation matters, the costing of policies, a rebuttal of monetarism, and the priorities for public spending policies. It drafted the economic and fiscal sections of *Labour's Programme 1982*.[63]

These internal policy-making committees, including Finance and Economic Affairs, were dominated by leftwingers during the period from the 1979 election until after *Labour's Programme 1982* was published. Judith Hart chaired several committees, including the public ownership working group, the new technology working group and the Financial Institutions Study Group as well as the Industrial Policy Sub-Committee.[64] After 1980 the Finance and Economic Affairs Sub-Committee was chaired by Doug Hoyle who also looked after the trade policy group. Benn chaired the EEC study group which developed the timetable by which the UK would leave the Common Market.

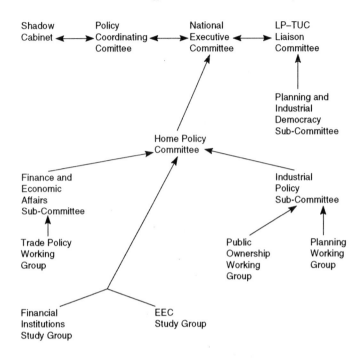

Figure 7.1 Labour Party policy-making 1979–83

Source: Derived from RD: 1148/November 1981

The left was well represented on these bodies both in terms of NEC members and those coopted onto them. The seemingly ubiquitous Stuart Holland was a member of all the committees referred to in the above paragraph. Membership of both the Finance and Economic Affairs and the Industrial Policy Sub-Committees was large. The former had forty-four members during 1981–82, the latter over fifty.[65] Of the NEC members who sat on Finance and Economic Affairs at least five were leftwingers (out of seven representatives). On Industrial Policy seven of the NEC representatives were from the left (out of nine). The NEC representation on other groups was similarly favourable to the left during the development of *Labour's Programme 1982*. Until 1982 rightwingers played little role in the discussions within Labour's policy committees.

Many of those involved in the original formulation and advocacy of the AES during 1972–73 were still at the centre of Labour's policy-making in this period. Geoff Bish, Stuart Holland, Judith Hart and Tony Benn had been involved in developing *Labour's Programme 1973*. So too had Michael Meacher, Margaret Beckett (who as Margaret Jackson had been secretary of the Public Sector Group) and Eric Heffer. All were active (to varying degrees) between 1979 and 1983. As well as Holland, other academic advocates of the AES, such as Michael Barratt Brown, Francis Cripps, John Hughes and Tony Millwood, served on policy-making committees. Given the personnel involved, the continuity of Labour's commitment to the AES is of little surprise.

Continued support for the AES came from Labour's leftwing research department. Researchers differed from some advocates of the AES in their support for some form of incomes policy. Geoff Bish, the research secretary moderated his views and by 1983 felt that modifications to the AES were necessary. But for the period after 1979 he articulated the AES in strong and robust terms as the drafts he produced, including those for the Liaison Committee document, *Economic Planning and Industrial Democracy*, indicate. Other members of the research department such as Roy Green and Adam Sharples were also strong supporters of the AES and active participants in the academic debate around it.

As during 1972–1973, Labour's policy-making committees and the party's research department were important in determining the content of policy documents. One official remembered: 'What was published was pretty much what we drafted.'[66] Policy was, he stated, 'driven by officials'. Tony Blair, then a parliamentary candidate for the first time, said later that Labour 'had allowed a small group of people to determine the agenda of the party'.[67] In 1983 Sam McCluskie, the party chair, complained, 'The impact of the research department was so overpowering that one could not even criticise drafts without the criticism being taken as personal.'[68] For the most part, there was a large measure of agreement over economic strategy between the party's officials and those who were active in the policy-making committees. One reason for this was that most members of the NEC were not that interested in the contents of policy documents and tended to accept the proposals of draft papers. One memo suggested that the NEC's commitment was in the broad direction of policy and not its fine detail.[69]

The Home Policy Committee and the NEC made few changes to draft documents. When the Financial Institutions Study Group was unable to reach agreement, the Home Policy Committee decided to go for nationalisation of the banks (a decision reversed by the NEC). The Home Policy Committee toughened the anti-incomes policy section of *Labour's Programme 1982*.[70] It had wanted a slightly stronger wording for Agreed Development Plans but there was usually harmony between the various committees and the party's research staff. The exception was anti-inflation strategy: research department staff wanted some form of incomes policy to be considered, something leftwingers on the NEC could not countenance.[71]

The constitutional concerns of leftwingers were evident in policy-making. Two policy documents produced by Labour in 1980 indicated the link between policy and the reform of Labour's structure. First, in May a set-piece occasion was held to discuss *Peace Jobs and Freedom*. Leftwingers wanted a one-day conference based around a new policy document in order to make clear to the leadership the policies to which they were expected to adhere.[72] According to the press, Callaghan did not want to be saddled with leftwing policy commitments and proposed, without success, that the conference should have the less important status of a rally.[73] *Peace, Jobs and Freedom* included a brief restatement of the AES. Benn wrote later, 'It contained most, though not all, of the policies for which I had been campaigning throughout the 1970s.'[74]

The second policy development in 1980 was the draft manifesto. The idea, promoted by Tony Benn and others, was that by producing such a document annually the party's manifesto would always be available and it would not be possible for a leader to railroad his or her own version through at short notice.[75] The Home Policy Committee and the NEC endorsed the proposal.[76] In April 1980 the draft of the rolling manifesto was presented as an important development in policy-making: Bish stated, 'The draft manifesto, in short, should become the focus for all serious policy-making in the party, and it would provide the firm basis of the work of the next Labour government.'[77] Unsurprisingly the shadow cabinet opposed the production of a rolling programme.[78] Both it and the PLP repeatedly resisted the use of the phrase 'draft manifesto' in the title of the document agreed by the Home Policy Committee.[79] Callaghan forced Benn to cancel a press conference launching the document on 9 July 1980.[80] The new 'manifesto' had not been agreed either with the PLP (who were unhappy about its contents) or the conference. The left's proposed amendment to Clause V to give control of the manifesto to the NEC alone had not been passed so it was premature for the NEC to publish a draft version.[81] Eventually it was agreed that the status of the manifesto would be clarified by the conference.[82] The composite to give the NEC control of the manifesto was lost and no further drafts were produced.[83]

Later documents such as *Labour's Programme 1982* remained straightforward in their articulation of the left's policy. This continuity in the content of policy is surprising given the move rightwards in the composition of the NEC from 1981 onwards. The shift was remarkably insignificant in its consequences for Labour's policy. In 1981 it may have given leftwingers an incentive to focus more closely on policy matters. At the 1982 conference the realignment became more apparent. Soon afterwards several leftwingers were taken off the Home Policy Committee by the rightwing majority on the NEC and Benn was removed as its chair by 12 votes to 4.[84] His replacement was a rightwing MP, John Golding, but he had no impact on the substance of the party's commitments. Labour's major policy documents had already been published and there was little motivation amongst either right or left to re-open discussions with an election approaching.[85] Moreover, Golding disliked the tendency of shadow cabinet members to issue policy statements, such as Peter Shore's *Programme for Recovery*, without consulting the NEC.[86] The continuity in Labour's economic proposals after the NEC had decisively shifted to the right is indicative of the persistent influence of the party's policy-making committees and of its research department officials such as Geoff Bish. As during 1972–1974, these bodies continued to be a key determinant of the content of economic policy.

Tony Benn suspected that rightwingers did not challenge Labour's policy proposals in 1982 (or earlier) because they intended to make a stronger attempt at moderation over the election manifesto.[87] In the event no challenge to the manifesto occurred and it was agreed at the shortest Clause V meeting between the NEC and the shadow cabinet on record.[88] Given that many shadow cabinet members apparently had 'grave reservations' about Labour's manifesto at the 1983 election and party policy more generally, the question arises as to why they accepted it without more of a fight.[89] It may be that John Golding and others, sensing that an election defeat could not be averted, decided to stick with radical policies so that the left would take the ensuing blame.[90] (In the same way that Callaghan's manifesto was blamed for the 1979 result.) Golding later said, 'If we weren't going to win, we may as well as lose on leftwing policies.'[91] *The Sunday Times* concluded, 'The desire to saddle the left with the blame should Labour lose outweighed the fear of what such a document would imply for government.'[92]

Labour's conference gave further support to the AES between 1979 and 1983 in a series of radical resolutions which were often moved and seconded by senior trade unionists. In 1982, the last conference before the 1983 general election formally passed *Labour's Programme 1982* and supported a proposal to nationalise 25 top companies. The same year's conference opposed proposals which were more sweeping and extreme than the AES.[93] The conference had less of a role in initiating policy developments with one exception. The 1980 conference voted to take the UK out of the EEC, altering the more qualified stance of *Labour's Draft Manifesto*. In other areas the conference responded to the lead given by party's policy-making committees.[94] The 1981 conference voted, against the NEC, for a ban on systematic overtime and a commitment not to tax benefits. Neither measure found its way into *Labour's Programme 1982*. In criticising that document, Stan Orme pointed out that some of its proposals owed more to internal groups than to the party's conference.[95]

The Role of Rightwingers in Policy Formation

Members of the PLP sat on the party's policy-making committees but they had little influence on the content of policy.[96]
Shadow cabinet spokespersons were often presented with
published proposals by the NEC as a *fait accompli* which they
were then called upon by the media to articulate and defend. Out of office, shadow ministers were in a weak position.[97] Many leftwingers saw Labour's formal policy-making
process as a way to bind them to party policy. They disputed the freedom for manoeuvre of Labour MPs, suggest-
ing that they should expound NEC policy regardless of their
own views. Geoff Bish spoke of the need to ensure that the
PLP 'became more committed to the policies as they
emerge'.[98] Minkin concluded, 'An assertive NEC, controlled
by a different faction from that of the majority in the shadow
cabinet, could greatly reduce the role of the PLP leadership in policy formation.'[99] One party official said of the
shadow chancellor, Peter Shore, that 'he didn't feel part of
the policy-making process.'[100]

The extra-parliamentary party did not want to exclude the
PLP and the shadow cabinet from policy formation altogether. Immediately after the 1979 election Bish suggested
that joint meetings be held between the NEC and the shadow
cabinet.[101] The objective was to find some means by which
policies could be arrived at which all sides in the party could
defend, without the PLP simply imposing their own views
(as many felt they had done while in office). One year later,
Bish spelt out at some length the need for a joint body:

> What we *must* avoid, however, in the years ahead, is the
> development of two separate, conflicting sets of policies
> – the NEC and the conference on the one hand, and the
> parliamentary leadership on the other. At the very least,
> we suggest, the two 'sides' should attempt to minimise
> their policy differences, as they arise, through proper dis-
> cussion.[102]

What the research department proposed was in essence the
reconstitution of the Policy Coordinating Committee, comprising equal numbers of representatives from the NEC and
the PLP. In November 1980 the NEC agreed and the first

meeting of the new committee was held in February 1981.[103]

The new body had little impact on policy-making. Few meetings were held, many focused on non-domestic issues, and at times major disagreements emerged in its discussions only to remain unresolved. Many in the PLP perceived it as an attempt to bind them to NEC proposals. In 1981 MP's raised doubts about the draft contents of *Labour's Plan for Expansion* and the published version was amended to make clear that it was an interim document still under review.[104] The PLP also wanted Labour to spell out the role of wages as a cause of inflation but this proposal was rejected by the NEC whose members perceived it as an attempt to introduce an incomes policy.[105] Benn commented later, 'It was one long struggle while the parliamentary side tried to water down policies they don't believe in, but there was no bitterness.'[106] The NEC retained overall control of policy-making: it finally agreed and published *Labour's Plan for Expansion* in April 1981.

When the Policy Coordinating Committee considered the draft of *Labour's Programme 1982*, several members of the shadow cabinet criticised its contents and status as a Labour document.[107] They disliked the sweeping commitments into which the party was entering – especially if they were to go into an election programme (as the title of the document suggested they might). John Smith argued that it was repetitive and had 'no clear sense of perception as to relative importance.'[108] Bruce Millan was concerned by the number of references to priorities in the document and claimed, 'Taken altogether these references are far more that could possibly be achieved in a single parliament either in terms of legislation or financially.'[109] Geoff Bish accepted later that 'not surprisingly, shadow cabinet members were extremely unhappy about having to agree so much so quickly.'[110]

Shadow cabinet members were not only concerned by the lack of consultations over the new document and its length: they disliked the fact that *Labour's Programme 1982* would be voted on by the party conference as a whole without the possibility of amendment.[111] Foot reassured them that this would not be the case. It would be possible, he suggested, to vote on the document section by section at the party conference. Such a manoeuvre would allow them to isolate those parts of the programme they especially disliked. There was even some consideration about attempting to abandon the document altogether as shadow cabinet members 'raised the whole question of the wisdom of proceeding with the Programme 1982'.[112] Foot had earlier insisted that the shadow cabinet should 'try to improve the programme rather than reject it'.[113] The voting procedure over *Labour's Programme 1982* led to another Foot–Benn clash when Benn wrote an article in *Tribune* claiming, apparently accurately, that the shadow cabinet wanted to avoid being committed to the contents of the document at conference.[114] In the event *Labour's Programme 1982* was voted on as a whole by the 1982 conference, only as amended indirectly by other votes at the conference. It was passed overwhelmingly.

Few amendments were proposed by the shadow cabinet either to the 1982 document or Labour's campaign document for the 1983 election at drafting meetings. The NEC decided matters which the Policy Coordinating Committee could not resolve and shadow cabinet members may have decided that they would have to live with the documents as best they could. In practice they may have hoped to ignore or put their own interpretation on many of the policies.[115] The main exception to this acquiescence was Peter Shore. At one meeting Benn recorded, 'Peter Shore just opposed every socialist measure – nationalisation of the banks, of industry, import controls, saying that devaluation would solve the problem.'[116] Two days later Benn claimed, 'Whenever public ownership is mentioned in the presence of the shadow cabinet they just go berserk.'[117]

The Policy Coordinating Committee did little to bridge the gap between the NEC and the PLP. It did not provide the basis for agreement over policy matters and Labour was still perceived as a divided party with a wide gulf between the policies to which left and right adhered. In 1982 when Geoff Bish analysed the party's difficulties, he blamed 'the reluctance of party spokesmen to agree a common platform, a common timetable and a common theme for their speeches and meetings'.[118] Bish wrote later, 'Senior spokesmen have sometimes felt little sense of real commitment to the detailed policies.'[119]

THE TRADE UNION CONTRIBUTION TO ECONOMIC POLICY-MAKING

The Liaison Committee remained the central means by which unions contributed to Labour's economic policy-making during 1979–83. It produced a series of documents which restated the case for the AES and two policy developments took place within it. First, the Liaison Committee was responsible for the concept of the National Economic Assessment as the main way to combat inflation – although to what it amounted remained unclear.[120] Second, a special sub-committee on planning and industrial democracy elaborated Labour's policy in these areas and made a set of explicit links between them.[121] Its proposals were published by the Liaison Committee as *Economic Planning and Industrial Democracy* in July 1982.

Although it was less obviously leftwing than Labour's own policy-making committees, the Liaison Committee advocated the strategy for which leftwingers also lobbied. The sub-committee on planning and industrial democracy endorsed measures similar to those of Labour. There were close links and an overlap of personnel between Labour's policy-making bodies and the Liaison Committee (and its sub-committee on planning). Both were serviced by the party's research department (the Liaison Committee was also backed by the TUC Economic Department). The joint secretaries of the Liaison Committee in this period were David Lea, a strong advocate of industrial democracy, and Geoff Bish. In 1982 changes did take place to the membership of the Liaison Committee as part of the shift rightwards within Labour.[122] These developments had little impact on the content of policy. The last document produced before the 1983 election simply put some flesh onto the NEA.[123]

Lewis Minkin challenges the view that the work of the Liaison Committee in 1982 was in agreement with the proposals of the leftwing Industrial Policy Sub-Committee. He questions the continuity of the Liaison Committee's plans with the contents of *Labour's Programme 1973*. Minkin argues that during the drafting of *Economic Planning and Industrial Democracy* a split emerged between leftwingers and other members of the Liaison Committee. The result was 'a discreet understanding between the TUC, NEC trade unionists, and party staff [which] redefined the policy emerging from the Industrial Policy Sub-Committee, which was a continuation of the party's industrial policy of the 1970s'.[124]

Some leftwingers noticed that Labour's divergent policy-making structure, split between the Liaison Committee and internal bodies, might lead to policy differences.[125] At various points Tony Benn, who was an active member of the Planning and Industrial Democracy Sub-Committee, expressed dismay at the draft contents of *Economic Planning and Industrial Democracy*. He suspected that Michael Foot might be using the new Liaison document to water down the proposals of *Labour's Programme 1982*.[126] Benn criticised papers produced by Bish and Lea as non-socialist, bureaucratic and bland.[127] He disliked their references to Japanese and French planning, fearing that some members of the Liaison Committee wanted to mimic such arrangements.[128] Benn felt, 'The objectives at the moment are purely technocratic. We must have some objectives involving social justice.'[129] After the next meeting he concluded: 'It was really just trying to make the national plan of 1964 work and I came away feeling there was absolutely no shift at all by the trade union leaders or by the shadow cabinet people there towards a socialist interpretation of the crisis or how to deal with it.'[130]

Benn's fears, recorded in his diary, may be overstated as many of his criticisms were accepted. One meeting noted: 'The planning objectives as set out [in the draft] were too technocratic. They did not pay sufficient attention to the need for planning to promote greater social efficiency.'[131] Benn was not alone in his doubts about France: 'The overall impression of the Joint Secretaries [Bish and Lea] was that the French planning mechanisms were not properly thought through and that there was a lack of coordination between the various ministers involved.'[132] A proposed appendix on planning in France and Japan was dropped and the final version made only an extremely brief reference to planning in other countries without mentioning any by name. In the final version planning was not conceived in purely economic terms but included references to social justice, accountability and the failure of the private sector. Public ownership was included and the objectives of the strategy remained far-reaching.[133] The minutes noted, 'In addition it was clear that public enterprise would have a key role in the new planning system.'[134]

During drafting the term 'planning agreement' was dropped and replaced by 'development contracts'. Benn opposed this phrase because it was reminiscent of corporatism and a voluntaristic approach. Supporters of the new term, such as Stan Orme and David Basnett, felt it was more realistic. Benn successfully ensured that the substance of the proposals was not moderated and the title was changed again to Agreed Development Plans (ADPs).[135] It was apparent that it would be very difficult for any company to avoid negotiating an agreement. Both Labour and Liaison documents produced in 1982 agreed a range of powers which the new planning department would have.[136] The Liaison sub-committee noted 'Considerable weight was placed in the paper upon the back-up powers for the planning authority.'[137] The apparent adequacy of the powers proposed explains why the Liaison document dropped Labour's reference to an Official Trustee – the main difference between the conception of ADPs in the two documents. The sub-committee felt however that the section setting out powers to issue directives 'adequately covered this point'.[138] There was no need for an Official Trustee. The differences on this issue between TUC documents and the NEC ones are minor and stylistic, as opposed to being substantive. Many leftwingers endorsed ADPs as far-reaching proposals, which were not in any way watered down from their earlier conception.[139]

Members of the Liaison Committee varied in their commitment to the AES, but the differences between the Labour party and the Liaison Committee should not be over-emphasised. There was considerable common ground over the kind of economic and industrial strategy that Labour should adopt. The leftwing Home Policy Committee, under Benn, accepted the work done by the Liaison Committee on economic planning during 1982 and proposed that it should feed into *Labour's Programme 1982*.[140] It considered and made few amendments to the draft of *Economic Planning and Industrial Democracy*.[141] The Industrial Policy Sub-Committee also discussed the proposals coming from the Liaison Committee. This accord between the TUC and Labour is unsurprising given the importance both bodies gave to the Liaison Committee and the influence that it had. When asked in 1980 whether new policies were required, Len Murray replied, 'No, but there are some very, very good old ideas.'[142]

The contents of *Economic Planning and Industrial Democracy* indicates the influence that leftwingers had on policy formation. Its substance does not suggest a moderation of Labour's commitment to the AES. The similarity between the detail of the proposals made by the Liaison Committee and those in *Labour's Programme 1982* must be noted – as well as the overall continuity with the arguments made in *Labour's Programme 1973*. In the economic strategy it articulated, the Liaison document remained remarkably similar to earlier Labour programmes. The development of policy during 1979–82 indicates neither a shift away from the proposals Labour elaborated during 1972–73 nor a split between the left and the Liaison Committee. One research official said later, 'There was no split between the left and the research department. There was no difference between the TUC and the Labour party – not over the broad content of policy.'[143] A TUC official echoed this claim: 'There was no difference between Liaison documents and Labour party ones.'[144]

In way of contrast, an example of an emphatic split between the NEC and the research department is given by Labour's attitude to car imports. In 1980 the NEC proposed that all cars sold in the UK should be assembled here.[145] The research department was scathing: it concluded that the NEC proposal ignored the reality of the present day motor industry, it did not consider the threat of retaliation and whether sufficient capacity existed in the economy. Benn, incidentally, agreed with the research department that the NEC's position was too tough.[146]

The TUC gave further endorsement to the AES through its own publications and statements. Its *Economic Review* outlined a moderate but identifiable version of the AES similar to that it had proposed during the Labour government.[147] TUC statements were often less radical than those of Labour and the Liaison Committee. This difference is not startling given that the trade unions had access to the Conservative government and hoped to have some influence on Tory policies.[148] One trade union leader, Alan Fisher, announced that unions should not 'sit back and wait' for a Labour government to be returned to office.[149] The more practical attitude of union leaders led on occasion to tension on the Liaison Committee. Some NEC members felt that the TUC was too compromising. At one meeting, 'the TUC pointed out that while the party was primarily interested in the policies on which the next election would be fought, the TUC also had to focus on influencing the current government's policies including the budget'.[150] At another Eric Heffer 'questioned the implication in the draft [*Trade and Industry* – a Liaison Committee document] that cooperation with the present government was possible. In response Mr Murray said that the TUC tried to seek a basis for cooperation with any government.'[151] As it became clear that the unions were unlikely to have any perceptible impact upon the Conservative government, so they came to focus less on immediate measures and more on maintaining their links with the Labour party.

The TUC also frequently supported the policies of the Labour left at its annual congress.[152] In 1980 *Tribune* claimed: 'The policies agreed at the TUC far more resemble the policies which Labour's National Executive Committee has been drafting than those of Mr. Callaghan and Mr. Healey.'[153] In commenting on the draft of *Labour's Programme 1982*, the Transport and General Workers Union stated: 'The first priority must be to implement a socialist economic strategy, including planned trade and investment, expansion of the public sector, fostering of new institutions and greater resources for training and re-training.'[154]

The role of trade unions in promoting radical economic policies should not be over-estimated. Many union leaders did not have a great involvement in initiating economic strategy – aside that is from the work of the Liaison Committee. A few unions produced pamphlets about aspects of economic strategy. Whilst some endorsed the left's interventionist proposals (often in a general and populist fashion), others actively opposed them.[155] Like the Labour conference, the contribution of most trade unions took the form of general support for restatements of the AES rather than the development of new ideas.[156] Minkin concludes, 'In general most unions (left and right) were neither resourced nor motivated to follow through the detailed exploration of macroeconomic policy.'[157] By 1982 many unions had tired of the policy disputes and civil war that had dominated Labour politics over the previous decade.

CONCLUSIONS

Between 1979 and 1983 activity within Labour was dominated by organisational concerns, especially over the party's constitutional structure. The demands for reform to the structure of Labour did not stem from a sudden desire by leftwingers to recast the nature of the party but from the frustration which had developed in office. There was, therefore, a direct link between the demands for constitutional reform and the party's policy stance. Many leftwingers felt that there was no point in pursuing policy matters if the constitution of the party remained unaltered. In such circumstances the leadership would simply side-step the policies formally agreed by the party.

The left became very bogged down in constitutional matters and the struggle to implement reforms, especially during 1979–81. The party was very internalised in this period. There was less activity with regard to economic policy than there had been during 1970–74. The left tended to take economic policy for granted and to reaffirm old strategies with a few additional elements. Labour's research department and the members of policy-making committees remained central in developing the detail of policy – even after the party's NEC had been captured by rightwingers. The party's institutional structure and policy-making process continued to be of paramount importance in determining Labour's policy commitments. Between 1979 and 1982 the Home Policy Committee, the NEC and the party conference were never seriously out of step over economic strategy.

Equally important were the policy and political legacies of 1979. The overwhelming characteristic of Labour's policy proposals is not their originality but the continuity they expressed with the measures developed in 1973. There were no major innovations. Leftwingers believed that an adequate policy existed, and that, for the most part at any rate, it did not require reformulation. In supporting a motion attacking the Labour government at the 1979 conference, Tony Benn made the case for existing policy and its persisting relevance: 'We said all this in 1973 and we put it in our 1974 manifesto, and we won two elections on it.'[158] Another delegate said, 'We require the kind of socialist interventionist policies that we set out in *Labour's Programme 1976*.'[159] Frank Allaun writing in *Tribune*, captured this view succinctly: 'I am not looking for new policies. I want to see the old ones carried out.'[160]

Labour remained a divided party between 1979 and 1983. A background paper for the Policy Coordinating Committee noted, 'For many years now, the party has had somehow to live with the fact that there are, *de facto*, two competing centres of authority in the party on questions of policy.'[161] The nadir was reached with the defection of the those who joined the Social Democrats. The disunity was extremely damaging electorally. Labour was unable to capitalise on the unpopularity of Margaret Thatcher's Conservative government. Far from it, once the Social Democrats left, Labour's support in the polls fell steadily. The split in the party fatally compromised Labour's election prospects.

8 Conclusions

INTRODUCTION

Labour experienced a crushing defeat in the general election on 9 June 1983. The party's share of the popular vote fell by 9.5 per cent from 1979 and it won only 209 seats. Labour's portion of the total vote was its lowest since 1918, and its lowest share per candidate since 1900. Within days of the election, Michael Foot announced his resignation as leader. In October, at the party conference, Neil Kinnock was overwhelmingly elected by the electoral college on the first ballot as his replacement. Tony Benn had lost his seat in Bristol at the general election and was unable to stand – it is, in any case, a matter of speculation as to how well he might have done. Soon after the election major changes were instigated by Neil Kinnock to Labour's internal structure, policy-making machinery and the content of its economic strategy. I discuss these developments, which dominated Kinnock's nine-year leadership of the party, in the Epilogue following.

In this chapter I look back at the Alternative Economic Strategy and the Labour party's policy-making experience between 1970 and 1983. In earlier chapters I have established four central themes. First, I have argued that the AES marked Labour's commitment to a new and radical social democracy. Second, I have indicated that many of Labour's leaders failed to endorse these innovative proposals. Third, I have demonstrated that Labour's institutional structure was of central importance in allowing such a divergence to arise. Fourth, I have noted the damaging consequences for Labour of such a split between its formal policy and the aspirations of the leadership, in terms of the struggle to reform the structure of the party after 1979.

In this chapter I consider five broad questions. The first two relate respectively to economic and electoral problems with the AES, central aspects of any party's policy for the economy. The last three return to the central themes of the book. The questions are as follows: First, what economic problems were identified with the AES? Second, why did Labour make the strategic choice that it did after 1970 and adopt an economic policy which many claimed was electorally unpopular? Third, what does Labour's choice indicate about the nature of British social democracy? Fourth, what does policy-making within Labour during this period suggest about the nature of the party? Fifth and last, what is the relationship of the Alternative Economic Strategy to Labour's decline and crisis?

ECONOMIC PROBLEMS WITH THE ALTERNATIVE ECONOMIC STRATEGY

Labour's defeat in the 1983 election removed the possibility of the AES being implemented. Whatever direct contribution the strategy may have made to the election result, it was clearly associated with the defeat. The electoral verdict explains in large part the party's later abandonment of the AES: for many, including some former advocates, the scale of defeat meant that radical changes were needed, including a drastic reformulation of economic strategy. Nevertheless, aside from its association with the electoral rebuff, theoretical problems emerged with the AES during 1979–83. When the AES was originally developed within the Labour party, there was limited academic support for it. The theoretical underpinnings were provided largely by Stuart Holland, and, to a lesser extent, the Cambridge Economic Policy Group. Few other economists advocated similar proposals. By the late 1970s a plethora of articles and books had appeared making the case for the AES.[1] This explosion of support was paradoxical. It indicated considerable breadth of support inside and outside the Labour party. But the debate resulted in different areas of the AES coming under scrutiny and many problems within it were identified, even by supporters. The debate also indicated that there were major disagreements over aspects of the strategy. There was considerable variation in the goals of different versions of the AES. Some doubted its economic potential: they saw it as a means either to generate support for a transition to a socialist society or to provoke an economic crisis in the capitalist system.

As the UK's economic recession intensified during 1979–81, doubts emerged about the scope for any government to reflate the economy because of the extent of deindustrialisation, capacity constraints and supply-side shortages. Concerns were expressed about the impact of any reflation on inflation, the value of sterling and the balance of payments. These problems led some leftwingers to conclude that a nationally-orientated economic strategy was unsustainable. The Mitterrand government's experience in France suggested limitations to any attempt to rely on national action alone. These difficulties were addressed in *Out of Crisis*, an international volume edited by Stuart Holland in 1983.[2] It proposed that reflation should be linked across nations throughout Europe. Labour's research department strongly rejected the pessimism of *Out of Crisis* and argued that its internationalism was impractical.[3]

The reliance of the AES on public ownership was questioned because nationalisation was unpopular and bureaucratic. Supporters doubted the extent of economic benefits that might come from competitive public enterprise. An example of such doubts came from Richard Pryke, one of the original architects of the NEB along with Stuart Holland. Pryke reversed his earlier pro-public ownership position and became extremely critical of the nationalised sector.[4]

Further disagreement emerged over planning and industrial democracy. Some advocates argued that planning should be based on social criteria, with workers making judgements about the production of 'socially useful' goods. Others felt that economic criteria should be used. They claimed that social criteria did not provide a viable or definite basis on which to make decisions. There were disputes over the mechanisms and the institutions that planning required. Some adherents, for example, those associated with the Institute for Workers' Control, wanted the AES to emphasise workers' plans. These were a radical form of planning agreement where workers would draw up alternative plans and use them as part of a challenge to management through the mobilisation of workers, independent of state action. The immediate objective was workers' control of the firm –

though what was involved in such a goal remained ambiguous. The advantage of workers' plans was that they did not require the election of a Labour government. Such proposals went well beyond Labour's planning measures and moderates regarded them as hopelessly impractical ideas.

The AES was poorly prepared to resolve conflicts of interest between planning and industrial democracy. In more radical versions, industrial democracy was meant to give workers control of a particular firm. Even in more moderate formulations, workers would have considerable influence. It was not apparent how the autonomy of workers in an individual firm could be made compatible with the objectives of national planning. How would conflicts of interest between groups and between different demands be resolved? How would national priorities be linked to local needs? If local demands had precedence then coordinating and planning the national economy would not be feasible. If national planning had pre-eminence then industrial democracy might amount to little. There was no obvious mechanism to reconcile the two goals. This problem was raised in discussions during the drafting of *Economic Planning and Industrial Democracy*. Academics also noted the difficulty of harmonising planning with industrial democracy. It was an acute dilemma for the radical supporters of the AES: the emphasis they placed on workers' plans left little scope for national decision-making. It remained a problem even for the more moderate versions of the AES. It was not a new issue. In 1947 Robert Dahl had argued that planning and workers' control involved 'two potentially contradictory doctrines'.[5] Dahl's claim was that Labour had resolved this conflict by abandoning workers' control and opting for planning.

Many academic supporters concluded – as members of Labour's research department had – that price controls alone were an inadequate basis for keeping inflation down. Some came to accept that an incomes policy was needed, though there was considerable uncertainty and disagreement over the form that it should take. Most proposed that any incomes policy must be radical in scope: wage restraint should only be agreed in exchange for greater control over firms' decision-making but little progress was made in the articulation of one. Many economists hinted at the kind of proposals that Ken Alexander and John Hughes had come up with in 1959 in *A Socialist Wages Plan*. There were disagreements over the extent and form of import controls. It was argued that selective import controls would restrict choice and promote inefficiency by sheltering industries from competition. Some supporters favoured tariffs while others wanted quotas and ceilings to be implemented. Doubts existed over the feasibility of import controls because of the retaliation that they could provoke. By 1982 even the Cambridge Group was less optimistic about the potential of import controls. It advocated a package of measures including European-wide reflation and devaluation.[6] Some supporters of the AES also doubted the wisdom of any commitment to leave the EEC.

Many advocates of the AES were critical of the detailed policies articulated by the Labour party. The collection *Planning the Planners* argued that the proposals of *Economic Planning and Industrial Democracy* were bland, unpopular and weak.[7] The result was a form of bureaucratic corporatism which did not encourage participation, was statist and too materially orientated in its objectives. Rightwing economists within Labour made similar criticisms to those articulated by Crosland a decade before – although few took an active part in the debate over economic policy.[8] Many noted that the success of the AES would depend upon its ability to mobilise popular support, yet there was little evidence that the proposals were able to do that. There was an absence of grassroots involvement. The strategy was also criticised as being far too optimistic: it contained 'significant elements of fantasy'.[9] A further problem concerned exactly how a Labour government would implement the measures it comprised.[10]

Feminists were critical of the AES on a number of grounds: it was too economic and too orientated around the objective of male employment. It failed to take up such issues as low pay for women, unequal access between the sexes for jobs and training, high hidden female unemployment, financial dependence, and the high share of unpaid work undertaken by women.[11] It was unsurprising, feminists claimed, that women were uninterested in the strategy. It was pointed out that it might be difficult for the AES to take on board female concerns: 'Men have to accept a loss in the relative economic privileges they have enjoyed.'[12]

Ever present in the debate surrounding the AES between 1979 and 1983 was the UK's economic crisis. The effect of the recession was to throw considerable doubt on the original assumptions on which the strategy was based. Firms did not appear to be enjoying abnormally high profits. Jim Tomlinson challenged Holland's claims about monopoly concentration, pricing and profits.[13] Holland continued to claim that the profits of some firms were buoyant but other economists were less certain.[14] The debate over profit levels was unresolvable given Holland's argument that the reported figures were inaccurate. But the severity of the recession – even more than the earlier economic crisis of 1974–75 – suggested limits to the economic gains that the strategy would achieve. It appeared unlikely that competitive public enterprise would bring about the benefits for which Holland and others hoped.

The debate over the AES and the UK's economic crisis did not lead to its automatic rejection. Labour's concentration on internal matters meant that the party did not pay enough attention to policy matters before 1983. However, members of Labour's research department and other advocates of the AES were aware of problems with the strategy. Despite these problems, they continued to argue that aspects of it were feasible. Instead of stopping firms siphoning off super profits, some suggested that the strategy would be able to promote changes in the decisions of private firms and so boost investment.[15] Such investment would lead to a higher national product. But doubts existed about the pace at which the strategy should be implemented and about the benefits that it would bring. As the economic environment changed with deindustrialisation and the privatisation programme of the Thatcher Government so support for the AES dwindled. By 1983 it was already apparent that any execution of the strategy would require adjustment.

LABOUR'S STRATEGIC CHOICE

The adoption of the Alternative Economic Strategy by the Labour party in 1973 marked the rejection of the Downsian approach to electoral competition. Revisionists had argued, in line with Anthony Downs, that the perceived moderate preferences of the electorate were paramount in developing any policy platform. Revisionists were horrified by Labour's left turn in the early 1970s, claiming that it went in the face of electoral rationality. Labour would, Revisionists claimed, be unelectable on such a radical programme – hence the importance of publicly distancing themselves from it.

If the adoption of the AES marked a rejection of the Revisionists' Downsian moderation, what was Labour's electoral perspective after 1970? One of Downs' basic assumptions was that politicians 'never seek office as a means of carrying out particular policies; their only goal is to reap the rewards of holding office per se'.[16] Such a strong postulate does not explain the motivation of Labour's policy-makers between 1970 and 1983. In this period the party's policy process produced a radical set of proposals. The economic objectives of those policies, a more efficient economy, greater accountability and increased equality, were the main considerations of policy makers. After Labour's dismal performance in office between 1964 and 1970, leftwingers wanted a social democratic strategy capable of overcoming the obstacles – as they identified them – to a revived economy. Policy-makers were motivated by ideological and economic considerations, not the electoral aspects of any strategy. They did not want simply to win office, they wanted to be in a position to implement a feasible and radical strategy which would achieve the goals they desired. Does Labour's commitment to such ideological policy formation mean that the party was defying electoral rationality after 1970? Ivor Crewe has illustrated how Labour's policies diverged from the preferences of its supporters.[17] Revisionists claimed that leftwingers were putting ideological dogma before political common sense and ignoring the realities of electoral competition. This conclusion is too strong and several points can be noted about the electoral nature of the AES.

First, aspects of Labour's strategy were popular. In July 1972, after the party's draft programme had been published, only 27 per cent of the electorate had heard of the proposals. Of these, 26 per cent said they were more likely to vote Labour. Only 17 per cent were less inclined to do so because of the new policies.[18] At various times between 1970 and 1983 such policies as trade controls, price controls, leaving the EEC, and industrial democracy were supported by substantial sections of the electorate.[19] Even in 1983 the electorate favoured Labour's emphasis on employment.[20] There was less support for public ownership, although in November 1974 more people endorsed nationalisation for North Sea Oil and development land than opposed it.[21] Some of the policies of the AES were not the electoral liability that Revisionists claimed they were. Germane evidence comes from the study of the 1983 election by Anthony Heath, Roger Jowell and John Curtice. They conclude that Labour's policies were not as unpopular as many asserted: 'If voters had decided between the parties according to their policy preferences, there would actually have been a dead heat between Conservative and Labour.'[22]

Second, Labour hoped to persuade the electorate of the necessity of those aspects of the strategy that they disliked. Rather than meeting the policy desires of the electorate, Labour wanted to convince the electorate of the desirability of its policy. Patrick Dunleavy and Christopher Husbands call this approach 'a preference shaping strategy'.[23] They argue that parties can attempt to change voters' perceptions of what is feasible and desirable. If the electorate's preferences are malleable, they may adjust in response to the arguments and policy proposals of a party. Policy preferences are likely to be especially volatile during a period of economic uncertainty such as the UK experienced during the 1970s and 1980s. Labour felt it could win over the electorate, partly by campaigning and partly by the impact of its policies. In October 1982 Geoff Bish noted that Labour had limited time 'to achieve a huge and sustained shift of opinion within the electorate'.[24] Labour needed 'to generate understanding and support for these policies'.[25] In government, supporters of the AES hoped, Labour would be able to shape preferences: successful economic management would provide the basis for increased electoral support. Labour's economic policy was ideological, but policy-makers felt that such an approach was compatible with winning elections because of the results it would achieve. Successful policy might create the kind of virtuous circle that the Swedish social democrats were perceived to enjoy.

There is evidence of fluctuating electoral preferences. During 1974–75 British public opinion about the common market changed decisively.[26] In March 1974, 51 per cent of the electorate opposed British membership. In January 1975 41 per cent wanted the UK to leave and only 33 per cent wanted to stay in. But by April that balance had shifted dramatically: only 31 per cent now favoured leaving and 57 per cent wanted the UK to stay. Opinion about membership of the EEC also indicates the importance of the government's role in shaping preferences. Even though only 33 per cent wanted to stay in the EEC in January 1975, that figure immediately shifted to 53 per cent if respondents were told that the government would recommend remaining in the common market.

Third, Labour also hoped to log-roll a coalition of support through its economic strategy and other measures. By offering individuals the policies they desired on those issues that they felt most strongly about, Labour could build up a winning coalition. Such log-rolling might allow a party to win despite unpopular policies – an argument first developed at length by Downs.[27] In 1981 Bish argued that Labour needed 'to get a much clearer idea about which groups we need to win over, by the time of the election'.[28]

Labour was not acting irrationally in electoral terms by adopting the AES.[29] Its policy-makers did not conform to the orthodox Downsian model of median voter policy formation. Labour's policy makers were motivated by ideological and economic factors. But at a time of economic crisis, their ideologically driven platform did not ignore popularity altogether. In retrospect, it did not succeed in winning the support of the electorate at the 1983 election – though many other factors were also responsible. But the defeat does not mean Labour was irrational to adopt the AES and hope to win an election on it. Labour won the February 1974 election on a radical manifesto (albeit largely due to increased third party voting) and Labour was ahead in opinion polls by a huge margin during 1980. The abandonment of the AES owes more to its intimate linkage with defeat in 1983 than to any inherent electoral (or economic) problems. What accounts for Labour's turn leftwards? The immediate cause was the failure of Revisionism to achieve the goals that the Labour party had adopted before 1964. Not only did Revisionism prove to be extremely disappointing as a strategy when Labour was in office, the deterioration in relations between the Labour government on the one hand and the trade unions, local activists and extra-parliamentary party on the other paved the way for the left's triumph. Trade unions reacted against Labour's performance by supporting leftwing initiatives. Revisionism's failure created an ideological vacuum and shifted the balance of power within the Labour party after 1970. Leftwingers were well placed to profit from such a situation. The combined work of Stuart Holland and Labour's research department was important in determining the content of the party's new policy proposals. Leftwingers were able to capitalise on the changed balance of power within the party.

The institutional structure of Labour was influential in determining the party's strategic choice after 1970.[30] Labour's open policy-making process based around the sub-committees of the NEC allowed leftwingers to exert considerable influence. It was within the network of committees set up after 1970 that Holland was able to secure support for his policies. The adoption of the AES did not reflect an explicit alliance within the Labour party to win over a majority of support so much as the work of leftwingers in committees. The strategy was forged within Labour's policy process. Later the policies were endorsed at the conference, but they did not originate there.

THE CHARACTER OF BRITISH SOCIAL DEMOCRACY

Labour's adoption of the Alternative Economic Strategy marked the abandonment, formally at any rate, of the party's adherence to Revisionism. The AES was a qualitatively different strategy, closer to the ideas of labour movement theorists, such as John Stephens and Gøsta Esping-Andersen, than those of Revisionists. By 1973 Labour was committed to radical proposals far in excess of those contained in its previous postwar documents. Labour had jettisoned the Keynesian social democracy which had been characteristic, at least since the 1950s, of its economic strategy. Labour embraced objectives which went well beyond the greater equality for which Revisionists persevered. These included a concern with economic efficiency and a desire to promote greater accountability. Such objectives challenged the balance between the private and public sectors. Labour's policies were based on a set of theoretical arguments which were very different to the consensual approach of the Revisionists. Crosland felt that taxation and demand management would provide a surplus for social spending. Supporters of the AES rejected such a harmonious argument: only direct action at the level of decision-making within the firm would produce the results to which social democrats aspired. Such intervention would involve considerable antagonism towards employers.

Production politics lay at the heart of the AES. It was no longer adequate, its supporters argued, to act at aggregate levels by manipulating the level of demand in the economy. Keynesian social democrats had claimed that indirect tools would be sufficient. Revisionist social democracy, in Pontusson's words (writing about Sweden), 'did not involve any sustained effort to reform the organisation of the corporate, commodity-producing sector of the economy'.[31] With the AES such reforms, whether through planning agreements, nationalisation, price controls or other measures, were at the centre of the strategy. It is of little surprise that Labour's Revisionist leadership was so hostile to the policies. Labour had adopted a fundamentally different form of social democracy.

There is one important contrast in Labour's adoption of the AES with the arguments of the labour movement theorists. Labour movement theorists suggest that policies are determined by coalitions within society and that the resources that workers can mobilise are a crucial variable in the development of strategy. The AES did not directly reflect a coalition of support amongst workers or even Labour party supporters. The development of the strategy owed more to the institutional structures of the internal party machinery than to pressure from Labour's wider constituent elements. The organisational framework of Labour, as earlier chapters have indicated, was a crucial determinant of the kind of policy that Labour endorsed. It was also a major factor in the abandonment of the AES during the 1974–79 Labour government. Developed within the party's internal policy-making committees, the strategy lacked wider support from the other elements of the party.

Critics of social democracy, especially those influenced by the structural constraints model, were extremely sceptical about the AES. They continued to argue that social democracy was compromised by the confines of capitalist society. Their arguments largely followed two lines of inquiry. First, some critics challenged the intentions of the AES and claimed that it did not amount to a radical programme. Second, some accepted that the AES was far-reaching in its objectives but questioned whether it was a viable policy package. Despite the inconsistency, some critics such as David Coates adopted both positions: he claimed that the AES was a moderate strategy, yet one which intense capitalist hostility would obstruct.[32]

Many critics continued to see Labour as a moderate party constrained by capitalism. David Howell emphasised the ambiguity of Labour's new policy after 1970.[33] He argued that the package was motivated by a desire for greater efficiency and not socialist objectives. David Coates stated that the new measures were a mixture of 'radical promise and verbal ambiguity'.[34] Coates maintained that Labour did not explain how redistribution and intervention would be made compatible with profit incentives. Labour would still depend upon the actions of private companies and the UK would remain a capitalist society. Leo Panitch claimed that the AES helped sustain Labour's task in integrating the working class within a capitalist society. Labour remained 'an agency of social control'.[35] Panitch stated that the shift leftwards within the party 'took place within the rubric of Labour's dominant ideology'.[36]

Such criticisms were repeated when Labour returned to opposition after 1979. Coates pointed to the diversity of arguments about what was the AES.[37] The party's objectives could not be regarded as socialist. Panitch felt that Labour's policy was ambiguous in its goals: it was unclear whether planning agreements were 'the centrepiece of a socialist economic strategy or of a modernised state capitalism'.[38] Panitch claimed that Labour policies were rooted within a moderate framework of class cooperation. In later work, Panitch modified his arguments somewhat: at times he repeated his earlier claims about Labour's integrative role but he was more sympathetic towards the Labour left.[39] He was especially critical of Neil Kinnock's leadership of the party and what he regarded as the deradicalisation of social democracy.

Far from emphasising the moderation of the AES, another line of criticism focused on the likely response of capitalists to the strategy. Some critics claimed that employers, seeing the AES as a threat, would use every means, economic and political, to oppose its successful implementation.[40] In economic terms it was argued that capitalists would disinvest, shift funds abroad and sell sterling. According to the critics, such actions would provoke an economic crisis and effectively derail Labour's strategy. Planning agreements would not work: companies would not negotiate or reach a formal deal.[41] Critics simply rejected the claim that the AES could ever increase investment: it would cut profits and lead to an economic crisis.[42] Capitalists would also promote a political crisis – possibly along the lines of that which had occurred in Chile in 1973.

Judgement can be passed on the criticism that with the AES Labour maintained its commitment to a moderate social democratic package. The claim that the strategy lacked a definite socialist content is harsh given the goals that Labour laid out in its policy documents. The AES was not the kind of mild strategy that Przeworski and others predicted social democrats would advocate. The strategy was explicit in its radical and far-reaching objectives. These objectives went beyond the promotion of economic efficiency. The AES was not developed within the framework of Labour's existing ideological commitments.

With its hostility to private industry, the AES did not look like a strategy aimed at integrating workers into capitalist society, as Panitch claimed it to be. At times Panitch presented the AES as a functional package for the benefit of capitalism: 'These parties [by moving leftwards] were in the process of reconstructing their viability as mediating agencies for the consensual reproduction of capitalism and the containment of industrial militancy and radical structural reform.'[43] Yet Panitch also charged Labour's more moderate policies with the same function of integrating workers. Likewise Ralph Miliband claimed that Labour's shift leftwards was as functional for capitalists as the party's earlier moderation.[44] The reasoning behind such conclusions remains unclear: exactly what is it that is functional for capitalists? Panitch and Miliband appear to suggest that, whatever the policies social democratic parties adopt, they are functional for capitalists. If the AES was functional for capitalists, their overt and extreme hostility towards it remains to be explained.

Supporters of the AES were divided in their response to criticisms about the likely reaction of capitalists. Some claimed that capitalists would not attempt to sabotage the strategy because they would realise that aspects of it were in their own interest, namely reflation and import controls. Others accepted that there would be opposition but claimed that the power of the state and workforces would be sufficient to counter it. (Ironically Crosland had made a similar claim in *The Future of Socialism* that the state and workers had adequate means with which to challenge the power of capitalists.) Supporters argued that capitalists would not wish to provoke either an economic or a political crisis from which they too would suffer. The mobilisation of workforces would challenge the authority of employers. Supporters of the AES emphasised the importance of mobilising popular support. There were few details about how such mobilisation might be achieved.

The debate between defenders of the AES and its critics over the likely response by capitalists remains unresolved. There are reasons for rejecting the sweeping claim of Przeworski's model that disinvestment and economic crisis must result from radical policies: some capitalists will, as advocates of the AES suggest, benefit from such policies; employers may be more concerned with the volume rather than the rate of profit (and trade-off higher taxation for increased demand); state spending may boost investment; even planning agreements might be acceptable to capitalists if they are assured of benefits (such as government grants or a stable fiscal environment) in exchange for increasing investment.[45] The state may also have measures with which to coerce capitalists: the threat of further intervention or nationalisation. The structural constraints model neglects the costs of disinvestment and the damage that economic crises do to employers as well as the rest of society. Relations between the state, capitalists and workers are not determined simply by the domination of employers. Both the state and workers may be in a position to bargain with employers over economic strategy. It is also unclear that the state must act in the interests of capitalists as many critics of the AES asserted.[46] There are reasons for rejecting this claim: most notably in some of the achievements of the 1945–51 Labour governments and in the concerns of capitalists towards the AES. Employers did not regard the state as their instrument.

These arguments do not mean that the AES would necessarily have realised the objectives laid down for it. There were undoubtedly problems with the measures it involved. But the one-sided nature of the structural constraints model over-emphasises the position of capitalists and is too categoric in its conclusion. The AES would have required adaptation but a reformed yet radical version might have been the basis for a feasible economic policy. Given that the strategy was never implemented by a government committed to it, the capitalist reaction to Labour's policies and their overall effectiveness cannot be determined. Had a radical Labour government attempted to implement the AES, the arguments of the structural constraints model might have been validated. The existing evidence does not confirm it: Labour's failure to implement the strategy between 1974 and 1979 owes more to the divide within the party than to the hostility of capitalists. The conflict between the optimism of the labour movement model and the pessimism of the structural constraints model in the circumstances of the 1970s means that the question of the AES meeting its objectives stays unanswered.

The critics of the AES are on stronger ground in doubting the intentions of the Labour party leadership. They were never reconciled to the AES and in government they made no real attempt to implement it. But many within the Labour party were convinced of the socialist content and desirability of the AES. For them the AES represented a new package embodying a radical social democracy. The attitude of the Labour leadership to the strategy and the party's experience in office may conform to Przeworski's thesis. Labour leaders were concerned by the impact that the AES would have on capitalists and private investment levels. By the late 1970s Revisionists had come to advocate a social democracy that was close to the arguments of the structural constraints model. But the failure to carry out the AES in office between 1974–79 owed more to the general and pragmatic antipathy of the Labour leadership than either the political hostility of capitalists or disinvestment by them. The Labour government was not coerced into moderation by capitalists. Its own leaders were simply antipathetic for a variety of reasons to the policies to which the party was formally committed and chose not to implement them.

Other actors within the Labour party did not conform to the structural constraints model. David Coates talked of the 'steady erosion of socialist purpose'.[47] Sven Steinmo claimed that social democrats progressively adapt their ideological position.[48] Yet between 1973 and 1983 leftwing social democrats in the UK did not adapt or moderate their proposals. They continued to uphold radical policies: if anything they strengthened their resolve. They did not react in the way predicted by the structural constraints model. Labour did not adopt a moderate social democracy. It remained committed to radical policies.

There is much in the debate about British social democracy in this period which remains indeterminate. Nevertheless, the formation of the AES does not support the structural constraints model and its predictions about the limitations of social democracy. The argument that the AES was not a radical strategy in its intentions is weak. The contention that it was not a viable package to implement remains indeterminate and probably overstated. Two points stand out about the character of the AES and British social democracy. First, the AES was a radical strategy. The theory it was based upon, its policy tools and its objectives were not moderate. With the AES Labour set itself far-reaching goals. As Pontusson concludes, Przeworski 'provides no explanation at all for the occasional (perhaps cyclical) re-emergence of anti-capitalist investment politics' of the kind that the AES represented.[49] Second, the AES was enthusiastically embraced by Labour leftwingers. They supported the strategy and saw it as a potential basis for economic regeneration and a socialist society. Both these points cast doubt on the arguments of the structural constraints model.

THE CHARACTER OF THE LABOUR PARTY

Between 1970 and 1983 the Labour party advocated an economic strategy that most of its leaders opposed. The result was disunity and conflict. How did such a situation come about? Robert McKenzie in his account of the Labour party stressed the power and autonomy of the leadership. McKenzie detailed a series of features of the Labour party which meant that its leaders dominated it and were able to control its policy-making process. The analysis presented here of Labour's economic policy-making from 1970–1983 indicates that Labour's leaders did not enjoy the authority that McKenzie claimed for them. McKenzie's argument rested on three features: the loyalty that Labour leaders could extract from the party and union leaders; the skills with which they could manipulate the party and its conference in particular; and their ability to dominate the NEC. Each of these three mechanisms underpinning the authority of the leadership broke down.

First, the Labour leadership was unable to extract an unconditional and all-encompassing loyalty from the party conference and from trade union leaders. Labour leaders could not win votes simply by appeals to dependable unions. There was no 'Praetorian guard' of union leaders who would unquestioningly back the PLP. Instead many trade union leaders supported an economic strategy which was at odds with that preferred by the Labour leadership. Many unions placed a higher priority on securing their policy desires at the conference than on sustaining the Labour leadership. At times the gaps between the PLP leadership and union leaders were patched over: during the Labour government some union leaders extended considerable loyalty to the cabinet and acquiesced in an incomes policy. But the 'bond of confidence' that McKenzie talked of did not exist. The result was that Labour leaders faced many conference resolutions with which they did not agree and policies over which they had major reservations.

The Labour leadership lost the confidence of senior trade union figures in the late 1960s. Revisionism as an economic strategy did not live up to expectations. The unions opposed the 1964–70 Labour government's wage restraint, deflation and the proposals of *In Place of Strife*. As Revisionists continued to promote an incomes policy to tackle inflation, so union leaders looked elsewhere for an economic strategy. The effect of Labour carrying out policies that were inimical to the interests of unions was that support was withdrawn and the pattern of authority in the party broke down. Revisionism lost its control of the Labour conference and leftwingers were able to generate support for more radical measures.

Second, Labour leaders did not enjoy skills and procedures with which to bolster their position. On occasion leaders were able to effect policy outcomes through procedural devices. The most important concerning economic policy was the decision of the Conference Arrangements Committee to link the proposal to nationalise 25 out of the top 100 companies with more radical ideas. This linkage ensured its defeat at Labour's 1973 conference. But overall the ability of Labour's leaders to manipulate the party conference was severely circumscribed. A steady stream of NEC documents with which the leadership disagreed came to the conference and were passed.

The period between 1970 and 1983 can be contrasted with the strength of the Labour leadership in the 1950s. Minkin attributes the dominance of Revisionism to several procedural devices.[50] Party leaders were able to rely on such factors as: vaguely worded statements which were open to interpretation; the inability of conference to amend NEC statements; the compositing process; the timing of proposals; the varied mandate interpretation of union leaders; and the three-year rule which debarred the immediate re-emergence of issues. These devices were of little use to a PLP leadership in the 1970s which was confronted with hostile policy statements from the NEC as well as radical conference resolutions. These statements were not vague, they could not be amended and they were not subject to compositing. The NEC determined their timing and PLP leaders could not get union bosses to bend their union mandates. The three-year rule was suspended in 1979 but had little effect in keeping issues off the agenda before then. The PLP leadership lacked the capacity to challenge NEC documents or amend their contents.

Last, PLP domination of the NEC broke down for a period after 1970. PLP leaders became extremely isolated on Labour's NEC: few rightwing MPs were elected to it. By the early 1970s unions were electing assertive and leftwing representatives alongside moderates. A new and fluid balance of power emerged as leftwingers were able to put together a coalition of MPs and others which could outvote Labour's moderate leadership. The PLP leadership was unable to prevent the NEC taking decisions with which it disagreed and publishing policy documents whose content it opposed. This last feature is important in explaining how the Labour party came to adopt policies with which its leaders were so uncomfortable. The NEC was responsible for the production of documents articulating an economic strategy that the PLP disliked. Had the PLP been able to sustain its dominance of the NEC it is unlikely that the AES would have emerged. The NEC encouraged and gave considerable freedom to Labour's policy-making committees.

McKenzie claimed that policy-making in the Labour party was controlled by the PLP leadership: 'It is abundantly clear that the real centre of day-to-day policy-making within the Labour party is to be found in the deliberations of the Parliamentary Committee and of the PLP.'[51] For McKenzie, Labour's policy process conformed to a strict hierarchy: The PLP dominated the NEC which in turn controlled the sub-committees and the research department. Between 1970 and 1983 there was no such hierarchy within Labour's policy-making. Measures, with few exceptions, did not stem either from the shadow cabinet or from the PLP. The centres of policy-making were the sub-committees of the NEC, the TUC–Labour Party Liaison Committee and the work of the research department. The sub-committees of the NEC were far removed from the influence, let alone control of the PLP. They were nominally under the control of the NEC, but usually the NEC granted the policy-making sub-committees and the party's research department considerable freedom. The detail of policy owed much to the policy desires of committee members and party officials. Usually the NEC simply endorsed the policy proposals that were produced by this process. The PLP leaders had little input and found themselves presented with a strategy with which they had grave reservations. The process by which Labour adopted the AES and the nature of relationships within the party between 1970 and 1983 throw considerable doubt on the McKenzie thesis. Any attempt to analyse Labour in this period from McKenzie's perspective would produce a distorted and one-sided account of the party and policy-making within it. To understand Labour's advocacy of the AES, the whole party must be studied and not the leadership alone.

Trade unions were important actors in Labour's policy process. The Liaison Committee developed the party's anti-inflation strategy and fleshed out proposals for industrial democracy. Many unions were committed advocates of the AES. The TUC in its annual *Economic Review* supported a moderate but identifiable version of it. But the contribution of trade unions should not be over-emphasised. Many trade unions remained concerned with more immediate industrial matters. One central concern was their determination to avoid an incomes policy. Union leaders often endorsed the left's policies and individual union conference passed motions in support of the measures contained in the AES. But trade unionists did not take a major part in the policy debate within Labour and by 1982, increasingly concerned by the bitter dispute, they were generally less supportive of the left. Apart from the work of the Liaison Committee, unions were rarely involved in the initiation of policy proposals. The role of trade unions in policy-making accords with that laid out by Lewis Minkin: they had a negative and covert influence.

The role of the Labour conference in policy-making should also not be overstated. It often enthusiastically approved party documents and resolutions picked up on many of the ideas of the AES. But conference rarely initiated proposals. The key to the development of the AES was the control by leftwingers of the NEC and the party's policy-making sub-committees. The proposals which originated in these committees were then presented to the conference and endorsed.

A further point to be noted from this discussion of policy-making is that Labour is a doctrinal party. Between 1970 and 1983 Labour engaged in a series of bitter disputes, the origins of which are to be found in disagreements over policy. Policy proposals, the party's objectives and the mechanisms by which they emerged provided the substance for these disputes. The disagreements went right to the heart of the party and questioned its fundamental goals. It is wrong to lay too much stress on Labour's ethos as the definitive characteristic of the party. Labour has been a party where different doctrines are bitterly contested – a conflict which has had major consequences for the party.

Between 1970 and 1983 it was of considerable importance for relationships within the party as to whether Labour was in office or in opposition. In opposition the PLP leadership, deprived of resources, was considerably weaker than it was in power. The 1974–79 Labour government was able, in large part, simply to ignore the policy demands of the Labour party. It had authority simply by virtue of its position in office. Out of government such power was not available to it. The status of the Labour party had important consequences for the authority of the leadership.

Between 1970 and 1983 the Labour party was much closer to the work of Lewis Minkin and Samuel Beer than Robert McKenzie. Economic policy-making in the Labour party highlights the diversity of sources and the limitations on the ability of Labour leaders to impose their own proposals on the party. There were major constraints on the autonomy of the leadership. After 1970 power within the Labour party was divided amongst its constituent elements. The PLP had influence but so too did the trade unions, the NEC and the party conference. If anything, Minkin's account under-estimates the importance of Labour's institutions – its sub-committees and research department – in determining the detail of the party's policy stance.

LABOUR'S DECLINE: FRACTURE AND FRATRICIDE IN
BRITISH SOCIAL DEMOCRACY

One over-riding feature of policy-making within the Labour
party between 1970 and 1983 was the inability of the different sections of the party to reach agreement over the economic strategy it should adopt. Although formally there was
a remarkable continuity in party policy from 1970 to 1983,
many leaders never reconciled themselves to the proposals
Labour advocated. Instead policy-making was marked by an
endemic disunity. One document stated, 'It was not at all
unusual for members of the NEC and the shadow cabinet
to publicly disassociate themselves from each other's policies at every opportunity.'[52] It would be mistaken to
characterise the whole party as taking sides in this debate.
Many elements, especially the unions, did not get involved
in policy disputes. It would also be wrong to depict left and
right as monolithic blocks. Nevertheless, a struggle between
two very different strategic packages based on contrasting
conceptions of social democracy dominated the Labour party
after 1970. The period was also marked by the severe electoral decline of the Labour party.

I argue that these developments, the disagreements over
policy and the party's electoral crisis, are causally linked.
The struggle for the Alternative Economic Strategy and the
consequent conflict to democratise the structure of the party
did great electoral damage to Labour. The conflicts which
began over policy in the early 1970s had broadened and
intensified by 1979. For three years from then on Labour
politics were marked by disunity and disagreement. The
bitterness and the factionalism meant that Labour ceased
to present a credible image to voters. The most damaging
split of all came in 1981 with the formation of the SDP.
The result was the split in the anti-Conservative vote at the
1983 election.

It would be wrong to attribute all Labour's problems since
1970 to policy disagreements and there are other important factors which help to explain Labour's decline. There
have also been other splits within the Labour party, notably
over UK membership of the EEC and over defence policy.
But Labour's division over the EEC was largely resolved by

the referendum of 1975 (though some rightwingers were concerned by the proposal passed at conference in 1980 to take the UK out of Europe). Labour's split over defence flared up predominantly in the early 1980s. Labour's divergence over economic strategy went to the heart of the ideology and the identity of the party. It concerned the fundamental objectives and the *raison d'être* of the party. It was a split which lasted longer than any other. In 1973 *The Spectator*'s political commentator called the differences over economic strategy the 'real Labour party split'.[53] A party document in 1977 said that economic strategy was 'obviously the most difficult of all the areas of disagreement'.[54]

The different sides within the party could not present a united and consistent set of arguments on economic policy, but engaged in a drawn-out and public display of hostility to each other. It is of little surprise that Labour lost electoral support. After 1979 Labour became very internalised as a party. Patrick Seyd comments that in 1981 'intra-party politics were at their most intense and the electorate were treated as mere bystanders'.[55] In fact the description is apt for much of 1970–83. Policy disputes presented a negative and divided image. Years earlier Richard Crossman had warned that the Labour party 'cannot survive a lengthy deadlock between its two axes of power'.[56] John Smith said later, 'The reason for that [credibility gap] is that the Labour party spent a good deal of its period in opposition fighting each other.'[57] After 1983 Denis Healey concluded, 'The election was lost, not in the three weeks of the campaign, but in the three years which preceded it. . . . In that period the party itself acquired a highly unfavourable public image, based on disunity, extremism, crankiness and general unfitness to govern.'[58] Throughout 1980, an average of 79 per cent of the public thought that Labour was divided.[59] In September 1980 when asked why Labour was not doing as well as it should, 50 per cent felt that it was because the party was divided – the most common response. Similar figures emerged in 1981: the party's disunity was the most frequently given reason for not voting Labour. 61 per cent of potential voters said it made them less likely to support the party in February 1981.[60]

Labour's right might blame the party's leftwing policies

rather than its internal dispute. But, as indicated earlier, it is unclear that the party was unelectable with such an economic strategy. At the height of the internal conflict within Labour between 1979 and 1982 there was some support for the party's policy. For the first two and half years in opposition, the Conservative government never had a lead in terms of overall policies of more than 6 per cent.[61] On several occasions Labour had a policy lead of 5 per cent over the Tories. Labour was more damaged by the divisions within it than by its extremism.[62]

Between 1970 and 1983 developing a genuinely united front over economic policy, agreed between all the factions and elements of the party, proved too great a task for Labour. The disunity over economic policy fuelled the conflict over the structure of the party. In turn that conflict led to the split as the SDP MPs left Labour. Ultimately Labour's disunity damaged the party's credibility with extremely detrimental electoral consequences. Labour's failure to implement the AES was not due to a lack of resources as labour movement theorists suggest but because the party was disunited. Moreover, the party's policy trajectory was decided by internal factors within Labour, rather than by external events.

In analysing Labour's decline and the crisis of social democracy more generally, many commentators have emphasised external structural factors. In the introduction to this book, I noted that Labour's declining electoral base has frequently been attributed to economic and social change. The difficulties social democratic parties have confronted have often been ascribed to developments in the environment in which they compete for votes and attempt to construct policies. My analysis of economic policy-making between 1970 and 1983 leads to the conclusion that key problems of British social democracy were internal to the party: Labour's failures were determined neither by external circumstances nor by structural causes but largely by the choices of its leading actors. The external environment in which Labour operates and the ability of the party to adapt and respond to changing circumstances are important factors in its decline. But my analysis suggests that Labour's problems in this period were also caused by the inability of the party to reach agreement over economic strategy. This failure to present a united front undermined its capacity to win votes. In analysing the decline of the Labour party attention needs to be given to internal and agency-orientated explanations of that crisis.

Several points can be noted from this analysis. I indicated in the introduction that there is a popular conception of the Labour left as a group of determined and narrow-minded individuals who manipulated the party after 1979. It has been suggested that these leftwingers unnecessarily provoked Labour into a conflict which was irrelevant to policy and irrational. The account presented here suggests that the origin of the pressures to democratise Labour (and the conflict which went with those pressures) is to be found in the frustration that developed when the leadership so obviously ignored the policy desires of the party. It was logical for leftwingers to seek answers as to why accepted party policy was not implemented by considering the role of the leadership. Given the degree of consensus within Labour's policy-making process, it was straightforward for leftwingers to look at the constitutional structures of the party as part of a continuation of policy disagreements with the Revisionists. It was manipulation on the part of the leadership, not the left, which promoted the post-1979 disputes within Labour. The policy choices of Labour's Revisionists during 1964–70 and 1974–79, alongside their failure to accept party policy, go a long way to explain the disagreements and disunity within Labour. Labour's rightwing leadership must accept some blame, at the very least, for the conflict within the party and for the damage that such conflict did. It was their hostility to much party policy and at the same time their apparent acceptance of some radical documents (such as the February 1974 election manifesto) which paved the way for the left's constitutional demands.

Rightwingers might of course respond that the party's activists were not representative of its members and so they were entitled to ignore leftwing demands. Recent research suggests that the views of activists and members do not diverge.[63] Moreover rightwingers only claimed autonomy from the party's structures once they found themselves to be at odds with the policies produced by Labour's internal policy-making process. By the late 1970s they criticised such structures as 'unrepresentative': previously they had been content to make use of the same organisations to ensure their policy preferences dominated the party.

Second, again as noted in the introduction, many accounts of Labour stress the constitutional struggle within the party after 1979. This period is presented as an abrupt and dramatic shift leftwards. Yet the argument that Labour was somehow hijacked by the left at this time is nonsensical. To characterise this period as a turning point or as a sensational shift leftwards, is mistaken. Labour moved decisively to the left after 1970 and well before 1979. What happened after 1979 was that the left looked for a means of implementing a policy that already existed. To understand the fracture that took place within Labour, attention needs to be focused at least as far back as the 1964–70 Labour Government.[64] It was then that the foundations for Labour's collapse were laid.

Third, Labour's failure to develop a strategy around which the party could unite represented a failure of social choice. Labour leftwingers and the party's largely Revisionist leadership were unable to agree on what form a socialist economic strategy should take. They refused to accept the proposals made by the others and when defeated, they continually attempted to have the decisions reversed. In such circumstances Labour's institutions were an important determinant of the party's policy positions. The party's organisational structure and divided constitutional authority between PLP and NEC were important causes of the divergence that occurred. With 'no single source of legitimate authority', Labour's democratic structure intensified and prolonged the conflict over strategy.[65] The institutions of the Labour party and their operation provide a crucial explanation of the crisis in the party.

Fourth, it may also be the case that, outraged at the attitude of the leadership, the left did not pay enough attention to the development of their strategy. Although theoretically coherent, it was based upon assumptions which, even by 1974, looked problematic. By the early 1980s, the left's strategy appeared increasingly implausible as the recession worsened. Yet leftwingers failed to adapt or reconsider its position because of its near-obsession with party democracy and constitutional struggle.

Could a compromise between Labour's left and right have been reached? It is difficult to conceive the form that a compromise might have taken in the circumstances of the 1970s and early 1980s to which both sides could have agreed. Any conjecture must be heavily qualified, but some form of radicalised corporatism might have provided a basis for agreement. The National Economic Assessment provided a framework in which short term economic benefits (immediately rising wages) could have been traded off against long term gains from higher investment and possibly increased social control within industry. But the Labour left could not accept an incomes policy and continued to hold a theory which assumed that re-appropriating monopolistic profits would provide near-instant benefits. Labour's right remained hostile to an interventionist industrial policy. The disengagement of unions from policy-making further limited the prospects for corporatism in the UK. A fragmented union movement was not prepared to undergo wage restraint. A more political union movement, coupled with an acceptance of longer term goals, might have permitted corporatism to develop. Political circumstances made an alternative strategic choice, perhaps a more realistic one given economic circumstances, difficult to realise.

By the mid-1980s the AES no longer seemed a feasible strategy given the deindustrialisation that had taken place and general antipathy to state intervention. It must remain an open question as to what impact the implementation of the AES would have had on the British economy. In the 1970s and the early 1980s, with a substantial industrial sector, and the revenue of North Sea Oil, an interventionist industrial strategy might have achieved a great deal. Four terms of Conservative government have not paved the way for industrial regeneration within the UK. The Alternative Economic Strategy may have been a missed opportunity: not just by a doctrinaire Labour party unable to agree on policy, but also by Britain as a whole.

Epilogue: The Development of Labour's Economic Strategy since 1983

Since 1983 the Labour party has undergone a fundamental transformation.[1] The origins of that transformation are to be found in the immediate aftermath of Labour's defeat in the 1983 general election and the detailed post-mortem which was launched soon afterwards. Many reasons were blamed for the party's dismal electoral performance including the Falklands War, the role of the Liberal–SDP Alliance in splitting the anti-Conservative vote, the hostile media, and Foot's poor leadership.[2] The research department noted Labour's bad campaign, lack of organisation, inadequate presentation, and the disunity in the party. Geoff Bish said of the shadow cabinet that they 'clearly felt they had been "bounced" into accepting a document they did not want. They *were* bounced. They did *not* like the policies. And it showed.'[3] The research department accepted that some of Labour's policies had not been popular – others, however, had been. More of a problem was that the party's economic programme was not perceived as credible but as a series of rash and expensive promises.[4] Its defence policy was even more of a vote loser. The result was that, while they liked aspects of Labour's strategy, voters felt that the Conservatives had the best overall package.

Soon after the election, Bish identified a series of problems with Labour's policy-making procedures. Most important of all, he argued that in future Labour had to be united over its policy proposals and the PLP had to be involved directly in their formation. Otherwise 'the result is confusion, lack of mutual commitment and distrust'.[5] His conclusion was stark: 'If we cannot agree, it's best that we say nowt.'[6] Another research department document stated, 'The party must learn to speak with one voice.'[7] Bish stated, 'We cannot simply go on as before.'[8]

210

Bish was not alone. Many of the party's leading figures accepted that a central cause of Labour's defeat was its internal structure with its division of authority between the PLP leadership and the NEC. The party's institutional structure was responsible, in part at any rate, for the policy divisions and disagreements which had marked the decade before 1983. Internal reorganisation and institutional reform were paramount among the objectives of the new Labour leader, Neil Kinnock. Although associated with the party's leftwing, Kinnock had distanced himself from Tony Benn and the 'hard left' at the time of the 1981 deputy leadership contest. The changes he initiated after 1983 reflected the political position he had adopted at that time. Kinnock said later, 'It was clear to me and to those associated with me that there would have to be profound change in the policies and in the organisation of the Labour party.'[9] In this chapter I examine the detail of Labour's transformation since 1983, the changes that have been made to the party's policy-making process and the development of its policy commitments.

THE TRANSFORMATION OF LABOUR'S INTERNAL STRUCTURE

Kinnock's election proved to be a watershed.[10] Over the next decade he instigated a series of fundamental reforms to the structure of the Labour party.[11] These reforms were introduced gradually. Kinnock proceeded particularly carefully after a proposal to modify the process by which the party's MPs were reselected was defeated in 1984. Later he lamented the leader's lack of an 'instrument for inaugurating and pursuing change.'[12] Nevertheless Kinnock proved to be a tough and forceful leader – in itself a contrast with his predecessor. For example, he was extremely vigorous and ultimately successful in expelling members of Militant from Labour. Over his nine-year leadership the cumulative impact of the reforms was dramatic. By the time Kinnock resigned as Labour leader in 1992 he had secured considerable authority within the party.

In October 1983 a Campaign Strategy Committee was established to oversee the party's campaigning activities. The new committee allowed the Labour leader to side-step the NEC on certain issues at a time when he was uncertain of its support. The committee indicated a new emphasis on campaigning amongst the electorate as opposed to internalised policy development. At the same time important reforms took place to Labour's policy-making process which integrated members of the PLP into the formation of the party's strategy. In 1985 Labour's headquarters at Walworth Road was reorganised and placed on a much more professional footing. Kinnock also increased the size of his office of Leader of the Opposition, employing twice as many staff as had Michael Foot. Extra resources were allocated to the PLP for research work.

In the late-1980s Kinnock introduced further reforms and marshalled support for them in the NEC. In 1987 an electoral college, which allowed individual members to participate directly, was introduced for the selection of MPs. The NEC encouraged and then insisted that, in elections to it, the constituencies' section representatives should be chosen by a ballot of individual party members and not by general management committees or delegates. In 1988 the NEC took control of candidate selection in by-elections. Two years later the NEC announced that the union block vote at the party conference should be reduced so increasing the relative weight of the constituency parties. A National Policy Forum was proposed to consider issues over a longer timeframe outside of the conference.

The full impact of some of these reforms was not immediately apparent – some of the changes, for example the new policy forum, were not introduced until after the 1992 election. They gave extra power to individual party members at the expense of its activists. They also helped to secure and subsequently bolster the dominant position of the party's leadership. The import of individual balloting for the NEC was manifest. The left had already lost ground in its constituency section. With the new mechanism, however, there was a marked alteration in its composition. By 1993 six of seven members of the CLP section were from the shadow cabinet. The seventh was ex-leader Neil Kinnock. No leftwinger was elected by party members to the NEC. (Since then the left has won back a couple of seats in the constituencies' section.)

Institutional reform within the Labour party was accompanied by important behavioural changes. The scale of 1983's defeat had a considerable impact on trade union leaders: one of the themes of that year's TUC annual congress was 'new realism' – the pragmatic need to take account of the economic changes that had occurred and the impact of the Conservative government on the labour movement. Over the next few years senior union figures extended considerable support to Kinnock's leadership: most notably when Labour abandoned its commitment to the closed shop and accepted some of the Conservative legislative reforms to industrial relations, trade unions leaders acquiesced.

Kinnock's position as party leader was reinforced by the continued fragmentation of Labour's left. Members of the soft left, including the Labour Coordinating Committee, became increasingly detached from the party's hard left. Shaken by the dimensions of defeat, moderate leftwingers felt it was important that there should be some form of rapprochement with the party's right. The hard left was uncertain what form Labour's economic strategy should take, and, racked by further internal disagreements, the coalition that had been organised around Tony Benn's deputy leadership challenge effectively broke up. The influence that the hard left enjoyed on party matters was steadily eroded. By the mid-1980s the Tribune group of MPs was firmly established as a centrist force within the party. Especially important was a realignment of the left during 1985 which strengthened Kinnock's base on the NEC: Tom Sawyer, an influential trade unionist, Michael Meacher and David Blunkett had, albeit somewhat equivocally, been regarded as allies of Tony Benn's. In 1983–84 they had voted with the hard left on the NEC. In 1984–85 they frequently broke ranks and voted with the leadership.[13] When elected, Kinnock had lacked majority support on the NEC. By 1986 he could be reasonably certain of winning votes on most issues. By 1992 he won them crushingly.

The main consequence of the institutional reforms and behavioural changes was that Neil Kinnock's immediate successor, John Smith, inherited a party structure in 1992 in which the authority of the leader was once again paramount. In chapter one I noted that the thesis which claimed that the parliamentary leadership of the Labour party was dominant and autonomous rested on three pillars. In the 1970s and early 1980s successive Labour leaders were unable to rely on any of these three mechanisms. By the late-1980s matters had been decisively reversed. First, Neil Kinnock was able to extract considerable loyalty from union leaders, the party conference and individual members. When Tony Benn challenged Kinnock for the party leadership in 1988 the result was a dismal failure. Whatever their doubts about policy change, most party members placed a high premium on winning elections and on loyalty to the leadership.[14] Second, Kinnock was able to make use of various devices and skills to ensure his autonomy. For example, in the first years of his leadership the Campaign Strategy Committee was important. Later Kinnock's large private office played an important part in his ascendancy within the party. Last, the PLP was able once again to dominate the NEC. An assertive leader, Kinnock was prepared to make full use of all three mechanisms in securing the outcomes he desired.

These developments were consequences of the institutional reforms and behavioural changes, which were motivated by the party's successive election defeats. They meant that Labour's leader was able to control the party's structure. The roles of the NEC and of the party conference were less important, both in formal constitutional terms and in the way that they operated in practice. Labour had come to resemble the kind of party that Robert McKenzie had argued it to be – one which the leadership was able to dominate. Such leadership domination was more contingent than McKenzie suggested it would be. It reflected the circumstances of Labour's electoral decline and successive Labour leaders and their staff worked intensively to generate support for their initiatives. Nevertheless, by the mid-1990s, the office of the Labour leader enjoyed an authority unparalleled in the party's history. Moreover, the distinction between Labour's status in government and opposition, identified by Lewis Minkin, was eroded. Labour leaders were no longer necessarily weaker in opposition than in office.

REFORMS TO THE POLICY-MAKING PROCESS

Changes to Labour's policy-making process predated some of the other institutional reforms to the party's structure. Kinnock later said that on becoming leader, 'I first had to replace the multitude of sub-committees, working parties and the like, which over the years had been spawned by the NEC.'[15] Bish was extremely critical of the party's policy making process: 'The most serious problem with these arrangements is that they have helped to cement the divisions between the NEC and the shadow cabinet on the development of policy and strategy, and its presentation to the electorate.'[16] Kinnock described the policy process that the party had established in the 1970s as 'a labyrinth of patronage, detached from electoral considerations with no guaranteed participation by parliamentary spokespeople and no strategic framework'.[17]

In December 1983 the sub-committees, which had carried out so much of the work in developing the Alternative Economic Strategy, were abolished by the NEC. Geoff Bish argued that they were too removed from the PLP and that their large memberships fluctuated too much so that policy also oscillated.[18] They were replaced by small committees made up equally of members of the NEC and senior PLP figures.[19] The central objective of these committee was to ensure that agreement could be reached: Bish stated bluntly, 'It is crucial for the credibility of the party that its leadership (both NEC and shadow cabinet) is able to speak with voice on all policy issues.'[20] MPs were formally integrated into the party's policy process. The research department also proposed that policy documents should be moderate in intentions and more general.[21] Fewer and less precise policy documents were produced after 1983. Labour published no more grandiose programmes with sweeping and precise commitments.

The result was a shift in influence over policy formation from party headquarters at Walworth Road to the PLP at Westminster. The development was evident in Labour's first initiative in terms of economic policy after the 1983 election, the Jobs and Industry Campaign, launched in April 1985. For the first time in over fifteen years, moderate members of the shadow cabinet played a central role in the formation of Labour party economic policy. As well as Neil Kinnock's own input, the new policies owed much to John Smith and Roy Hattersley as employment spokesperson and shadow chancellor respectively. Research department staff worked closely with them in drafting documents – another new development, but they were less important than the personal political advisers employed by shadow ministers. John Eatwell who worked in Neil Kinnock's private office was especially influential in the formation of party policy, drafting many of Kinnock's speeches and liaising directly with members of the shadow cabinet. Indeed, by 1985 members of the shadow cabinet took much more interest in economic policy generally than they had during the 1979–83 parliament.

Other changes were evident in the Jobs and Industry Campaign. It indicated Labour's concern not just with internal policy development but with securing electoral support for the party's programme: it was a *campaign*, involving a variety of events and rallies to get the party's message across to voters. Labour accepted the importance of meeting the policy desires of the electorate. The party now made intensive and detailed use of opinion polls. It adopted a Downsian-type electoral strategy and attempted to match the preferences of the median voter. Especially important in this regard was Peter Mandelson, appointed director of the party's campaigns and communications in 1985. At the same time the Liaison Committee became less important. It met infrequently and no major policy initiatives were developed within it.

After its 1987 election defeat Labour launched a formal Policy Review. Seven policy committees were set up in place of the Joint Policy Committees. Each had a convenor from the shadow cabinet and one from the NEC. Neil Kinnock chose the convenors and a member from his office sat in on each group in order to monitor and coordinate the whole process. In 1988 a shadow cabinet economics committee was established and soon afterwards a new Economic Secretariat to serve frontbenchers was constituted. By 1990 economic policy initiatives stemmed from the leaders of the PLP.

Labour's policy-making process changed dramatically between 1983 and 1990. The PLP became much more assertive and policy development became orientated towards the preferences of the electorate. By the time of the 1992 election members of the party's policy directorate (as the research department was now termed) had little impact on the development of original policies. Documents were drafted by shadow ministers and their advisers. When Labour decided to endorse the European Exchange Rate Mechanism in 1990 the key figures behind the decision were Neil Kinnock and John Eatwell along with John Smith, as shadow chancellor, and Gordon Brown, the trade and industry spokesperson.

LABOUR'S ECONOMIC POLICY COMMITMENTS

The content of Labour's economic policy was altered gradually but dramatically. Senior figures were quick to distance themselves in 1983 from the party's existing proposals. After the defeat, Roy Hattersley concluded, 'Last June our economic policy. . . . was a net vote loser. Nobody believed that our theories could be put into practice. The whole strategy lacked two essential ingredients: a coherent plan for investment and a scheme to confront inflation.'[22] In October *The Economist* commented that Kinnock's intention was to shift Labour away from the 1983 manifesto in a series of stages.[23] One TUC official said later, 'It was clear that you could not carry on with the same policies'.[24] Another concluded, 'There was no credibility left in simply repeating the prescriptions of the Liaison documents.'[25] One policy adviser, John Eatwell, noted later that much about the context that shaped economic strategy had changed.[26] A new environment led inevitably to different proposals. The first modification to Labour's AES concerned its attitude to the EEC. Even before the 1983 election, research staff accepted that leaving the common market was 'a loser' and stated that 48 per cent of the population opposed withdrawal.[27] Labour soon dropped the proposal.[28]

Labour's manifesto at the 1987 general election can be contrasted sharply in terms of economic strategy with that produced four years earlier. *Britain Will Win* contained few remnants of the AES.[29] The National Economic Assessment remained as a vague kind of corporatist economic summit. There was a commitment to reflation and a promise to extend social ownership towards high technology industries and some other unspecified parts of the economy. Planning agreements, the sweeping proposals for industrial democracy, price controls, and protection had all gone. No case was made for profitable public ownership and there were no proposals for new institutions to plan the economy. Social ownership appeared to be concerned with increased investment through limited strategic equity. Altogether it was a very different package which did not envisage greatly increased control in the economy. It was neither so antipathetic to private industry nor so sweeping in intentions. Labour accepted that private industry would play the central role in economic recovery – a marked departure from the Alternative Economic Strategy. The main task of a Labour government would be to persuade private firms to invest more resources in the economy. In a speech drafted for Kinnock in 1985, John Eatwell argued, 'The main task of modernising British industry will fall to the private sector.' Later Eatwell claimed that five changes had occurred in the party's economic policy after 1983: i) Labour had abandoned its macroeconomic commitment to full employment; ii) it had shifted to a pro-European outlook; iii) it had renounced public ownership as a key means of affecting economic outcomes; iv) it had abandoned the idea that the state should interfere in private firms' decision-making; and v) the party had shifted from advocating discretionary policy-making to proposing rules in economic management.[30] Each of these five changes indicates a shift from the AES. The party had moved a long way from *Labour's Programme 1982*.

The party's new industrial strategy owed much to the resurgent leadership of the PLP. In his first parliamentary speech as shadow minister for trade and industry John Smith emphasised the need for a supply side strategy which tackled problems of low investment, poor skills, limited research and development, and regional inequalities through the construction of a new partnership between government and industry. He outlined the same approach to the party conference a year later. Smith's views were shared by John Eatwell, a proponent of continental-style industrial intervention. Their argument was that, while markets worked well enough for the most part, there were some goods and services they did not provide satisfactorily. Firms did not invest because of short-termism and they did not train their work-forces because of fears that skilled employees would be poached by other companies. Tackling these problems required considerable intervention and Labour's long term objective was to create in the UK the kind of organised capitalism that so benefited the German economy (amongst others). A Labour government would coordinate markets through a variety of incentives and interventions to ensure that firms invested sufficient capital (by protecting them from take-overs amongst other measures), trained their workforces and sank resources into research and development. Where possible, co-ordinated capitalism would be constructed with the support of industry. These themes were clear in the Jobs and Industry Campaign: it emphasised measures to boost investment, to stimulate research and development and to increase training – all with the cooperation of industry.

In 1989 the result of the two-year Policy Review were published by the party. Though heralded as a set of original developments, the review largely confirmed the existing industrial strategy and its objectives. Some changes took place later. Most notably Labour endorsed the European Exchange Rate Mechanism and gave a strong commitment to macro-economic stability. Nevertheless the core of the party's economic and industrial policy remained focused on moderate reforms to the supply side of the economy. The central objective of these interventions was to coordinate economic activities and so raise private sector investment. Despite Gordon Brown's adoption of the label 'new economics', this supply-side strategy has been reaffirmed in his economic proposals and Labour party policy documents since the 1992 election defeat.

Some commentators have taken Labour's moderate industrial strategy to characterise a return to Revisionist social democracy. The party's modest objectives, including improved equality and social justice, resemble those of the Revisionists. But, in attempting to raise investment and increase capacity, Labour's industrial strategy remains focused on the supply-side of the economy. 'Production politics', albeit in a mild form, continues to be at the centre of the party's social democratic strategy and immediate objectives. Economic

policy is concentrated upon shaping the investment decisions that firms make and organising the environment in
which they operate. The party's ultimate goals represent a
retreat from those of the labour movement theorists – though
many of them have toned down their own commitment to
radical aims. Labour no longer proposes to transform capitalist society. Indeed some observers were quick to conclude
that this moderation represents a break with the party's
existing social democratic promises altogether.

The new strategy is manifestly less radical than the Alternative Economic Strategy. Whether it marks the abandonment of social democracy is another matter. Labour's
post-1983 economic strategy can be contrasted with the
political economy of successive Conservative governments.
The latter's strategy embodies a free market approach based
on a casualised workforce, contractual relationships, weakened collective bargaining, and reduced institutional interventions. Coordinated capitalism as an approach involves
social cohesion, consultation of workforces, forms of participation and discussion, long term relationships and the
development of associational relationships. State intervention, in creating incentives and forming the economic environment, has an important role to play. The party's central
objective is economic regeneration but the means to achieve
an improved economic performance include participation,
negotiation, collective action and egalitarian measures – all
features which lend themselves to social democratic goals.
Economic regeneration was a central feature of the party's
policies in successive Revisionist and leftwing programmes.
Moreover, characteristics of Labour's strategy are desirable
in themselves as well as in order to promote economic regeneration. Since 1992 Gordon Brown has emphasised that
measures to promote equality are efficient and therefore
welcome additions to Labour's economic strategy as a means
of securing an improved economic performance. But others in the party, such as John Prescott, have argued that
the same measures, currently in the party's economic strategy, are desirable precisely because they promote equality
and participation. As such they are ends in themselves. John
Eatwell's claim is that the coordinated model is inherently
social democratic. The party has drawn heavily from the

experience of European social democratic parties in the last decade. It is certainly not evident that the strategy is incompatible with a commitment to social democratic objectives of economic efficiency, accountability and increased equality.

Labour's social democracy now represents a curious hybrid. It has abandoned the transformative objectives of labour movement theorists but retains their concern with production and the decisions made by firms. It has accepted some of the limited goals of Revisionists but rejects their focus on distribution. It accepts the importance of private profit identified by the structural constraints model but rejects the limited conclusions reached by its theorists. Labour's policy commitments mark a fresh, limited, pragmatic and reformist trajectory. They amount to a new interpretation of social democracy which can be distinguished from the three I outlined in chapter one. In abandoning the labour movement approach, Labour has neither returned to Revisionism nor accepted the limitations of the structural constraints model.

It is worth noting that the Alternative Economic Strategy was not immediately abandoned by all its supporters in 1983. Some continued to advocate its measures and Andrew Glyn, a previous critic, proposed a package of policies close to the AES in his 1985 pamphlet for the Campaign Group of Labour MPs, *A Million Jobs a Year*.[31] Others came to focus on certain aspects of the strategy which would not require the election of a Labour Government for their implementation. Stuart Holland stressed a European dimension for intervention.[32] Other advocates emphasised the local dimension of any strategy where a Labour local authority might use local enterprise boards to influence economic activity.[33] These initiatives represented a departure in their scope and goals from the AES and they had limited impact upon the Labour party. Gradually, even academic interest in the AES faded. By 1986 one erstwhile supporter suggested that the AES belonged in the past.[34]

CONCLUSIONS

Despite the institutional reforms and substantial developments in policy, Labour lost further successive general elections in 1987 and 1992. Neil Kinnock resigned after his second defeat and was succeeded by John Smith. Smith died of a heart attack two years later in 1994 and was replaced by Tony Blair. In many ways 1987's election outcome was expected given the dimensions of defeat four years earlier and the legacies of the party's civil war during 1979–83. The 1992 result was more of a surprise: the party's institutions had been transformed and its new policies were well established. Arguably Labour was more united than at any time since the war and much less internalised that it had been between 1970 and 1983. The party had performed well in opinion polls from 1989 onwards. The election result suggested that institutional reform was a necessary condition for a future Labour general election victory but not a sufficient one. Structural changes to the economy and to society continue to undermine the party's electoral base. Labour's adaptation to such changes through the development of a popular policy programme proved problematic. The party's moderate proposals ran into trouble over Conservative claims about their impact on taxation. Labour attempted to establish an image of fiscal prudence. During the election campaign it proved a difficult position to sustain at the same time as offering some positive spending commitments.

Nevertheless the institutional reforms and the policy changes under Neil Kinnock's leadership have had a remarkable impact on the party's electoral fortunes. When Kinnock became leader, Labour was a disunited party desperately fighting for second place with the Liberal-SDP Alliance. Six years later, in June 1989, Labour beat the Conservatives decisively in the elections to the European parliament. In psychological terms it was an important result: for the first time in nearly fifteen years, the party had won a national electoral contest. But the transformation to Labour may have been achieved at a cost in terms of the participation of its members. Patrick Seyd and Paul Whiteley found that members had become less active during the late 1980s.[35] Seyd concluded that 'a sense of disengagement prevailed' amongst the party's activists.[36] Such a lack of activism had important consequences. Whiteley and Seyd concluded that if constituency membership had been double its actual size the Labour vote would have increased by 5 per cent in 1992.[37] Had either party members been as active as they had been five years previously or membership levels been slightly higher in a dozen crucial marginal constituencies, it would have been sufficient to deny the Conservative government re-election as a majority administration. In the aftermath of defeat, it appeared as if there might be a trade-off between institutional reform and an active membership. Particularly problematic was that, although they undermined each other, both centralisation of Labour's structures and mass participation by party workers might be necessary for electoral victory.

Since 1994, however, Labour's membership figures have shown a dramatic increase. By the time of the next election over half the party's members will have joined since 1992. The rise in membership is associated by many with Tony Blair's leadership of the party. Overall, Blair has had a remarkable two years as Labour leader. Labour secured a consistent lead in the opinion polls and he proved to be an exceptionally popular Leader of the Opposition. With his theme of 'New Labour', Blair has presented an image of the party as being transformed almost beyond recognition through a far-reaching process of modernisation. The ideas and economic proposals of the Alternative Economic Strategy seem far removed from those put forward by the party he leads. The institutional reforms of the 1980s and 1990s have established a powerful position for whoever is Labour leader. Fundamental obstacles to a Labour election victory – the party's divided structure and the internal conflict that structure generated – have been resolved. While a future Labour government will have to ensure that relations within the party do not deteriorate as they did between 1974 and 1979, Blair has been just as dominant as were Kinnock and Smith before him. As a result he has been able to turn from internal matters and focus largely on electoral issues. The most important task facing him before the next election will be to mobilise those new members around an economic strategy that is coherent, plausible, distinctive and attractive to the electorate.

References

INTRODUCTION: ECONOMIC STRATEGY AND THE LABOUR PARTY

1. Labour party, *Labour's Programme 1973* (1973).
2. Tony Benn, *Against the Tide* (London, Hutchinson, 1989), pp. 42–3.
3. From the private political diaries of Tony Benn, 14 May 1973, in the Benn archives, (henceforth, Benn diary).
4. Anthony Crosland, 'The Prospects of Socialism – Nationalisation?', *Encounter*, XLI (September 1973), pp. 60–1, p. 61.
5. Labour party, *New Hope for Britain* (1983), p. 11.
6. Labour party, *Labour's Programme 1982* (1982), p. 9.
7. See Paul Whiteley, *The Labour Party in Crisis* (London, Methuen, 1983).
8. See, for example, Peter Jenkins, *Mrs Thatcher's Revolution* (London, Jonathan Cape, 1987), pp. 102–28.
9. On Labour's 'shift to the left' see Anthony King, 'Margaret Thatcher's First Term' in Austin Ranney, *Britain at the Polls, 1983* (Durham, Duke University Press, 1985), pp. 15–22.
10. See the discussion in BBC, *The Wilderness Years*, 3 December 1995; David Kogan and Maurice Kogan, *The Battle for the Labour Party* (London, Kogan Page, 1982); and Austin Mitchell, *Four Years in the Death of the Labour Party* (London, Methuen, 1983).
11. Kevin Jeffreys, *The Labour Party since 1945* (London, Macmillan, 1993), p. 108.
12. Peter Dorey, *British Politics since 1945* (Oxford, Blackwell, 1995), p. 181. See also David Dutton, *British Politics since 1945* (Oxford, Blackwell, 1991), p. 89.
13. Eric Shaw, 'Towards Renewal? The British Labour Party's Policy Review', in Richard Gillespie and William Paterson (eds), *Rethinking Social Democracy in Western Europe* (London, Frank Cass, 1993), pp. 112–32, p. 115.
14. A strong statement was Eric Hobsbawm's *The Forward March of Labour Halted?* (London, Verso, 1981), pp. 1–19. See also Ivor Crewe, 'Labour Force Changes, Working Class Decline, and the Labour Vote: Social and Electoral Change in Postwar Britain' in Frances Fox Piven (ed.), *Labor Parties in Postindustrial Societies* (Oxford, Polity, 1991), pp. 20–46. Similar, though not so pessimistic, arguments had been developed in the 1950s by Labour's Revisionist thinkers – they are discussed in chapter 1.
15. I. Crewe, 'Labour Force Changes, Working Class Decline, and the Labour Vote: Social and Electoral Change in Postwar Britain', p. 25.
16. Ivor Crewe, 'Why the Conservatives Won', in Howard Penniman, *Britain at the Polls, 1979* (London, AEI, 1981), pp. 263–305; and Ivor Crewe 'Labour and the Electorate', in Dennis Kavanagh, *The Politics of the*

Labour Party (London, George Allen and Unwin, 1982), pp. 9–49.

17. A more up-beat assessment is given by Wolfgang Merkl, 'After the Golden Age Is Social Democracy Doomed to Decline?', in Christiane Lemke and Gary Marks (eds), *The Crisis of Socialism in Europe* (Durham, Duke University Press, 1992), pp. 136–70. Labour movement theorists, whose work is discussed in chapter 1, are also more optimistic about the potential of social democratic parties.

18. Perry Anderson, 'Introduction', in Perry Anderson and Patrick Camiller (eds), *Mapping the West European Left* (London, Verso, 1994), pp. 1–22. See also Christopher Pierson, *Socialism After Communism* (Oxford, Polity, 1995), pp. 7–52.

19. Adam Przeworski, *Capitalism and Social Democracy* (Cambridge, Cambridge University Press, 1985).

20. Frances Fox Piven, 'The Decline of Labor Parties: An Overview', in Frances Fox Piven (ed.), *Labor Parties in Postindustrial Societies*, pp. 1–19, p. 8.

21. Jonas Pontusson, 'Explaining the Decline of European Social Democracy', *World Politics*, vol. 47 (1995), pp. 495–533, p. 496.

22. See Stephen Haseler, *The Gaitskellites* (London, Macmillan, 1969), pp. 1–15; and Patrick Seyd, *The Rise and Fall of the Labour Left* (London, Macmillan, 1987), pp. 1–17.

23. P. Seyd, *The Rise and Fall of the Labour Left*, pp. 2–3. See also Lewis Minkin, *The Labour Party Conference* (Manchester, Manchester University Press, 1980), pp. 9–11 and p. 383, ft. 42.

24. L. Minkin, *The Labour Party Conference*, p. 11.

25. Labour's left consists of an ethos as well as a commitment to a doctrine. It also embodies a commitment to internationalism. These features are not as distinctive as its objectives of transforming society. Labour's right also embodies an ethos (though different) and an internationalism.

26. T. Benn, *Against the Tide*, pp. 34–8; and NEC-PC minutes, 16 May 1973.

27. Benn's words. T. Benn, *Against the Tide*, p. 36.

28. NEC-PC minutes, 16 May 1973, p. 25.

29. T. Benn, *Against the Tide*, p. 34; and NEC-PC minutes, 16 May 1973, p. 7.

CHAPTER 1: THE NATURE OF SOCIAL DEMOCRACY AND THE LABOUR PARTY

1. These two typologies are not intended to be either exhaustive or all-inclusive – though much of the literature concerning social democracy and Labour can be found within their categories. My objective is to establish a setting within which to locate subsequent analysis. I do not think Labour's present social democratic commitments can be found within this framework – as I make clear in the epilogue.

2. Adam Przeworski, *Capitalism and Social Democracy* (Cambridge, Cambridge University Press, 1985), p. 3.

3. Gøsta Esping-Andersen, *Politics Against Markets* (Princeton, Princeton University Press, 1985), p. 10. He suggests that reforms will cumulatively be transformative.

4. Stephen Padgett and William Paterson, *A History of Social Democracy in Post War Europe* (London, Longman, 1992), p. 1.

5. For discussions of Revisionism see Geoff Foote, *The Labour Party's Political Thought A History* (London, Croom Helm, 1985), pp. 193–234; Stephen Haseler, *The Gaitskellites* (London, Macmillan, 1969), pp. 61–97; David Howell, *British Social Democracy* (London, Croom Helm, 1976) pp. 191–4; David Lipsey and Dick Leonard (eds), *The Socialist Agenda Crosland's Legacy* (London, Jonathan Cape, 1981); John Mackintosh, *Parliament and Social Democracy* (London, Longman, 1982), pp. 222–32; David Marquand, *The Progressive Dilemma* (London, Heinemann, 1991), pp. 166–78; and Alan Warde, *Consensus and Beyond* (Manchester, Manchester University Press, 1982), pp. 43–74.

6. Anthony Crosland, *The Future of Socialism* (London, Jonathan Cape, 1964, originally 1956); Anthony Crosland, 'The Transition from Capitalism', in Richard Crossman (ed.), *New Fabian Essays* (London, Dent, 1970, originally 1952), pp. 33–68; Anthony Crosland, *The Conservative Enemy* (London, Jonathan Cape, 1962); and Anthony Crosland, 'The Private and Public Corporation in Great Britain', in E. Mason (ed.), *The Corporation in Modern Society* (Cambridge, Harvard University Press, 1960), pp. 260–76. A detailed account of Crosland's political thought is contained in Andrew Martin, 'The Revision of Gradualist Socialism: C. A. R. Crosland and the Ideology of the British Labour Party' (Columbia University PhD thesis, 1967). Crosland was a Labour MP from 1950–55 and 1959–1977.

7. R. Crossman (ed.), *New Fabian Essays*; and Socialist Union, *Twentieth Century Socialism* (Harmondsworth, Penguin, 1956). Both the Fabian Society and Socialist Union promoted Revisionist ideas within the Labour party. On the development of Revisionist thought and disagreements between its theorists see Nicholas Ellison, *Egalitarian Thought and Labour Politics* (London, Routledge, 1994), pp. 73–108.

8. Douglas Jay, *The Socialist Case* (London, Faber and Faber, 1937); and Evan Durbin, *The Politics of Democratic Socialism* (London, Labour Book Service, 1940). See Elizabeth Durbin, *New Jerusalems The Labour Party and the Economics of Democratic Socialism* (London, Routledge and Kegan Paul, 1983). Durbin became a Labour MP in 1945, Jay in 1946.

9. See Susan Crosland, *Tony Crosland* (London, Jonathan Cape, 1982), p. 67.

10. Socialist Union, *Twentieth Century Socialism*, p. 66.

11. There are surprisingly few references to Keynes in *The Future of Socialism* and it may be that Crosland (and others) came to take Keynesian economic policy for granted. See G. Arnold, 'Britain: The New Reasoners', in L. Labedz (ed.), *Revisionism* (London, George Allen and Unwin, 1962), pp. 299–312, p. 300; and G. D. H. Cole, *Capitalism in the Modern World* (Fabian Tract 310, 1957), p. 18.

12. A. Crosland, *The Future of Socialism*, p. 316.
13. A. Crosland, *The Conservative Enemy*, p. 56.
14. Hugh Gaitskell, *Socialism and Nationalisation* (Fabian Tract 300, 1956), p. 11. See also A. Crosland, *The Conservative Enemy*, p. 56; and A. Crosland, 'Burnham and the Managerial Revolution', unpublished draft chapter 6 from *The Future of Socialism*, Crosland papers, 13/7, p. 11.
15. A. Crosland, 'Burnham and the Managerial Revolution', p. 7.
16. A. Crosland, *The Future of Socialism*, p. 15.
17. Managers – unlike shareholders – would not be worried by increased taxation of dispersed profits: D. Jay, *The Socialist Case*, p. 266.
18. A. Crosland, *The Conservative Enemy*, p. 87.
19. A. Crosland, *The Future of Socialism*, pp. 29–32; and A. Crosland, 'The Transition from Capitalism', p. 38.
20. Socialist Union, *Twentieth Century Socialism*, p. 66.
21. A. Crosland, *The Future of Socialism*, p. 318. See also Austen Albu, 'The Organisation of Industry' in R. Crossman, *New Fabian Essays*, pp. 121–42.
22. H. Gaitskell, *Socialism and Nationalisation*, p. 7. See also Hugh Gaitskell, 'The Economic Aims of the Labour Party', *Political Quarterly*, 24 (1953), pp. 5–17.
23. Socialist Union, *Twentieth Century Socialism*, p. 127.
24. A. Crosland, *The Conservative Enemy*, p. 42.
25. A. Crosland, *The Future of Socialism*, pp. 319–33; and H. Gaitskell, *Socialism and Nationalisation*, pp. 23–9. See also W. A. Robson, *Nationalized Industry and Public Ownership* (London, George Allen and Unwin, 1960), pp. 133–5, 460–8.
26. Rita Hinden, 'The Lessons for Labour', in Mark Abrams and Richard Rose, *Must Labour Lose?* (Harmondsworth, Penguin, 1960), pp. 99–121, p. 119.
27. A. Crosland, *The Future of Socialism*, p. 324; and Mark Abrams 'The Socialist Commentary Survey', in M. Abrams and R. Rose, *Must Labour Lose?*, pp. 11–58.
28. A. Crosland, *The Future of Socialism*, p. 324.
29. A. Crosland, *The Conservative Enemy*, p. 43.
30. A. Crosland, *The Future of Socialism*, p. 341–3; and H. Gaitskell, 'The Economic Aims of the Labour Party', pp. 12–13.
31. A. Crosland, *The Future of Socialism*, pp. 257–62.
32. Socialist Union, *Twentieth Century Socialism*, p. 102.
33. A. Crosland, *The Conservative Enemy*, p. 225.
34. Anthony Crosland, *The New Socialism* (Melbourne, Dissent, 1963), p. 5.
35. Anthony Downs, *An Economic Theory of Democracy* (New York, Harper and Row, 1957).
36. A. Crosland, *The New Socialism*, p. 8. See also Anthony Crosland, *Can Labour Win?* (Fabian Tract 324, 1960), and M. Abrams and R. Rose, *Must Labour Lose?*.
37. See A. Crosland, *The Future of Socialism*, pp. 79–80; Evan Durbin, *Problems of Economic Planning*, (London, Routledge and Kegan Paul,

1949), pp. 4–13; Roy Jenkins, 'Equality', in R. Crossman (ed.), *New Fabian Essays*, pp. 69–90; Socialist Union, *Socialism A New Statement of Principles* (London, Lincolns-Prager, 1952); Socialist Union, *Twentieth Century Socialism*, p. 61; and D. Lipsey, 'Crosland's Socialism', in D. Lipsey and D. Leonard (eds), *The Socialist Agenda Crosland's Legacy*, pp. 21–43.

38. A. Crosland, draft introduction to *The Future of Socialism*, Crosland papers, 13/9.

39. Key texts include Gøsta Esping-Andersen, *Politics Against Markets*; W. Korpi, *The Democratic Class Struggle* (London, Routledge and Kegan Paul, 1983); and John Stephens, *The Transition from Capitalism to Socialism* (Chicago, University of Illinois Press, 1986, originally 1979).

40. For critical discussion see James Fulcher, 'Labour Movement Theory Versus Corporatism: Social Democracy in Sweden', *Sociology*, 21 (1987), pp. 231–252; G. Olsen, *The Struggle for Economic Democracy in Sweden* (Aldershot, Avebury, 1992), pp. 1–20; J. Pontusson, 'Behind and Beyond Social Democracy in Sweden', *New Left Review*, 143 (1984), pp. 69–96.

41. J. Stephens, *The Transition from Capitalism to Socialism*, p. 71.

42. W. Korpi, *The Democratic Class Struggle*, p. 208.

43. J. Stephens, *The Transition from Capitalism to Socialism*, pp. 54 and 72.

44. W. Korpi, *The Democratic Class Struggle*, pp. 18–19. See also G. Esping-Andersen and W. Korpi, 'Social Policy as Class Politics in Post-War Capitalism', in John Goldthorpe (ed.), *Order and Conflict in Contemporary Capitalism* (Oxford, Oxford University Press, 1984), pp. 179–208; and E. H. Stephens and J. Stephens, 'The Labor Movement, Political Power and Workers' Participation in Western Europe', *Political Power and Social Theory*, 3 (1982), pp. 215–250.

45. Gøsta Esping-Andersen and Roger Friedland, 'Class Coalitions in the Making of West European Economies', *Political Power and Social Theory*, 3 (1982), pp. 1–52, p. 45. A similar theoretical framework is adopted by Peter Gourevitch, *Politics in Hard Times* (Cornell, Cornell University Press, 1986).

46. J. Stephens, *The Transition from Capitalism to Socialism*, pp. 50–51; and W. Korpi, *The Democratic Class Struggle*, p. 21.

47. G. Esping-Andersen, *Politics Against Markets*, p. 22.

48. Conflict in society need be neither overt nor de-stabilising and periods of agreement may occur. They are not permanent.

49. Christopher Pierson, *Beyond the Welfare State* (Cambridge, Polity, 1991), p. 30; and Andrew Martin, 'Is Democratic Control of Capitalist Economies Possible?', in Leon Lindberg et al (eds), *Stress and Contradiction in Modern Capitalism* (Lexington, D. C. Heath, 1975), pp. 13–56.

50. Rudolf Meidner, 'Why did the Swedish Model Fail?', *Socialist Register* (1993), pp. 211–28, p. 218.

51. J. Pontusson, 'Behind and Beyond Social Democracy in Sweden', p. 72.

52. G. Esping-Andersen, 'From the Welfare State to Democratic Social-

ism', *Political Power and Social Theory*, 2 (1981), pp. 111–140, p. 113.
53. J. Stephens, *The Transition from Capitalism to Socialism*, pp..146, 182–83.
54. Especially important as the potential bases for social democratic economic strategy were the various proposals in the mid-1970s for Scandinavian wage earner funds (associated with the Swedish economist Rudolf Meidner). Such funds would increase worker participation, restore economic growth by increasing investment, trade wage restraint for greater control of capital, and last, go beyond welfare state socialism and the problems it had encountered. See G. Esping-Andersen, *Politics Against Markets*, pp. 296–306; J. Stephens, *The Transition from Capitalism to Socialism*, pp. 182–92; W. Korpi, *The Democratic Class Struggle*, pp. 209–11. See also Rudolf Meidner, *Employee Investment Funds* (London, George Allen and Unwin, 1978).
55. See Francis Castles, *The Social Democratic Image of Society* (London, Routledge and Kegan Paul, 1978), pp. 124–31.
56. G. Esping-Andersen, 'Single Party Dominance in Sweden: The Saga of Social Democracy', in T. J. Pempel (ed.), *Uncommon Democracies* (Cornell, Cornell University Press, 1990), pp. 33–57, pp. 48–9; and J. Pontusson, 'Conditions of Labour Party Dominance: Sweden and Britain Compared', in T. J. Pempel (ed.), *Uncommon Democracies*, pp. 58–82, pp. 61–2.
57. See Michael Newman, *John Strachey* (Manchester, Manchester University Press, 1989), pp. 131–53.
58. John Strachey, *Contemporary Capitalism* (London, Victor Gollancz, 1956), p. 180; John Strachey, 'Tasks and Achievements of the Labour Party', in R. Crossman (ed.), *New Fabian Essays*, pp. 181–215, p. 188; and John Strachey, 'The Object of Further Socialisation', *Political Quarterly*, 24 (1953), pp. 68–77.
59. Hugh Thomas, *John Strachey* (London, Eyre Methuen, 1973), p. 278.
60. Aneurin Bevan, *In Place of Fear* (London, Quartet, 1978, originally 1952), p. 23.
61. Przeworski's fullest statement is *Capitalism and Socialism Democracy*. See also Adam Przeworski, *The State and the Economy under Capitalism* (New York, Harwood, 1990), pp. 92–6. In recent work Przeworski has modified his stance: see Adam Przeworski and Michael Wallerstein, 'The Structural Dependence of the State on Capital', *American Political Science Review*, 82 (1988), pp. 11–30.
62. For discussion see W. Higgins and N. Apple, 'How Limited is Reformism? A Critique of Przeworski and Panitch', *Theory and Society*, 12 (1983), pp. 603–30; Desmond King and Mark Wickham-Jones, 'Social Democracy and Rational Workers', *British Journal of Political Science*, 20 (1990), pp. 387–413; and Duane Swank, 'Politics and the Structural Dependence of the State in Democratic Capitalist Nations', *American Political Science Review*, 86 (1992), pp. 38–54.
63. See Adam Przeworski and John Sprague, *Paper Stones* (Chicago, University of Chicago Press, 1986); and A. Przeworski, *Capitalism and Social Democracy*, pp. 24–35.
64. A. Przeworski, *Capitalism and Social Democracy*, pp. 133–70.
65. A. Przeworski, *Capitalism and Social Democracy*, p. 35.

66. A. Przeworski, *Capitalism and Social Democracy*, p. 40.
67. A. Przeworski, *Capitalism and Social Democracy*, p. 41.
68. A. Przeworski, *Capitalism and Social Democracy*, p. 42.
69. See Sven Steinmo, 'Social Democracy versus Socialism: Goal Adaptation in Social Democratic Sweden', *Politics and Society*, 16 (1988), 403–47.
70. A. Przeworski, *Capitalism and Social Democracy*, p. 46.
71. Charles Taylor, 'What's Wrong with Capitalism', *New Left Review*, 2 (1960), pp. 5–11, p. 11.
72. Ralph Miliband, *Parliamentary Socialism* (London, Merlin, 1972, originally 1961), pp. 356 and 373–4.
73. Ralph Miliband, *Capitalist Democracy in Britain* (Oxford, Oxford University Press, 1982), p. 94.
74. David Coates, *The Labour Party and the Struggle for Socialism* (Cambridge, Cambridge University Press, 1975), pp. 221 and 223. Coates talks of 'limits that are rooted in the general requirements of capitalist private enterprise as a system', p. 157.
75. D. Coates, *The Labour Party and the Struggle for Socialism*, p. 161.
76. R. Miliband, *Parliamentary Socialism*, p. 356.
77. D. Howell, *British Social Democracy*, p. 298.
78. Leo Panitch, *Social Democracy and Industrial Militancy* (Cambridge, Cambridge University Press, 1976), p. 236. See also Leo Panitch, *Working Class Politics in Crisis* (London, Verso, 1986).
79. L. Panitch, *Social Democracy and Industrial Militancy*, p. 238.
80. Ralph Miliband, 'The Politics of Contemporary Capitalism', *New Reasoner*, 5 (1958), pp 39–52, p. 46.
81. See, for example, Clause VII (1), *LPACR* (1979), p. 468; and Clement Attlee, *The Labour Party in Perspective* (London, Left Book Club, 1937), p. 93.
82. Clause IX (1), *LPACR* (1979), p. 469.
83. Robert McKenzie, *British Political Parties* (London, Heinemann, 1967, originally 1955). See also Dennis Kavanagh, *Politics and Personalities* (London, Macmillan, 1990), pp. 16–39; and Henry Drucker, *Doctrine and Ethos in the Labour Party* (London, George Allen and Urwin, 1978), pp. 1–8.
84. R. McKenzie, *British Political Parties*, p. 455.
85. See Lewis Minkin, *The Labour Party Conference* (Manchester, Manchester University Press, 1980).
86. See L. Minkin, *The Labour Party Conference*, pp. 85–93.
87. R. Michels, *Political Parties* (New York, Free Press, 1968, originally 1911), pp. 81–106.
88. R. McKenzie, *British Political Parties*, pp. 313, 423–5, 490–2, 510.
89. R. McKenzie, *British Political Parties*, p. 597.
90. R. Michels, *Political Parties*, p. 70, see also pp. 61–80 and 107–14.
91. L. Minkin, *The Labour Party Conference*, pp. 66–81, 141–6, 239–41.
92. R. McKenzie, *British Political Parties*, pp. 414–6.
93. R. McKenzie, *British Political Parties*, p. 527.
94. R. McKenzie, *British Political Parties*, p. 570.
95. L. Minkin, *The Labour Party Conference*; and Lewis Minkin, *The Con-*

tentious Alliance Trade Unions and the Labour Party (Edinburgh, Edinburgh University Press, 1991); and Samuel Beer, *Modern British Politics* (London, Faber and Faber, 1965). See also Samuel Finer, *The Changing British Party System 1945–1979* (Washington, AEI, 1980) and Martin Harrison, *Trade Unions and the Labour Party since 1945* (London, George Allen and Unwin, 1960), pp. 335–8.

96. L. Minkin, *The Labour Party Conference*, pp. 53–5.
97. A central theme of L. Minkin, *The Contentious Alliance*.
98. L. Minkin, *The Labour Party Conference*, pp. 24–5.
99. L. Minkin, *The Labour Party Conference*, p. 146.
100. Minkin's analysis predates the recent reform to constituency parties voting procedure for the NEC.
101. S. Finer, *The Changing British Party System 1945–1979*, p. 79.
102. R. Crossman, *New Statesman*, 23 June 1961, p. 1010.
103. S. Beer, *Modern British Politics*, p. 188. See also R. McKenzie and S. Beer, 'Book Section – Debate', *Parliamentary Affairs*, 19 (1967), pp. 373–84.
104. L. Minkin, *The Labour Party Conference*, p. 11.
105. L. Minkin, *The Labour Party Conference*, p. 53.
106. L. Minkin, *The Labour Party Conference*, p. 39.
107. L. Minkin, *The Labour Party Conference*, p. 50.
108. S. Finer, *The Changing British Party System 1945–1979*, p. 95.
109. L. Minkin, *The Labour Party Conference*, p. 52.

CHAPTER 2: THE REVISIONIST ASCENDANCY

1. Hugh Dalton, *High Tide and After* (Muller, London, 1962), p. 412.
2. *New Statesman*, 20 July 1957, p. 73. It noted that compromises had been made within the drafting committee.
3. *The Spectator*, 19 July 1957.
4. *The Times*, 29 July 1957.
5. See Vernon Bogdanor, 'The Labour Party in Opposition 1951–1964', in Vernon Bogdanor and Robert Skidelsky (eds), *The Age of Affluence 1951–1964* (London, Macmillan, 1970), pp. 78–116; David Coates, *The Labour Party and the Struggle for Socialism* (Cambridge, Cambridge University Press, 1975), pp. 75–96; David Howell, *British Social Democracy* (London, Croom Helm, 1976), 174–244.
6. Samuel Beer, *Modern British Politics* (London, Faber and Faber, 1965), pp. 188–200; David Butler, *The British General Election of 1955* (London, Macmillan, 1955), pp. 13–15, 24–5; Stephen Haseler, *The Gaitskellites* (London, Macmillan, 1969), pp. 48–67; Ralph Miliband, *Parliamentary Socialism* (Merlin, London, 1972, originally 1962), pp. 315–36; and Patricia Pugh, *Educate, Agitate, Organise* (London, Methuen, 1984), p. 232.
7. Denis Healey, *Socialism with a Human Face* (London, 1981), p. 6.
8. Robert Currie, *Industrial Politics* (Oxford, Oxford University Press, 1979), pp. 179–90; S. Haseler, *The Gaitskellites*, pp. 99–107; W. A. Robson, *Nationalised Industry and Public Ownership* (London, George

Allen and Unwin, 1960), pp. 474–85; and H. Weiner, *British Labour and Public Ownership* (London, Stevens, 1958), pp. 78–95.

9. Labour party, *Industry and Society* (1957), p. 16.
10. *Industry and Society*, pp. 16–17.
11. *Industry and Society*, p. 57.
12. Labour party, *Labour Believes in Britain* (1949), pp. 12–13.
13. *LPACR* (1949), p. 155.
14. 'Report to Policy Committee of Sub-Committee on Privately Owned Industry', RD: 236/December 1948, p. 3.
15. Labour party, *Challenge to Britain* (1953), p. 11.
16. 'The Future of Private Industry', RE: 113/November 1956, p. 4.
17. Labour party, *Plan for Progress* (1958), p. 12.
18. *Industry and Society*, p. 48.
19. Labour party, *Signposts for the Sixties* (1961), p. 10.
20. W. A. Robson, *Nationalized Industry and Public Ownership*, p. 478.
21. Labour party, *Britain Belongs to You* (1959).
22. Lewis Minkin, *The Labour Party Conference* (Manchester, Manchester University Press, 1980), pp. 237–41 and 325–6.
23. See D. Howell, *British Social Democracy*, 186–90; David Howell, *The Rise and Fall of Bevanism*, (ILP, no date); Mark Jenkins, *Bevanism Labour's High Tide* (Nottingham, Spokesman, 1979); and Alan Warde, *Consensus and Beyond* (Manchester, Manchester University Press, 1982), pp. 75–97.
24. S. Haseler, *The Gaitskellites*, p. 20; D. Howell, *British Social Democracy*, pp. 139–49.
25. Barbara Castle, 'The Socialist Alternative', *Fabian Journal*, 5 (1952), pp. 13–17, p. 15.
26. Quoted by M. Jenkins, *Bevanism*, p. 83.
27. Susan Crosland, *Tony Crosland* (London, Jonathan Cape, 1982), p. 68.
28. Petronius, *Fabian Journal*, 6 (1952), p. 27.
29. Richard Crossman, *Planning for Progress* (London, Hamish Hamilton, 1965).
30. As well as *Contemporary Capitalism* (London, Victor Gollancz, 1956), see Strachey's review of Crosland's *The Future of Socialism*, 'The New Revisionist', *New Statesman*, 6 October 1956.
31. Michael Newman, *John Strachey* (Manchester, Manchester University Press, 1989), p. 146.
32. See Lin Chun, *The British New Left* (Edinburgh, Edinburgh University Press, 1993); Michael Kenny, *The First New Left* (London, Lawrence and Wishart, 1995), pp. 119–67; and David Widgery (ed.), *The Left in Britain* (Harmondsworth, Penguin, 1976), pp. 509–14.
33. See John Hughes, 'New Left Economic Policy', in Robin Archer et al (eds), *Out of Apathy* (London, Verso, 1989), pp. 95–106.
34. *The Insiders*, in *Universities and Left Review*, 3 (1958), pp. 24–64, p. 31.
35. Michael Barratt Brown, 'The Controllers', parts I–III, *Universities and Left Review*, 5, 6, 7 (1958–9), pp. 53–61, 38–41, 43–9.
36. Michael Barratt Brown, 'Plan for Progress', *Universities and Left Review*, 6 (1959), pp. 12–18, p. 16.
37. John Hughes, 'The Commanding Heights', *New Left Review*, 4 (1960), pp. 11–19.

38. John Hughes, 'The British Economy: Crisis and Structural Change', *New Left Review*, 21 (1963), pp. 3–20.

39. John Hughes, 'Steel Nationalisation and Political Power', New Reasoner, 2 (1957), pp. 6–29; and John Hughes, *Plan for Steel Re-Nationalisation* (Fabian Research Series 198, 1958).

40. Clive Jenkins, 'Retreat: The Labour Party and the Public Corporations', p. 58, *The Insiders*; and Clive Jenkins, *Power at the Top* (London, MacGibbon and Kee, 1959).

41. Michael Artis and Peter Sedgewick, 'The Scope of Nationalisation', in *The Insiders*, pp. 38–41, p. 39.

42. John Hughes, 'An Economic Policy for Labour', *New Left Review*, 24 (1964), pp. 5–32.

43. Ken Coates, 'Workers' Control', *New Left Review*, 23 (1964), pp. 69–71, p. 70.

44. Ken Alexander and John Hughes, *A Socialist Wages Plan* (New Left discussion booklet, 1959), p. 7. For a discussion see H. Turner et al, 'A Polemic on the Wages Plan', *New Reasoner*, 10 (1959), pp. 73–106.

45. See Ralph Miliband, 'The Politics of Contemporary Capitalism', *New Reasoner*, 5 (1958), pp. 39–52; Ralph Miliband, 'The Transition to the Transition', *New Reasoner*, 6 (1958), pp. 35–48; and John Saville, 'The Welfare State', *New Reasoner*, 2 (1957), pp. 5–25.

46. Notably John Hughes. See also Ken Alexander, 'Premier Wilson's Plan', *New Left Review*, 9 (1961), pp. 53–6.

47. Quoted by Philip Williams, *Hugh Gaitskell* (London, Jonathan Cape, 1979), p. 389. See Anthony Crosland, *The Conservative Enemy* (London, Jonathan Cape, 1962), pp. 68–96 and M. Barratt Brown, 'Crosland's Enemy', *New Left Review*, 19 (1963), pp. 23–31. See also Michael Kenny, *The First New Left*, pp. 129–36.

48. Ralph Samuel, 'Born Again Socialism', in R. Archer et al, *Out of Apathy*, pp. 39–58, p. 49. John Hughes is dubious about the impact of these proposals on Labour; interview, February 1994.

49. *New Reasoner*, 3 (1957–58), p. 3.

50. Peter Sedgewick, 'The Two New Lefts', in D. Widgery (ed.), *The Left in Britain*, p. 135.

51. Anthony Crosland, *The New Socialism* (Dissent, Melbourne, 1963), p. 12.

52. An early critique of economic policy, which stressed the UK's commitments abroad, was Andrew Shonfield, *UK Economic Policy Since the War* (Harmondsworth, Penguin, 1958).

53. Following Alan Warde's term 'technocratic-socialism', see A. Warde, *Consensus and Beyond*, pp. 94–109. See also Paul Foot, *The Politics of Harold Wilson* (Harmondsworth, Penguin, 1967); S. Haseler, *The Gaitskellites*, pp. 243–9; D. Howell, *British Social Democracy*, pp. 236–40; and R. Miliband, *Parliamentary Socialism*, pp. 353–60.

54. Harold Wilson, *The New Britain: Labour's Plan* (Harmondsworth, Penguin, 1964), p. 14.

55. Harold Wilson, *Purpose in Politics Selected Speeches* (London, Weidenfield and Nicolson, 1964), pp. 14–28. See also Tony Benn, *Out of the Wil-*

derness (London, Hutchinson, 1987), pp. 82–3; and Labour party, *Labour and the Scientific Revolution* (1963).

56. A. Warde, *Consensus and Beyond*, p. 98.
57. See J. Sargent, *Out of Stagnation* (Fabian Tract 343, 1963), p. 29; and M. Stewart and R. Winsbury, *An Incomes Policy for Labour* (Fabian Tract 350, 1963), pp. 22–3.
58. See, for example, the unabridged version of Crosland's *The Future of Socialism* (London, Jonathan Cape, 1956), pp. 444–5.
59. H. Wilson, *The New Britain: Labour's Plan*, p. 18.
60. M. Stewart and R. Winsbury, *An Incomes Policy for Labour*.
61. Contrast A. Crosland, *Can Labour Win?*, p. 19; and A. Crosland, *The Conservative Enemy*, pp. 158–159. See also David Butler and Anthony King, *The British General Election of 1964* (London, Macmillan, 1965), p. 62.
62. A. Crosland, *The Future of Socialism*, preface.
63. See Harold Wilson, *Post-War Economic Policies in Britain* (Fabian Tract 309, 1957); and Harold Wilson, 'A Four Year Plan for Britain', *New Statesman*, 24 March 1961, pp. 462–8. See also Ben Pimlott, *Harold Wilson* (London, Harper Collins, 1992), p. 227.
64. D. Butler and A. King, *The British General Election of 1964*, pp. 57–76.
65. Labour party, *Labour in the Sixties* (1960).
66. *Signposts for the Sixties*, pp. 12–14.
67. Labour party, *Let's Go with Labour for the New Britain* (1964).
68. See Wilfred Beckerman (ed.), *The Labour Government's Economic Record 1964–1970* (London, Duckworth, 1972); David Butler and Michael Pinto-Duschinsky, *The British General Election of 1970* (London, Macmillan, 1971), pp. 1–46; P. Foot, *The Politics of Harold Wilson*; Brian Lapping, *The Labour Government 1964–70* (Harmondsworth, Penguin, 1970); Clive Ponting, *Breach of Promise* (Harmondsworth, Penguin, 1989); Michael Stewart, *The Jekyll and Hyde Years* (London, Dent, 1977), pp. 21–118; and Phillip Whitehead, *The Writing on the Wall* (London, Michael Joseph, 1985) pp. 1–28.
69. Michael Artis, 'Fiscal Policy for Stabilisation', in W. Beckerman (ed.), *The Labour Government's Economic Record 1964–1970*, pp. 262–99, p. 265.
70. D. Howell, *British Social Democracy*, p. 254.
71. See G. Dorfman, *Government Versus Trade Unionism in British Politics Since 1968* (London, Macmillan, 1979), pp. 8–49; W. Fishbein, *Wage Restraint by Consensus* (London, Routledge and Kegan Paul, 1984), pp. 53–6; and Leo Panitch, *Social Democracy and Industrial Militancy*, (Cambridge, Cambridge University Press, 1976), pp. 165–203;
72. The leftwing Tribune group tended towards negative criticisms of the Wilson government, with a few positive proposals added on briefly without any theoretical basis. See Tribune group, 'Never Again', *Tribune*, 20 July 1967; and Tribune group, 'A New Economic Strategy for Labour', *Tribune*, 12 January 1968.
73. Michael Foot, 'Credo of the Labour Left', *New Left Review*, 49 (1968), pp. 19–34, p. 25.
74. Stuart Hall, Raymond Williams, and E. P. Thompson, *May Day Manifesto* (May day pamphlet, 1967).

75. Raymond Williams (ed.), *May Day Manifesto 1968* (Harmondsworth, Penguin, 1968), pp. 41–4.
76. Another source of opposition to the Labour government was the Institute for Workers' Control which had been founded in 1964 to lobby for industrial democracy.
77. Labour party, *Labour's Economic Strategy* (1969).
78. The demands for industrial democracy had surfaced at Labour's conference in 1967. *Labour's Economic Strategy*, p. 59.
79. Labour party, *Agenda for a Generation* (1969).
80. Labour party, *Now Britain's Strong – Let's Make It Great to Live in* (1970).
81. See T. Burgess et al, *Matters of Principle Labour's Last Chance* (Harmondsworth, Penguin, 1968); and Peter Townsend and Nicholas Bosanquet (eds), *Labour and Inequality* (London, Fabian Society, 1972).
82. For a defence see A. Crosland, *Socialism Now* (London, Jonathan Cape, 1975); R. Crossman, *Socialism and Planning* (Fabian Tract 375, 1967); and Wilson's own mammoth volume, *The Labour Government 1964–1970* (London, Weidenfield and Nicolson, 1971).
83. A. MacIntyre, 'The Strange Death of Social Democratic England', in D. Widgery (ed.), *The Left in Britain*, pp. 235–40.

CHAPTER 3: LABOUR'S ALTERNATIVE ECONOMIC STRATEGY

1. *Tribune*, 2 March 1973.
2. *Tribune*, 18 June 1973.
3. *The Times*, 1 October 1973.
4. Stuart Holland, *The Socialist Challenge* (London, Quartet, 1975). Holland also produced a brief summary, *Strategy for Socialism* (Nottingham, Spokesman, 1975). In 1979 he became a Labour MP.
5. Between 1972 and 1982 Holland wrote over twenty-five papers about economic policy for the Labour party. The most important were 'A State Holding Company' RD: 271/February 1972, (co-authored with Richard Pryke); 'Planning and Policy Coordination', RD: 315/March 1972; 'Planning Strategy, Tactics and Techniques', RD: 442/October 1972; and 'The New Economic Imperatives', RD: 473/November 1972.
6. Holland's articles include: Stuart Holland, 'State Entrepreneurship and State Tradition', in Stuart Holland (ed.), *The State as Entrepreneur* (London, Weidenfield and Nicolson, 1972), pp. 5–44; Stuart Holland, 'Economic Crisis, New Public Enterprise and Democratic Planning', *Public Enterprise*, 6 (1974), pp. 3–12; Stuart Holland, 'Planning Disagreements', in Stuart Holland (ed.), *Beyond Capitalist Planning* (Oxford, Blackwell, 1978), pp. 137–164; Stuart Holland, 'An Alternative Economic Strategy', in Michael Barratt Brown et al (eds), *Full Employment – Priority* (Nottingham, Spokesman, 1978), pp. 133–6; Stuart Holland, 'New Public Enterprise and Economic Planning', in Ken Coates (ed.), *How to Win?* (Nottingham, Spokesman, 1981), pp. 111–46; and Stuart Holland, 'Economic Objectives', in Jon

Lansman and Alan Meale (eds), *Beyond Thatcher The Real Alternative* (London, Junction Books, 1983), pp. 17–38.

7. TUC–Labour Party Liaison Committee, *Economic Planning and Industrial Democracy* (1982).

8. See also Tony Benn, *Speeches* (Nottingham, Spokesman Books, 1974); Tony Benn, *Arguments for Socialism* (Harmondsworth, Penguin, 1980); Michael Meacher, *Socialism with a Human Face* (London, George Allen and Unwin, 1982); and Brian Sedgemore, *The How and Why of Socialism* (Nottingham, Spokesman, 1977).

9. Tribune group, 'The Crisis – And the Only Way in Which the Labour Government Can Solve It!', *Tribune*, 31 January 1975. See also Tribune group, 'Back from the Brink', *Tribune*, 27 June 1975.

10. LCC, *There is an Alternative* (1980).

11. There was considerable discussion of the proposals involved in the AES in two fora during the early 1970s; the IWC publication *Workers' Control Bulletin*, and the Public Enterprise Group journal, *Public Enterprise*.

12. The components of the AES were not the only economic measures developed by Labour between 1970 and 1983. Policy documents contained a host of other proposals including taxation, regional policy, and training. The measures of the AES were at the heart of Labour's strategy as an integrated package.

13. Detailed theoretical backgrounds were provided by two Labour party documents in the mid-1970s: Labour party, *The National Enterprise Board* (1973); and Labour party, *International Big Business* (1977). This section draws especially from them as well as the work of Stuart Holland.

14. S. Holland, *The Socialist Challenge*, pp. 14–15, 48–52; S. Holland, 'The New Economic Imperatives', pp. 2–3; and S. Holland, 'Planning Strategy, Tactics and Techniques', p. 4.

15. Labour party, *Labour's Programme 1973* (1973), p. 13.

16. *International Big Business*, p. 11.

17. S. Holland, *The Socialist Challenge*, pp. 49–50; and *International Big Business*, p. 110.

18. S. Holland, *The Socialist Challenge*, p. 187.

19. IPSC minutes, 31 October 1972, p. 1.

20. *Tribune*, 25 May 1973.

21. TUC, *Annual Report* (1972), p. 521.

22. S. Holland, *The Socialist Challenge*, p. 26.

23. S. Holland and R. Pryke, 'A State Holding Company', p. 14; and S. Holland, 'Coping with Multinational Companies', RD: 437/October 1972.

24. Tribune group, 'The Crisis – And the Only way in which the Labour Government Can Solve It!'.

25. S. Holland, *New Statesman*, 15 June 1973, p. 882.

26. S. Holland, *The Guardian*, 24 May 1973.

27. S. Holland, 'Planning Strategy, Tactics and Techniques', p. 5. See also 'Prices, Profit and Investment', RD: 447/October 1972, p. 2.

28. *International Big Business*, pp. 11 and 26.

29. Regional problems were a special interest of Holland: see S. Holland, *The Socialist Challenge*, pp. 95–117; S. Holland, *The Regional Problem* (London, Macmillan, 1976); and S. Holland, *Capital Versus the Regions* (London, Macmillan, 1976).

30. Robin Murray, *Multinational Companies and Nation States* (Nottingham, Spokesman, 1975).

31. See W. Kennet, L. Whitty and S. Holland, *Sovereignty and Multinational Companies* (Fabian Tract 409, 1971); S. Holland, *The Socialist Challenge*, pp. 75–8 and S. Holland, 'Coping with Multinational Companies'.

32. S. Holland, *The Socialist Challenge*, p. 27.

33. *Labour's Programme 1973*, p. 30.

34. *Labour's Programme 1973*, p. 13.

35. S. Holland, *The Socialist Challenge*, p. 61; and F. Archibugi, J. Delors, and S. Holland, 'Planning for Development', in S. Holland (ed.), *Beyond Capitalist Planning*, pp. 184–202.

36. RD: 356/May 1972, p. 21.

37. Tony Benn, Frances Morrell, and Francis Cripps, *A Ten Year Industrial Strategy for the UK* (Spokesman Pamphlet 49, 1975), p. 3. See also Labour party, *Labour and Industry* (1975), p. 1.

38. See, for example, Stuart Holland, 'Retrospect on the National Enterprise Board', RD: 528/September 1980; and Stuart Holland, 'Economic Policy and Public Enterprise', RD: 896/May 1981.

39. Labour party, *Labour's Programme 1982* (1982), p. 9.

40. *Labour's Programme 1982*, p. 38.

41. *Economic Planning and Industrial Democracy*, p. 8.

42. *Labour's Programme 1973*, p. 7.

43. *Labour's Programme 1982*, p. 4.

44. *Labour's Programme 1982*, p. 17.

45. RD: 2287/April 1982, p. 5.

46. *Labour's Programme 1982*, p. 6.

47. *Labour's Programme 1982*, p. 9.

48. See, for example, Labour party, *The Socialist Alternative* (1981), p. 12; and *Labour's Programme 1982*, p. 9.

49. 'National Planning', RD: 1046/September 1981, p. 6.

50. Labour party, *Labour's Plan for Expansion* (1981), section 6.

51. T. Benn, 'Interview with Eric Hobsbawm', Marxism Today (October 1980), pp. 5–13, p. 12.

52. *Labour's Programme 1973*, p. 15.

53. TUC, *Economic Review* (1972), p. 16.

54. *Labour and Industry*, p. 5.

55. TUC–Labour Party Liaison Committee, *Economic Issues Facing the Next Labour Government* (1981), p. 4.

56. 'National Planning', RD: 1046/September 1981, p. 6.

57. *Labour's Programme 1973*, p. 13.

58. *Labour's Programme 1973*, p. 33.

59. Tribune group, 'The Crisis – And the Only Way in Which the Labour Government Can Solve It!'.

60. Richard Pryke was also associated with demonstrating the positive

benefits of existing public ownership. See Richard Pryke, *Public Enterprise in Practice* (London, MacGibbon and Kee, 1971); and Richard Pryke, 'Productivity, Performance and Ownership', *Public Enterprise,* 1 (1971), pp. 6–10.

61. *Tribune,* 6 July 1973.
62. *The National Enterprise Board,* p. 16; and S. Holland, *The Socialist Challenge,* pp. 199–204.
63. S. Holland and R. Pryke, 'The State Holding Company', p. 11.
64. TUC, *Annual Report* (1972), p. 529.
65. S. Holland, 'State Entrepreneurship and State Intervention', p. 7.
66. M. Barratt Brown, *From Labourism to Socialism* (Nottingham, Spokesman, 1972), p. 233. It remained ambiguous as to what a social audit amounted.
67. S. Holland, 'Planning Strategy, Tactics and Techniques', p. 17. Elsewhere Holland was more equivocal. On occasion he advocated a form of social audit either as means of obtaining information or as a wider set of criteria for decision-making. See S. Holland, *The Socialist Challenge,* pp. 234–7; and S. Holland, 'Social Cost and the Crisis', *Workers' Control,* 2 (1978), pp. 4–6.
68. S. Holland, 'Planning Strategy, Tactics and Techniques', p. 6.
69. S. Holland, 'The New Economic Imperatives', p. 7.
70. See *The National Enterprise Board.* The idea was developed by M. Posner and R. Pryke, *New Public Enterprise* (Fabian Research Series 254, 1966), pp. 13–14. See also S. Holland, 'Towards a State Holding Company', *Socialist Commentary* (December 1971), pp. 10–12; S. Holland and R. Pryke, 'A State Holding Company'; and RD: 422/ August 1972. The regional objectives for the state holding company remained important; see S. Holland, 'Regional Policy', RD: 644/February 1973.
71. PSG minutes, 2 November 1972; and IPSC minutes, 5 April 1973.
72. M. Meacher, 'Industrial and Financial Strategy', in J. Lansman and A. Meale (eds), *Beyond Thatcher The Real Alternative,* pp. 39–52, p. 47.
73. Labour party, *Labour's Programme 1976* (1976), p. 28.
74. *Labour's Programme 1973,* p. 35.
75. TUC, *Annual Report* (1973), pp. 606–7; and *LPACR* (1971), p. 298.
76. 'Prices, Profits and Investment', RD: 447/October 1973; and 'Profits and Investment', RD: 917/November 1973.
77. Labour party, *Capital and Equality* (1973), pp. 41–2.
78. *Labour's Programme 1973,* pp. 36–7. See also 'The Institutions, Profits and Investment', RE: 97/March 1975; J. Hughes, 'A Possible Application of the Swedish "Investment Funds" System', RE: 91/March 1975; and J. Hughes, *Funds for Investment* (Fabian Research Series 325, 1976).
79. See, for example, M. Barratt Brown, 'Capital and Equality', *Workers' Control Bulletin* (October 1973), pp. 8–9.
80. *Labour and Industry,* pp. 9–10.
81. An exception was John Hughes, an enthusiastic supporter of such proposals.

82. Labour party, *Banking and Finance* (1976), p. 22. See also 'Financial Institutions: the Policy Options', RE: 551/March 1976.
83. Ian Mikardo's pledge on behalf of the NEC, *LPACR* (1976), p. 314.
84. WPBI minutes 28 March 1977, 26 April 1977, and 9 November 1977; RE: 1729/June 1978; and 'Banking and Insurance A Summary of Trade Union Views', RE: 1730/June 1978. ASTMS and NUBE were amongst those concerned by Labour's plans.
85. USDAW, 'Statement on Banking and Finance', RE: 1012/February 1977.
86. APEX, 'The Banking and Finance Sector', RE: 1034/March 1977.
87. WPBI minutes, 11 December 1978. See also *Interim Report from the Working Party on Banking and Insurance, LPACR* (1978), pp. 450–459; and 'The Final Report of the Working Group', RE: 2061A/March 1979.
88. Labour party, *Labour's Draft Manifesto* (1980), pp. 8–10.
89. RD: 386/May 1980, p. 8.
90. 'Programme for Work', RD: 576/November 1980, p. 7.
91. Tony Benn, *Parliament, People, and Power* (London, Verso, 1982), p. 80.
92. Benn diary, 12 July 1982; and *The Times*, 13 July 1982.
93. Letter, 15 July 1982, NEC minutes.
94. Labour party, *The Financial Institutions* (1982). See also Labour party, *The City* (1982).
95. *Labour's Programme 1973*, pp. 17–18; and S. Holland, *The Socialist Challenge*, pp. 227–34.
96. In 1970 the TUC's Economic Committee had proposed 'that investment incentives and government contracts should be on the basis of bargains struck between the government and large companies in relation to national objectives'. TUC, *Annual Report* (1970), p. 438. Nothing came of this fore-runner of planning agreements.
97. S. Holland, 'Planning Strategy, Tactics and Techniques', p. 3.
98. S. Holland, 'The New Economic Imperatives', p. 3.
99. See 'The Planning Agreements System', RD: 697/March 1973; Labour party, *The Community and the Company* (1974); and S. Holland, 'Multinationals Working Party', RE: 992/February 1977.
100. See Ken Coates and Tony Topham, *Trade Unions in Britain* (London, Fontana Books, 1988), pp. 280–2.
101. RD: 2313/April 1982, p. 9.
102. 'National Planning', RD: 1046/September 1981, p. 6.
103. 'National Planning, Corporate Plans and Industrial Democracy', RD: 1097/October 1981, p. 3.
104. PIDSC minutes, 26 January 1982, p. 3.
105. S. Holland, *The Socialist Challenge*, pp. 255–93; and S. Holland, 'Industrial Democracy', RD: 930/November 1973.
106. See Labour party, *Industrial Democracy Working Party Report* (1967).
107. TUC, *Industrial Democracy*, Interim Report, in TUC, *Annual Report* (1973), pp. 383–430; and TUC, *Industrial Democracy*, in TUC, *Annual Report* (1974), pp. 292–339.
108. See, for example, M. Barratt Brown and S. Holland, *Public Ownership*

and Democracy (IWC pamphlet 38, 1973); and T. Benn, 'A New Policy for Labour', *Workers' Control Bulletin* (5 January 1974), p. 6.

109. *Labour's Programme 1973*, p. 73.
110. *Labour's Programme 1982*, pp. 46–8.
111. *Economic Planning and Industrial Democracy*, p. 11. See Francis Cripps, 'Public Ownership: Organisation and Structure', RD: 645/December 1980; John Eatwell and Roy Green, 'Economic Theory and Political Power', in B. Pimlott (ed.), *Fabian Essays in Socialist Thought* (London, Heinemann, 1984), pp. 185–204; and Roy Green and Andrew Wilson, 'Economic Planning and Worker's Control', *Socialist Register* (1982), pp. 21–46.
112. PIDSC minutes, 26 January 1982. See also PIDSC minutes, 26 October 1981, p. 23.
113. 'Planning Negotiations – the Link Between Industrial Democracy and National Planning', RD: 2005/December 1981, pp. 6–7.
114. S. Holland, 'Planning Strategy, Tactics and Techniques', pp. 21–7. See also *Labour's Programme 1973*, pp. 22–24; and Francis Cripps, 'Planning Agreements and the Industry Act', RES: 2/March 1974. Holland drew on the French experience in this regard. See S. Holland, 'Inflation and Price Control', RD: 605/February 1973.
115. S. Holland, 'Whose Inflation?', *Workers' Control Bulletin*, 28 (October 1975), pp. 15–16, p. 16.
116. T. Balogh, *Labour and Inflation* (Fabian Tract 403, 1970), p. 60.
117. See J. Boston, 'The Theory and Practice of Voluntary Incomes Policies with Particular Reference to the British Labour Government's Social Contract 1974– 1979' (Oxford University DPhil thesis, 1983), p. 175; and W. Fishbein, *Wage Restraint By Consensus* (London, Routledge and Kegan Paul, 1984).
118. *Labour's Programme 1973*, p. 22.
119. TUC-Labour Party Liaison Committee, *Economic Policy and the Cost of Living* (1973), p. 4.
120. *Labour Weekly*, 2 March 1973.
121. Some supporters of the AES wanted an incomes policy. See, for example, B. Sedgemore, *The How and Why of Socialism*, pp. 38–41.
122. *Labour's Programme 1973*, pp. 22 and 24–5.
123. S. Holland, *Strategy for Socialism*, p. 79.
124. *Labour's Draft Manifesto*, p. 7; and *Labour's Plan for Expansion*, section 23.
125. RD: 576/November 1980, p. 6. See also Geoff Bish, 'Party Policy: Some Gaps in Labour's Programme', RD: 148/November 1979.
126. *Economic Issues Facing the Next Labour Government*, p. 13.
127. See *The Economy, the Government and Trade Union Responsibilities*, in TUC, *Annual Report* (1979), pp. 392–7, p. 395; and *The Daily Telegraph*, 15 February 1979.
128. Interview, August 1993.
129. PLP minutes, 14 February 1979, p. 4.
130. TUC-Labour Party Liaison Committee, *Partners in Rebuilding Britain* (1983), p. 16.

131. RD: 314/March 1972; and RD: 447/October 1972.
132. *Economic Issues Facing the Next Labour Government*, p. 12.
133. Party research official, Adam Sharples emphasised that price controls would effect wage levels; FEASC minutes, 16 May 1981. The same point had been made earlier in RD: 439/October 1972, p. 2.
134. 'A Socialist Counter Inflation Policy', RD: 900/May 1981, p. 10.
135. 'Inflation – Towards a Socialist Approach', RD: 1165/December 1981, p. 38. The document concluded 'some understanding must be reached on wage bargaining', p. 47.
136. Interview, August 1993; FEASC minutes, 9 April 1981 and 25 March 1982; Patrick Wintour, *New Statesman*, 27 February 1981; and Leo Panitch, 'Hard Pounding', *New Socialist* (September/October 1982), pp. 18–21. Many economists who supported the AES came to the same conclusion. See, for example, John Grahl, 'Discussion: Government, Trade Unions and Inflation', *Socialist Economic Review*, 1 (1981), pp. 209–213.
137. 'Inflation – Towards a Socialist Approach', RD: 726/February 1981, p. 27.
138. RD: 859/May 1981, p. 15.
139. HPC minutes, 8 June 1981, pp. 2–3.
140. HPC minutes, 6 July 1981; and NEC minutes, 21 July 1981. Leftwingers were concerned by the status given to the NEA in *Partners in Rebuilding Britain*; NEC minutes, 23 March 1983.
141. *LPACR* (1981), p. 75.
142. FEASC minutes, 18 May 1981, p. 2. See also Stuart Holland and Paul Ormerod, 'Corporation Tax and Economic Policy Issues', RD: 434/June 1980.
143. HPC minutes, 10 May 1982, p. 4.
144. *Labour's Programme 1982*, p. 24.
145. S. Holland, 'An Alternative Economic Strategy', p. 136.
146. 'The Economic Outlook', RE: 57/February 1975, p. 2.
147. 'The Economic Outlook', RE: 82/March 1975, p. 2.
148. 'Economic Report', RE: 231/July 1975, p. 6.
149. 'Economic Report', RE: 336/November 1975, p. 6.
150. *Labour and Industry*, p. 3. The same point was made in Labour's *Jobs and Prices* (1975), p. 2.
151. Two TUC documents in 1973 advocated controls on manufactured items. See TUC, *Economic Policy and Collective Bargaining* (1973), pp. 37–8; and TUC, 'The Oil Situation and Economic Prospects' (November 1973). See also LC minutes, 14 November 1973. Further support for import controls was given in the TUC, *Economic Review* (1974), p. 16.
152. CEPG, *Cambridge Economic Policy Review*, 1 (1975), p. 3.
153. *Labour's Programme 1976*, p. 13.
154. See, for example, TUC, *Economic Review* (1976), pp. 47–9.
155. *Labour's Programme 1982*, p. 20–2. See also 'Towards Planned Trade', RD: 517/September 1980.
156. 'Import Controls: the Issue of Retaliation', RE: 363/November 1975.

See also *Cambridge Economic Policy Review*, 1 (1975), p. 10; and *Cambridge Economic Policy Review*, 5 (1979), p. 6.

157. See Stuart Holland, 'Trade Agreements', RD: 2002/January 1982.
158. See, for example, Wynne Godley, 'Interview', *Marxism Today* (July 1981), pp. 12–18.
159. *Tribune*, 23 May 1980.
160. TUC, *Economic Policy and Collective Bargaining*, p. 378.
161. LC minutes, 17 December 1979, p. 228. See also Moss Evans, 'Import Controls Are The Key To Industrial Planning', *Public Enterprise*, 19 (Autumn 1980), pp. 3–4, p. 3. Import controls were linked to reflation and industrial intervention in AUEW-TASS, *Import Controls Now!* (1980).
162. TUC-Labour Party Liaison Committee, *Trade and Industry* (1980), p. 13. See LC minutes, 21 January 1980 and 19 May 1980.
163. LC minutes, 23 June 1980, p. 253.
164. LC minutes, 19 May 1980, p. 3.
165. S. Holland, 'British Public Enterprise and the EEC', *Public Enterprise*, 2 (1972), pp. 1–9. See also S. Holland et al, 'Competition and the Containment of the Meso-Economic (Multinational) Firm', RE: 1115/April 1977; and S. Holland, 'Power in the Community: A Critique of Federalism', RE: 1118/April 1977.
166. See S. Holland *Uncommon Market* (London, Macmillan, 1980); S. Holland, 'The EEC and UK Industrial Policy', RE: 961/January 1977; S. Holland, 'International Aspects', in J. Lansman and A. Meale (eds), *Beyond Thatcher The Real Alternative*, pp. 64–80.
167. *Labour's Programme 1976*, pp. 109–12. See also 'The EEC and UK Industrial Policy', RE: 828/November 1976; and 'EEC Industrial Policy', RE: 1201/June 1977.
168. S. Holland, 'The EEC and UK Industrial Policy', p. 7.
169. *Labour's Programme 1982*, p. 230.
170. Interview, Labour party research official, August 1993.
171. *LPACR* (1980), p. 183.
172. M. Meacher, 'Industrial and Financial Strategy', p. 47.
173. S. Holland, 'Economic Objectives', p. 27.
174. IPSC minutes, 29 June 1978.
175. *Financial Times*, 2 June 1980.
176. RD: 235/April 1980.
177. *The Times*, 25 July 1981.
178. RD: 728A/March 1981, p. 1.
179. RD: 2429/May 1982. There were over thirty attributions on industrial strategy alone.
180. For example, *The Times*, 6 May 1981 and 16 March 1982.
181. Interview, TUC Official, August 1993.
182. Interview, March 1992. A point also made by party research official, interview, September 1993.
183. *The Guardian*, 27 May 1981.
184. Roy Green, 'Bridging the Industrial Divide', *New Socialist*, (September/October 1982), pp. 22–3, p. 22.
185. RD: 2660/February 1983.

186. *Financial Times*, 14 July 1982.
187. *LPACR* (1982), p. 204.
188. *Tribune*, 15 June 1973.
189. *Socialist Commentary* (July 1970), p. 2.
190. S. Holland, 'The New Economic Imperatives', p. 1.
191. Tribune group, 'The Crisis – And the Only Way in Which the Labour Government Can Solve It!'.
192. Philip Williams, *Hugh Gaitskell* (London, Jonathan Cape, 1979), p. 448; Douglas Jay, *Change and Fortune* (London, Hutchinson, 1980), p. 264; and Noel Tracey, *The Origins of the Social Democratic Party* (London, Croom Helm, 1983), p. 22.
193. Labour party, *Industry and Society* (1957), p. 57.
194. A point emphasised by Patrick Seyd, *The Rise and Fall of the Labour Left* (London, Macmillan, 1987), p. 27.
195. See Nicholas Ellison, *Egalitarian Thought and Labour Politics* (London, Routledge, 1994), pp. 40–3; and Robert Skidelsky, *Oswald Mosley* (London, Macmillan, 1980).
196. Perry Anderson and Stuart Hall, 'Politics of the Common Market', *New Left Review*, 10 (1961), pp. 1–14.
197. John Hughes, 'An Economic Policy for Labour', *New Left Review*, 24 (1964), pp. 5–32.
198. Jonas Pontusson, *The Limits of Social Democracy* (Cornell, Cornell University Press, 1992), p. 20.
199. Adam Przeworski, *Capitalism and Social Democracy* (Cambridge, Cambridge University Press, 1985), p. 40.

CHAPTER 4: THE POLICY DEBATE WITHIN LABOUR

1. The phases are distinguished by two factors. First, the attitude of the right to policy-making (predominantly engaged as in 1970–74 or largely disengaged as in 1979–83) and second, the political status of Labour in terms of being in opposition or government.
2. Interview, David Lipsey, October 1993.
3. Interview with Llew Gardner, April 1974, Crosland papers, 13/28, p. 16.
4. Anthony Crosland, *Socialism Now* (London, Jonathan Cape, 1975), p. 33.
5. Wilfred Beckerman, 'Labour's Plans for Industry', *New Statesman*, 8 June 1973, pp. 836–840. See also Holland's response, *New Statesman*, 15 June 1973, p. 882; and Beckerman's reply, *New Statesman*, 29 June 1973, p. 961.
6. Interview, David Lipsey, October 1993.
7. Roy Jenkins, *What Matters Now* (London, Fontana, 1972), p. 26.
8. John Mackintosh, *Parliament and Social Democracy* (London, Longman, 1982), p. 177.
9. A. Crosland, *Socialism Now*, p. 34.
10. A. Crosland, *Socialism Now*, p. 29; and Andrew Glyn and Bob Sutcliffe, *British Capitalism, Workers and the Profits Squeeze* (Harmondsworth, Penguin, 1972).

11. Austen Albu, 'Labour's Future', *Socialist Commentary* (June 1972), p. 4.
12. A. Crosland, 'Policies for the People, by the People', *Socialist Commentary* (November 1971), pp. 3–5, p. 4. Crosland argued, 'Profits are crucial to high investment and high investment is crucial to economic growth.'
13. A. Crosland, *Socialism Now*, p. 247.
14. Denis Healey, 'Labour's Programme: Financing the Expenditure', RD: 841/July 1973. See also Tony Benn, *Office Without Power* (London, Hutchinson, 1988), p. 344.
15. S. Holland, *New Statesman*, 15 June 1973, p. 882.
16. 'Economic Outlook', RE: 57/February 1975, p. 22. See also John Hughes, 'Trends in Profits and Productivity 1971–2', in Michael Barratt Brown and Ken Coates (eds), *Trade Union Register*, 3 (1973), pp. 98–106; and J. Hughes, *Profit Trends and Price Controls* (Spokesman pamphlet 41, 1974).
17. Letter, 17 November 1973, Crosland papers, 13/17.
18. Interview, David Lipsey, October 1993.
19. W. Beckerman, 'Labour's Plans for Industry', p. 840.
20. A. Crosland, *Socialism Now*, p. 37.
21. R. Jenkins, *Labour Weekly*, 17 March 1973.
22. A. Crosland, *Socialism Now*, pp. 57, 82–3, 248–9. See speeches, Crosland papers, 13/24 and 13/28. See also R. Jenkins, *What Matters Now*, pp. 92–3.
23. A. Crosland, 'True Answers or Easy Answers?', *Encounter*, XLII (February 1974), pp. 94–5, p. 94. See also Shirley Williams, 'Promises and Priorities', *Socialist Commentary* (November 1973), pp. 5–8; and Reg Prentice, 'What Kind of Labour Party?', *Socialist Commentary* (April 1973), pp. 4–6.
24. Benn diary, 9 July 1973. See also NEC-PC minutes, 25 January 1973.
25. Speech, 20 September 1975, Crosland papers, 13/32.
26. Roy Jenkins, 'Socialist Priorities in Public Spending', *Socialist Commentary* (July 1973), pp. 4–5, p. 4; and *The Times*, 2 June 1973.
27. *Observer*, 21 January 1973; reprinted in A. Crosland, *Socialism Now*, pp. 103–8.
28. Interview. Public ownership was a 'liability'; 'The Secretary of State's Political Position', 13 January 1976, Crosland papers, 13/27.
29. T. Benn, *Against the Tide* (London, Hutchinson, 1989), p. 38. See also NEC-PC minutes, 16 May 1973, pp. 36–7.
30. A. Crosland, *Socialism Now*, p. 252.
31. A. Crosland, *Socialism Now*, p. 43.
32. 'The Secretary of State's Political Position', p. 4.
33. *LPACR* (1973), p. 184.
34. J. Mackintosh, *Parliament and Social Democracy*, p. 177.
35. Speech, 1 November 1974, Crosland papers, 13/24.
36. Interview, October 1993.
37. Eric Heffer, *Labour's Future* (London, Verso, 1986), p. 14.
38. Interview, October 1993.
39. Roy Jenkins, 'Socialism and the Regions', *Socialist Commentary* (May

1972), pp. 15–18. Edmund Dell also supported a limited form of holding company. See Edmund Dell, 'The British Experience', *Socialist Commentary* (December 1971), pp. 12–13; and Edmund Dell, *Political Responsibility and Industry* (London, George Allen and Unwin, 1973), pp. 72–4, 218–20.

40. IPSC minutes, 12 June 1972, and 5 April 1973; and T. Benn, *Against the Tide*, p. 17. Such doubts were raised by others.

41. David Marquand, 'Problems of Economic Growth', RD: 153/July 1971, p. 5.

42. Speech, 9 June 1973, Crosland papers, 13/24.

43. See Benn diary, 14 May 1973, 16 May 1973, 30 May 1973, 12 June 1973, and 20 June 1973; NEC-PC minutes, 25 January 1973 and 16 May 1973; and IPSC minutes, 31 October 1972 and 5 April 1973.

44. *LPACR* (1973), p. 184.

45. *The Guardian*, 20 June 1973. He had earlier stated that the NEB 'will be the most powerful body in the country', *The Guardian*, 6 June 1973.

46. PLP minutes, 11 July 1973.

47. W. Beckerman, 'Labour's Plans for Industry', p. 836.

48. Roy Hattersley, *The Times*, 4 June 1973.

49. Roy Hattersley, *The Times*, 4 June 1973.

50. Anthony Crosland, *Social Democracy in Europe* (Fabian Tract 438, 1975), p. 11.

51. William Rodgers, *Socialist Commentary* (December 1973), p. 3.

52. Interview, October 1993.

53. IPSC minutes, 30 April 1973.

54. Interview, Edmund Dell, March 1994.

55. A. Crosland, 'Policies for the People, by the People', p. 4.

56. Healey's words. NEC-PC minutes, 16 May 1973, p. 39.

57. S. Williams, 'Promises and Priorities', p. 6. A similar point was made by Crosland, NEC-PC minutes, 16 May 1973, p. 6.

58. *The Times*, 4 June 1973.

59. *The Times*, 25 June 1973. See also *Tribune*, 25 May 1973; *The Times*, 1 October 1973; and NEC-PC minutes, 16 May 1973, pp. 31–3.

60. *New Statesman*, 8 June 1973. See also Michael Meacher, 'Chronic Boom', *The Guardian*, 5 June 1973.

61. *The Times*, 7 June 1973. See also Ian Mikardo, NEC-PC minutes, 16 May 1973, p. 29; and S. Holland, *New Statesman*, 29 June 1973, p. 882.

62. Stuart Holland, 'Editorial', *Public Enterprise*, 5 (September–October 1973), p. 1. Michael Hatfield gives different data; *The House the Left Built* (London, Victor Gollancz, 1978), pp. 228–9.

63. Peter Shore, *Leading the Left* (London, Weidenfeld and Nicolson, 1993), p. 4.

64. B. Castle, *The Castle Diaries 1974–76* (London, Weidenfeld and Nicolson, 1980) p. 11.

65. PLP minutes, 11 July 1973.

66. Anthony Crosland, 'Open Letter to Grimsby Constituency Labour Party', *Socialist Commentary* (September 1974), pp. 1–2, p. 2.

67. Harold Wilson, *Final Term* (London, Weidenfeld and Nicolson and Michael Joseph, 1979), p. 28.
68. M. Hatfield, *The House the Left Built*, p. 211.
69. IPSC minutes, 28 November 1972, p. 2; and Tribune group minutes, 25 June 1973.
70. David Wood, *The Times*, 3 October 1973.
71. *The Times*, 13 December 1973. See also W. Rodgers, *Socialist Commentary* (December 1973), pp. 2–3.
72. *The Times*, 1 October 1973.
73. J. Boston, 'The Theory and Practice of Voluntary Incomes Policies with Particular Reference to the British Labour Government's Social Contract 1974–1979' (University of Oxford DPhil thesis, 1983), p. 176.
74. *The Times*, 6 September 1974.
75. Interview, July 1989. See also B. Castle, *The Castle Diaries 1974–76*, p. 149.
76. Interview, July 1989.
77. Letter, *The Times*, 18 October 1974. See also S. Holland, *The Socialist Challenge* (London, Quartet, 195), p. 40.
78. Interview, TUC Official, September 1993.
79. NEC-PC minutes, 16 May 1973, p. 40. He went on 'the instrument [of intervention] should be the IRC'.
80. NEC minutes, 25 July 1973; and *The Times*, 12 July 1973.
81. *The Times*, 9 and 11 January 1974.
82. Michael Meacher, 'Interview', *Politics and Power*, 2 (1980), pp. 5–14, p. 8.
83. Philip Ziegler, *Wilson* (London, Weidenfeld and Nicolson, 1993), p. 402.
84. David Butler and Dennis Kavanagh, *The British General Election of February 1974* (London, Macmillan, 1974), p. 125.
85. B. Castle, *The Castle Diaries 1974–76*, p. 13.
86. Bernard Donoughue, *Prime Minister* (London, Jonathan Cape, 1987), p. 51.
87. See Denis Healey, *The Time of My Life* (London, Michael Joseph, 1989), pp. 406–9; and Edmund Dell, *A Hard Pounding* (Oxford, Oxford University Press, 1991), pp. 88–102.
88. LC minutes, 20 May 1974; and B. Castle, *The Castle Diaries 1974–76*, p. 103.
89. *The Times*, 23 May 1974.
90. Barbara Castle, *Fighting All the Way* (London, Macmillan, 1993), p. 478.
91. *The Economist*, 6 April 1974.
92. He said 'the private sector is likely to be responsible for the greater part of our economic activity for as far ahead as I can see'. Interview with *Investor's Chronicle*, 29 September 1974, p. 1206.
93. Quoted by Michael Hatfield, *The House the Left Built*, p. 235. *The Guardian* noted Benn's plans to be 'surprisingly at odds' with Healey's; 18 May 1974.
94. Interview, March 1994.

95. T. Benn, *Against the Tide*, pp. 168 and 175; M. Hatfield, *The House the Left Built*, p. 231; Robert Jenkins, *Tony Benn* (London, Writers and Readers, 1980); and Phillip Whitehead, *The Writing on the Wall* (London, Michael Joseph, 1985), p. 130.
96. T. Benn, 'The Alternative Economic Strategy in Outline', reproduced in T. Benn, *Against the Tide*, pp. 725–7.
97. Shirley Williams et al, 'Comment on a Ten Year Strategy', RE: 198/June 1975, p. 3.
98. B. Castle, *The Castle Diaries 1974–76*, p. 355.
99. M. Hatfield, *The House the Left Built*, p. 245. The anti-market case was made by many supporters of the AES. See, for example, Michael Barratt Brown, 'The Common Market and Workers' Control', *Workers' Control Bulletin*, 22 (December 1974), pp. 3–5.
100. *Tribune*, 16 May 1975.
101. Quoted by M. Hatfield, *The House the Left Built*, p. 248.
102. Quoted by Robert Jenkins, *Tony Benn*, p. 223. See also Roy Jenkins, *A Life at the Centre* (London, Macmillan, 1992), pp. 410–1.
103. Speech, 23 May 1975, Crosland papers, 13/27.
104. Tony Benn, *A New Course for Labour* (IWC Pamphlet 51, 1976), p. 3.
105. See K. Burk and A. Cairncross, *'Goodbye Great Britain'* (London, Yale University Press, 1992), pp. 20–110.
106. Benn was supported by the party's research department. See 'Public Expenditure Cuts: A Supplementary Note', RE: 726/July 1976.
107. J. Barnett, *Inside the Treasury* (London, Andre Deutsch, 1982) p. 79.
108. Susan Crosland, *Tony Crosland* (London, Jonathan Cape, 1982), p. 354.
109. T. Benn, *Against the Tide*, p. 381.
110. For example, LC minutes, 23 February 1976; and RE: 728/July 1976. The latter details a meeting with the Home Policy Committee where Healey rejected import controls and defended spending cuts.
111. R. Bacon and W. Eltis, *Britain's Economic Problem: Too Few Producers* (London, Macmillan, 1976).
112. Quoted by N. Bosanquet, 'Has Manufacturing Been "Crowded Out"?', *Socialist Commentary* (January 1977), pp. 4–5, p. 4. Bacon and Eltis's arguments had been summarised in *The Sunday Times*. Hugh Scanlon, leader of the AUEW, was also much influenced by Bacon and Eltis.
113. *The Times*, 28 May 1976.
114. *The Times*, 5 May 1976.
115. *The Times*, 20 May 1976.
116. Michael Foot, *Loners and Loyalists* (London, Collins, 1986), p. 49.
117. Stephen Fay and Hugo Young, 'The Day the Pound Nearly Died', *Sunday Times*, 14, 21 and 28 May 1978. See also T. Benn, *Against the Tide*, pp. 661–79.
118. S. Crosland, *Tony Crosland*, pp. 381–2.
119. See K. Burk and A. Cairncross, *'Goodbye Great Britain'*, pp. 85–102.
120. Revisionists continued to oppose protection. See, for example, S. Williams, 'Principles and Policies for the Next Election', *Socialist Commentary* (February 1978), pp. 12–14, p. 13; S. Williams, 'Jobs

for the World', *Socialist Commentary* (June 1978), pp. 9–10; and E. Dell, 'Politics of Protection', *Socialist Commentary* (June 1978), pp. 7–9.

121. 'Medium Term Prospects for the UK Economy 1976–1980', RE: 813/ November 1976; and 'Economic Report November 1976: the Economic Policy Outlook', RE: 816/November 1976.

122. Quoted by Phillip Whitehead, *The Writing on the Wall*, p. 187.

123. See Anthony Arblaster, 'Anthony Crosland: Labour's Last "Revisionist"?', *Political Quarterly*, 48 (1977), pp. 416–28.

124. Quoted by John Campbell, *Roy Jenkins* (London, Weidenfield and Nicolson, 1983), p. 175.

125. Speech, 9 May 1975, Crosland papers, 13/32.

126. Speech, 24 January 1976, Crosland papers, 13/27. David Lipsey suggests that Crosland may have been limited by the doctrine of collective responsibility; interview, October 1993. A more upbeat assessment was contained in A. Crosland, 'Equality in Hard Times', *Socialist Commentary* (October 1976), p. 3.

127. A. Crosland, *Social Democracy in Europe*. See also 'The Secretary of State's Political Position', p. 13.

128. Manifesto group, *What We Must Do A Democratic Socialist Approach to Britain's Crisis* (1977), p. 17.

129. Nick Bosanquet, *Economic Strategy: A New Social Contract* (Fabian Research Series 333, 1977), pp. 28–29, 43. Elsewhere Bosanquet was more critical of crowding out; 'Has Manufacturing Benn "Crowded Out"?', pp. 4–5.

130. *LPACR* (1976), p. 188. See also Noel Tracey, *The Origins of the Social Democratic Party* (London, Croom Helm, 1983), pp. 27–30.

131. 'The Manifesto: A Note on Some of the Items Left Out', RD: 58/ September 1979, p. 1. See also *The Daily Telegraph*, 29 September 1979.

132. RD: 58/September 1979, p. 1.

133. T. Benn, *Conflicts of Interest*, p. 508.

134. *The Times Guide to the House of Commons May 1979* (London, Times Books, 1979), p. 297; and *The Times Guide to the European Parliament* (London, Times Books, 1979), p. 251.

135. *The Times Guide to the House of Commons May 1979*, p. 295.

136. *Labour Weekly*, 27 February 1981.

137. Chris Mullin, Campaign letter (10 January 1982, Benn archive).

138. Ivor Crewe and Anthony King, *The SDP* (Oxford, Oxford University Press, 1995), p. 24.

139. Quoted by N. Tracey, *The Origins of the Social Democratic Party*, p. 34.

140. *Tribune*, 6 June 1980.

141. *Labour Activist*, quoted by *The Times*, 26 September 1980.

142. D. Healey, 'A Note on Economic Policy in the 1980s', (unpublished paper, 1979), p. 5.

143. *Tribune*, 21 March 1980.

144. *The Sunday Times*, 1 June 1980

145. Geoffrey Sinclair, *Tribune*, 6 June 1980; and *Financial Times*, 31 May 1980.

146. *The Times*, 16 June 1981.

147. *LPACR* (1981), pp. 57–8.
148. D. Healey, *Socialism with a Human Face* (1981), p. 13.
149. *The Times*, 18 June 1981.
150. David Watt, *The Times*, 5 June 1981.
151. See, for example, LC minutes, 21 January 1980, p. 3; 25 February 1980, p. 4; 19 May 1980, p. 3; and Benn diary, 21 January 1980.
152. D. Healey, 'A Note on Economic Policy in the 1980s', p. 3.
153. LC minutes, 21 January 1980, p. 3.
154. L. Minkin, *The Contentious Alliance Trade Unions and the Labour Party* (Edinburgh, Edinburgh University Press, 1991), p. 423.
155. T. Benn, *The End of an Era* (London, Hutchinson, 1992), p. 60.
156. LC minutes, 21 July 1980.
157. *The Times*, 1 June 1981.
158. LC minutes, 21 January 1980; PC minutes, 17 March 1982; and T. Benn, *The End of an Era*, p. 87.
159. PC minutes, 30 April 1980.
160. *LPACR* (1981), p. 73.
161. G. Kaufman, *How to be a Minister* (London, Sidgewick and Jackson, 1980), p. 53; and T. Benn, *The End of an Era*, p. 60.
162. D. Owen, *Face the Future* (London, Jonathan Cape, 1981), pp. 112, 132–4, 173–80 and 186–8.
163. Benn diary, 16 April 1981.
164. *The Times*, 11 July 1980.
165. PLP minutes, 17 February 1982. Leftwing MPs supported the strategy against these criticisms.
166. PLP minutes, 13 April 1983.
167. Roy Hattersley, 'The Pursuit of Power', interview with Robert McKenzie, 28 May 1981, p. 9.
168. *Labour Weekly*, 23 January 1981. He laid out a very cautious set of measures in *Signposts for the Eighties* (London, CLV, 1981).
169. See Roy Hattersley, 'The Doers Versus Dreamers for Democracy', *New Statesman*, 24 September 1982.
170. Roy Hattersley, 'Why a Labour Government needs an incomes policy', 1980, in *A Duty to Win* (1983), pp. 28–32, p. 29.
171. When members of the shadow cabinet did support aspects of the AES it was often in a lukewarm and disaggregated way. Occasional support was given to import controls but they were presented as an isolated and limited strategy and not as part of a package of measures; see, for example, PC minutes, 30 April 1980.
172. Benn diary, 24 May 1982. See also Orme's overall defence of the AES in *Labour Weekly*, 6 February 1981 and 5 February 1982.
173. M. Rees, 'New Horizons for Industrial Planning', in G. Kaufman (ed.), *Renewal* (Harmondsworth, Penguin, 1983), pp. 41–5, p. 42.
174. Peter Shore, 'The Purpose of Labour's Economic Programme', in G. Kaufman (ed.), *Renewal*, pp. 27–39, p. 35.
175. P. Shore et al, *Programme for Recovery A Statement by the Shadow Chancellor and Treasury Team* (1982). Named as authors were Peter Shore, Robert Sheldon, Robin Cook and Jack Straw: *Financial Times*, 27 November 1982.

176. Other measures included: public sector investment, cuts in VAT and the National Insurance Surcharge, price controls and the introduction of some import controls.
177. Patrick Wintour, *The Guardian*, 24 March 1983.
178. L. Minkin, *The Contentious Alliance*, p. 424.
179. *The Sunday Times*, 28 November 1982.
180. *The Times*, 24 November 1982.
181. *Financial Times*, 24 November 1982.
182. Benn diary, 25 November 1982.
183. PLP minutes, 8 December 1982.
184. *Financial Times*, 27 November 1982.
185. 'Policy Development', RD: 2902/November 1983, p. 4.
186. Roy Green, 'The Economy: Has Labour bought the Treasury line?', *Tribune*, 31 December 1982.
187. Austin Mitchell, *Four Years in the Death of the Labour Party* (London, Methuen, 1983), pp. 62–3.
188. *The Guardian*, 24 November 1982.
189. *Tribune*, 28 May 1982.
190. Benn diary, 24 May 1982.
191. PC minutes, 4 May 1983 and 10 May 1983.
192. *The Times*, 12 May 1983; and Michael Foot, *Another Heart and Other Pulses* (London, Collins, 1984), pp. 30–6.
193. T. Benn, *The End of an Era*, pp. 286–7.
194. Interview, party researcher, September 1993.
195. See, for example, PC minutes, 19 March 1980.
196. Benn diary, 21 January 1980.
197. R. Hattersley, 'Why a Labour Government needs an incomes policy', *How to Win*, p. 29.
198. LC minutes, 21 January 1980.
199. LC minutes, 21 January 1980, p. 4.
200. See, for example, PCC minutes, 8 April 1981; and RD: 832/April 1981.
201. Interview, party researcher, September 1993.
202. *The Times*, 16 March 1982.
203. PLP minutes, 8 December 1982, p. 2.
204. Benn diary, 14 December 1981.
205. 'Economic Planning and Industrial Democracy: Regional Conferences', NEC paper, p. 3.
206. David Basnett, *The Future of Collective Bargaining* (Fabian Tract 481, 1982); David Basnett, 'Pay Checks', *New Socialist*, (November/December 1982), pp. 14–15; and *The Times*, 1 June 1982.
207. LC minutes, 21 February 1983.
208. *The Times*, 11, 18 and 21 April 1983. In September 1982 the General Council of the TUC tied on whether even to discuss pay policy with Labour. The annual congress voted against discussions, although it also endorsed the NEA. See *The Times*, 8 September 1982. On the general hostility of many union figures to incomes policy see Andrew Taylor, *Trade Unions and the Labour Party* (London, Croom Helm, 1987), pp. 115–23 and 262–8.

209. *The Times*, 24 January 1983.
210. *The Times*, 9 May 1983.
211. *The Times*, 19 May 1983.
212. RD: 2539/November 1982, p. 2.
213. *Tribune*, 3 June 1983.
214. Letter, 31 March 1981.
215. 'Special Conference on the Economy: Draft NEC Statement', RD: 330/April 1980, p. 1; and *The Times*, 24 April 1980.
216. Neil Kinnock, 'Personality, Policies and Democratic Socialism', *Tribune*, 18 September 1981.
217. 'Policy Coordination Committee', RD: 719/February 1981, p. 4.

CHAPTER 5: THE ADOPTION OF THE ALTERNATIVE ECONOMIC STRATEGY

1. *Tribune*, 26 June 1970.
2. *Tribune*, 3 July 1970.
3. *Tribune*, 31 July 1970.
4. Patrick Seyd, *The Rise and Fall of the Labour Left* (London, Macmillan, 1987), p. 78.
5. See, for example, Jack Jones, Hugh Scanlon and John Forrester (later of Labour's NEC), *LPACR* (1970), pp. 114–6, 120–1, 176 and 220–1. See Warren Fishbein, *Wage Restraint by Consensus* (London, Routledge and Kegan Paul, 1984), pp. 116–7.
6. Jack Jones, *Union Man* (London, Collins, 1986), p. 196.
7. The NEC was defeated by the conference on both issues. See NEC minutes, 27 September 1970 and 30 September 1970.
8. Robert Taylor, *The Fifth Estate* (London, Routledge and Kegan Paul, 1978), pp. 197–228.
9. See R. Taylor, *The Fifth Estate*, pp. 199, 212–3, 247–50 and 272.
10. Stephen Bornstein and Peter Gourevitch, 'Unions in a Declining Economy: the Case of the British TUC', in Peter Gourevitch et al, *Unions and Economic Crisis* (London, George Allen and Unwin, 1984), pp. 13–88, pp. 37–41.
11. See, for example, Ken Coates and Tony Topham, *The New Unionism* (London, Peter Owen, Penguin, 1972); and Ken Coates, 'Converting the Unions to Socialism', in Michael Barratt Brown and Ken Coates (eds), *Trade Union Register*, 3 (1973), pp. 9–46.
12. Samuel Finer, *The Changing British Party System* (Washington, AEI, 1980), p. 114. Patrick Seyd estimates that there were 14 Leftwingers on the NEC in 1973; *The Rise and Fall of the Labour Left*, p. 101.
13. Ian Mikardo, *Back-bencher* (London, Weidenfeld and Nicolson, 1988), pp. 182–3.
14. See Jad Adams, *Tony Benn* (London, Macmillan, 1992), pp. 312–37; and Robert Jenkins, *Tony Benn* (London, Writers and Readers, 1980), pp. 151–94.
15. *LPACR* (1970), p. 180.
16. Many PLP and shadow cabinet meetings were dominated by the

European issue and how Labour should respond. See PLP minutes and PC minutes 1970–1972.

17. NEC minutes, 28 October 1970 and 25 November 1970; and RD: 12/September 1970, p. 4.
18. 'The Need for Standing Advisory or Sub-Committees', RD: 26/November 1970; HPC minutes, 9 November 1970; Michael Hatfield, *The House the Left Built* (London, Victor Gollancz, 1978), p. 42; and William Stallard, 'The Labour Party in Opposition and Government 1970–1979' (University of Keele PhD thesis, 1985), pp. 99–101.
19. RD: 47/January 1971.
20. RD: 5/July 1970; M. Hatfield, *The House the Left Built*, pp. 34–6; and W. Stallard, 'The Labour Party in Opposition and Government 1970–1979', pp. 97–9.
21. RD: 5/July 1970, p. 1.
22. RD: 47/January 1971, pp. 2–3; RD: 94/April 1971; and IPSC minutes, 28 April 1971 and 18 May 1971.
23. Michael Meacher, 'Interview', *Politics and Power*, 2 (1980), pp. 5–14, p. 8.
24. Peter Shore, *Leading the Left* (London, Weidenfield and Nicolson, 1993), p. 104.
25. *The Times*, 5 July 1972.
26. FEASC minutes, 29 April 1971, 15 June 1971, and 14 December 1971.
27. 'The Public Sector', RD: 216/December 1971; IPSC minutes, 21 December 1971; Phillip Whitehead, *The Writing on the Wall* (London, Michael Joseph, 1985), p. 120; and M. Hatfield, *The House the Left Built*, pp. 88–9.
28. PSG minutes, 25 January 1972. Holland was coopted at the second meeting.
29. S. Holland and R. Pryke, 'A State Holding Company', RD: 271/February 1972.
30. IPSC minutes, 21 March 1972; and M. Hatfield, *The House the Left Built*, pp. 121–5.
31. IPSC minutes, 5 April 1972.
32. Labour party, *Labour's Programme for Britain* (1972).
33. RD: 336/April 1972.
34. IPSC minutes, 25 April 1972.
35. IPSC minutes, 18 April 1972, and 25 April 1972.
36. *The Times*, 16 November 1970.
37. *Sunday Express*, quoted by *Tribune*, 17 July 1970; and Anthony Crosland, 'Policies for the People, by the People', *Socialist Commentary* (November 1971), pp. 3–5. See also M. Hatfield, *The House the Left Built*, p. 51; and W. Stallard, 'The Labour Party in Opposition and Government 1970–1979', pp. 122 and 155.
38. See Crosland papers, 13/24. Dick Leonard wrote in the Foreword to *Socialism Now* 'no longer has he the leisure or the freedom to range as widely as his whim takes him'; Anthony Crosland, *Socialism Now* (London, Jonathan Cape, 1975), p. 10. See also NEC minutes, 30 May 1973.

39. Quoted by M. Hatfield, *The House the Left Built*, p. 57.
40. IPSC minutes; and M. Hatfield, *The House the Left Built*, pp. 44–5.
41. *The Times*, 5 July 1972.
42. PC minutes, 29 March 1972; and *The Times*, 11 April 1972.
43. See Roy Jenkins, *A Life at the Centre* (London, Macmillan, 1991), pp. 344–53; and David Owen, *Time to Declare* (London, Michael Joseph, 1991), pp. 193–205.
44. Denis Healey, *The Time of My Life* (London, Michael Joseph, 1989), p. 367.
45. M. Hatfield, *The House the Left Built*, p. 57.
46. Interview, October 1993.
47. See *The Times*, 16 September 1971; and *Labour Weekly*, 29 December 1972.
48. Speech, 9 December 1972, Crosland papers, 13/24.
49. NEC minutes, 24 November 1971.
50. See Martin Sloman, *Socialising Public Ownership* (London, Macmillan, 1978), pp. 14–15.
51. Interview, March 1994.
52. In Crosland's absence! IPSC minutes, 31 October 1972.
53. S. Holland, 'Planning Strategy, Tactics and Techniques', RD: 442/October 1972; and S. Holland, 'The New Economic Imperatives', RD: 473/November 1972.
54. IPSC minutes, 28 November 1972.
55. Interview, David Lipsey, October 1993.
56. Interview, March 1994.
57. PSG minutes, 15 March 1973, 29 March 1973, and 10 April 1973.
58. IPSC minutes, 5 April 1973; and Tony Benn, *Against the Tide* (London, Hutchinson, 1989), p. 17. See also HPC minutes, 9 April 1973; and NEC minutes, 18 April 1973.
59. NEC-PC minutes, 16 May 1973.
60. M. Hatfield, *The House the Left Built*, pp. 183–6.
61. *The Times*, 14–17 May 1973; *The Guardian*, 14 May 1973; and M. Hatfield, *The House the Left Built*, pp. 193–5.
62. *The Times*, 17 May 1973; and *The Guardian*, 17 May 1973.
63. NEC-PC minutes, 16 May 1973, p. 44.
64. *The Times*, 31 May 1973; M. Hatfield, *The House the Left Built*, pp. 195–8; and P. Whitehead, *The Writing on the Wall*, p. 122.
65. NEC minutes, 30 May 1973.
66. *The Times*, 1 June 1973.
67. Benn diary, 7 July 1973. Tony Benn, *Parliament, People and Power* (London, Verso, 1982), p. 26.
68. P. Shore, *Leading the Left*, p. 104. See PLP minutes, 11 July 1973.
69. A. Crosland, 'The Prospects of Socialism – Nationalisation?', *Encounter*, XLI (September 1973), pp. 60–61. The journalist Nora Beloff claimed that his view was shared by the majority of the shadow cabinet, *Observer*, 4 June 1973.
70. *New Statesman*, 8 June 1973, p. 839.
71. P. Whitehead, *The Writing on the Wall*, p. 121.
72. *The Times*, 2 and 4 June 1973.

73. NEC minutes, 28 September 1973; and *The Times*, 29 September 1973.
74. Patrick Cosgrave, *The Spectator*, 6 October 1973.
75. Lewis Minkin, *The Labour Party Conference* (Manchester, Manchester University Press, 1980), p. 342.
76. *The Times*, 3 October 1973.
77. W. Fishbein, *Wage Restraint by Consensus*, pp. 117–20; G. Dorfman, *Government Versus Trade Unionism in British Politics since 1968* (London, Macmillan, 1979), pp. 108–12; M. Hatfield, *The House the Left Built*, pp. 48–9; L. Minkin, *The Labour Party Conference*, p. 337; William Stallard, 'Policy-Making in the Labour Party: the Liaison Committee in Opposition and Government 1970–1979', *Teaching Politics*, 16 (1987), pp. 42–55; and Andrew Taylor, *Trade Unions and the Labour Party* (London, Croom Helm, 1987), pp. 6–9.
78. See RD: 199/November 1971.
79. LC minutes, 25 September 1972.
80. LC minutes, 21 February 1972, 20 March 1972, 22 May 1972, 19 June 1972 and 24 July 1972.
81. LC minutes, 22 January 1973 and 29 January 1973. See the account given by S. Bornstein and P. Gourevitch, 'Unions in a Declining Economy: the Case of the British TUC', pp. 42–45; Jonathan Boston, 'The Theory and Practice of Voluntary Incomes Policies with Particular Reference to the British Labour Government's Social Contract 1974–1979' (Oxford University DPhil thesis, 1983); W. Fishbein, *Wage Restraint by Consensus*, pp. 117–132; and Andrew Taylor, *Trade Unions and the Labour Party*, pp. 22–30.
82. See, for example, TUC, *Collective Bargaining and the Social Contract* (1974).
83. See, for example, Philip Ziegler's judgement; *Wilson* (London, Weidenfeld and Nicolson, 1993), p. 392.
84. Barbara Castle, *The Castle Diaries 1974–76* (London, Weidenfeld and Nicolson, 1980), p. 10.
85. See, for example, David Basnett, 'Working Out the Social Contract', *Socialist Commentary* (October 1974), pp. 3–5.
86. TUC-Labour Party Liaison Committee, *Economic Policy and the Cost of Living* (1973), p. 6.
87. Interview, TUC Official, August 1993.
88. Ben Pimlott, *Harold Wilson* (London, Harper Collins, 1992), p. 604.
89. Interview, TUC Official, August 1993.
90. S. Bornstein and P. Gourevitch, 'Unions in a Declining Economy: the Case of the British TUC', p. 44.
91. M. Meacher, 'Interview', p. 7.
92. J. Boston, 'The Theory and Practice of Voluntary Incomes Policies with Particular Reference to the British Labour Government's Social Contract 1974–1979', p. 178; and W. Fishbein, *Wage Restraint by Consensus*, pp. 124 and 131.
93. LC minutes, 4 January 1974; and B. Castle, *The Castle Diaries 1974–76*, pp. 18–20.
94. Interview, October 1993.

95. TUC, *Annual Report* (1973), pp. 606–7.
96. See RD: 900/October 1973 on policies of the TGWU; and RD: 897/ October 1973 on the GMWU. Both supported public ownership.
97. RD: 438/October 1972, p. 1.
98. Interview, TUC Official, August 1993.
99. For accounts see P. Whitehead, *The Writing on the Wall*, pp. 51–98; Martin Holmes, *Political Pressure and Economic Policy* (London, Butterworth, 1982); and Colin Leys, *Politics in Britain* (London, Verso, 1986), pp. 79–84.
100. S. Holland, 'Planning and Policy Coordination', RD: 315/March 1972, pp. 6–7; T. Benn, 'Industrial Power and Industrial Policy', RD: 722/April 1973; and IPSC minutes, 12 June 1972.
101. Quoted by R. Jenkins, *Tony Benn*, p. 164.
102. Benn diary, 9 July 1973; and *LPACR* (1973), p. 47. An inconclusive Opposition Green Paper was eventually produced proposing nationalisation, although members of the Banking and Insurance Group were dissatisfied with it. See Labour party, *Banking and Insurance* (1973).
103. PSG minutes, 2 May 1972 and 15 March 1973.
104. E. Heffer, 'Labour's Policy Making Process', *New Statesman*, 1 June 1973, pp. 796–8, p. 798.
105. Interview, March 1994.
106. *LPACR* (1972), p. 257.
107. *LPACR* (1971), pp. 298 and 300–1.
108. Coventry Trades Council et al, *State Intervention in Industry* (Nottingham, Spokesman, 1982), p. 74.
109. S. Bornstein and P. Gourevitch, 'Unions in a Declining Economy: the Case of the British TUC', p. 43.
110. Minkin qualifies union support for leftwing policies. Most union leaders had other priorities. See *The Contentious Alliance Trade Unions and the Labour Party* (Edinburgh, Edinburgh University Press, 1991), pp. 165–73.
111. A. Budd, *The Politics of Economic Planning* (London, Fontana, 1978), p. 133.
112. M. Hartley Brewer, *The Guardian*, 3 November 1975, quoted by S. Wilks, 'Planning Agreements: the Making of a Paper Tiger', *Public Administration*, 59 (1981), pp. 399–421, p. 402.
113. Interview, October 1993.
114. G. Jones 'A Left House Built on Sand', *Socialist Commentary* (November 1978), pp. 12–13, p. 12. See also B. Pimlott, *Harold Wilson*, p. 665.

CHAPTER 6: LABOUR IN OFFICE, 1974–1979

1. See T. Evans, 'A Strategy for Government Industrial Policy', *Public Enterprise*, 8 (1978), pp. 17–20; Tom Forester, 'Neutralising the Industrial Strategy', in Ken Coates (ed.), *What Went Wrong* (Nottingham, Spokesman, 1979), pp. 74–94; Daniel Kramer, *State Capital and Private En-*

terprise (London, Routledge, 1988), pp. 1–15; and M. Sawyer 'Industrial Policy', in M. Artis and D. Cobham (eds), *Labour's Economic Policies 1974–79* (Manchester, Manchester University Press, 1991), pp. 158–75.

2. Labour party, *Let Us Work Together – Labour's Way Out of the Crisis* (1974).
3. Tony Benn, 'The Current Work Programme of the Department of Industry' (May 1974), p. 4.
4. Cmnd 5710, *The Regeneration of British Industry* (London, HMSO, 1974). See *The Economist,* 17 June 1974. The Labour MP Brian Sedgemore notes the accuracy and detail of *The Economist's* reporting about industrial policy in this period: evidence, he claims, that leaks were coming from inside the Department of Industry. See *The Secret Constitution* (London, Hodder and Stoughton, 1980), p. 137.
5. 'The Industry Bill Two Steps Forward – One Step Backwards?', Tribune group papers.
6. *The Regeneration of British Industry,* p. 1.
7. Labour party, *Britain Will Win with Labour* (1974).
8. See *Tribune,* 15 November 1974; and Ken Coates, 'Labour's Turning Point', *Workers' Control Bulletin,* 25 (July 1975), pp. 2–3.
9. 'Industry Bill', RE: 84/March 1975; Robert Taylor, 'The Pragmatic Industry Bill', *Socialist Commentary* (June 1975), pp. 12–14; Political Economy Collective, *Workers and the Industry Bill* (Newcastle, 1975); and D. Hobson and J. Stuttard, 'A Guide to the Industry Act 1975', *Accountant's Digest,* 27 (1976).
10. Labour Party Research Department, 'Labour's Industrial Policy and the Industry Bill', Information Paper no: 2/March 1975, p. 35.
11. *The Economist,* 15 February 1975.
12. Stephen Wilks, 'Planning Agreements: the Making of a Paper Tiger', *Public Administration,* 59 (1981), pp. 399–420, p. 405.
13. HMSO, *Industry Act 1975* (London, 1975), clause 21, pp. 2006–7.
14. Department of Industry, *The Contents of a Planning Agreement* (London, HMSO, 1975), p. 3. Planning agreements would be 'wholly voluntary, based on consent'; p. 2.
15. A similar conception of planning agreements was contained in Peter Shore's *Programme for Recovery* (1982).
16. Denis Healey and Eric Varley, 'Industrial Strategy', RE: 1532/February 1978.
17. Cmnd. 6315, *An Approach to Industrial Strategy* (London, HMSO, 1975), p. 3. See also *The Economist,* 1 November 1975; and T. Benn, *Against the Tide* (London, Hutchinson, 1989), pp. 455–7;
18. Quoted by S. Wilks, 'Planning Agreements the Making of a Paper Tiger', p. 407. See also 'Industrial Strategy: Government and Party', RE: 381/December 1975, p. 5.
19. Quoted by S. Wilks, 'Planning Agreements: the Making of a Paper Tiger', p. 405.
20. See 'The National Enterprise Board', RE: 668/June 1976; M. Parr, 'The National Enterprise Board', *National Westminster Bank Review* (February 1979), pp. 51–62; and N. Vann, 'Negotiating Planning

Agreements', *Studies for Trade Unionists*, 3 (March 1977), pp. 3–11.
21. Coventry Trades Council et al, *State Intervention in Industry* (Nottingham, Nottingham, 1982), pp. 80–98.
22. M. Sawyer, 'Industrial Policy', p. 160.
23. Harold Wilson, *Final Term* (London, Weidenfield and Nicolson, 1979), p. 35.
24. Quoted by D. Kramer, *State Capital and Private Enterprise*, p. 8.
25. T. Forester, 'Neutralising the Industrial Strategy', p. 85.
26. Department of Industry, *National Enterprise Board Guidelines* (London, HMSO, 1977), p. 2.
27. D. Kramer, *State Capital and Private Enterprise*, p. 14.
28. Coventry Trades Council et al, *State Intervention in Industry*, pp. 99–112; and S. Wilks, 'Planning Agreements: The Making of a Paper Tiger', p. 406–416. See 'A Note on Planning Agreements: Progress and Policy', RE: 933/January 1977.
29. TUC, *The Trade Union Role in Industrial Policy* (1977), p. 94.
30. Cmnd. 6706, *Report of the Committee of Inquiry on Industrial Democracy* (London, HMSO, 1977). See also John Elliott, *Conflict or Cooperation?* (London, Kogan Page, 1978), pp. 205–64.
31. Some Leftwingers were also unhappy. See Ken Coates and Tony Topham, 'Bullock What's Wrong?', *Workers' Control Bulletin*, 35 (1977), pp. 2–3; Ken Coates, 'Holding the Line Against Bullock', *Workers' Control*, 1 (1978), pp. 3–4; and Ken Coates and Tony Topham, *The Shop Steward's Guide to the Bullock Report* (Nottingham, Spokesman, 1977).
32. See T. Benn, *Against the Tide*, p. 158; and Joel Barnett, *Inside the Treasury* (London, Andrew Deutsch, 1982), pp. 35–7.
33. M. Sawyer, 'Prices Policies', in M. Artis and D. Cobham (eds), *Labour's Economic Policies 1974–79*, pp. 176–89.
34. *The Economist*, 16 November 1974 and 21 December 1974. Some Leftwingers were more positive about the impact of price controls on inflation; interview, John Hughes, February 1994.
35. See Shirley Williams, 'Review of the Price Code' (paper, 12 November 1974); and Shirley Williams, 'Investment and Other Cut-Backs in Industry' (paper, November 1974).
36. H. Wilson, *Final Term*, pp. 29–36, 135–43.
37. Phillip Whitehead, *The Writing on the Wall* (London, Michael Joseph, 1985), p. 129.
38. Barbara Castle, *The Castle Diaries 1974–76* (London, Weidenfield and Nicolson, 1980), pp. 145–46. See also Tony Benn, *Against the Tide*, p. 159.
39. Quoted by Coventry Trades Council et al, *State Intervention in Industry*, p. 37. *The Times*, 23 May 1974; and B. Castle, *The Castle Diaries 1974–76*, p. 103.
40. Michael Hatfield, *The House the Left Built* (London, Victor Gollancz, 1978), pp. 235–8; Eric Heffer, *Labour's Future* (London, Verso, 1986), p. 12; Austen Morgan, *Harold Wilson* (London, Pluto Press, 1992), pp. 438–9; and Robert Jenkins, *Tony Benn* (London, Writers and Readers, 1980), pp. 207–9.

41. H. Wilson, *Final Term*, p. 33.
42. See Eric Heffer, *Never a Yes Man* (London, Verso, 1989), p. 154; T. Benn, *Against the Tide*, pp. 187–9; and Edmund Dell, *A Hard Pounding* (Oxford, Oxford University Press, 1991), pp. 94–5.
43. *The Economist*, 20 July 1974.
44. H. Wilson, *Final Term*, p. 33.
45. P. Whitehead, *The Writing on the Wall*, p. 130.
46. B. Donoughue, *Prime Minister* (London, Jonathan Cape, 1987), p. 52.
47. R. Day, . . . *But with Respect* (London, Weidenfield and Nicolson, 1993), p. 112.
48. Michael Meacher, 'Interview', *Politics and Power*, 2 (1980), pp. 8–14, p. 10.
49. P. Whitehead, *The Writing on the Wall*, p. 131.
50. *The Economist*, 15 June 1974.
51. T. Benn, *Against the Tide*, p. 193.
52. T. Benn, *Against the Tide*, p. 209.
53. B. Castle, *The Castle Diaries 1974–76*, p. 167. See also I. Mikardo, *Back-bencher* (London, Weidenfield and Nicolson, 1988), p. 197.
54. *The Economist*, 17 August 1974.
55. *The Guardian*, 3 August 1974. The result was 'a major victory for rightwing members of the cabinet'.
56. Interview, T. Benn, July 1989.
57. R. Jenkins, *Tony Benn*, p. 212.
58. Quoted by Jad Adams, *Tony Benn* (London, Macmillan, 1992), p. 355.
59. Quoted by Coventry Trades Council et al, *State Intervention in Industry*, p. 43.
60. Ben Pimlott, *Harold Wilson* (London, Harper Collins, 1992), p. 665.
61. *The Guardian*, 16 August 1974.
62. P. Whitehead, *The Writing on the Wall*, p. 131.
63. B. Donoughue, *Prime Minister*, p. 53.
64. *The Guardian*, 16 August 1974.
65. P. Whitehead, *The Writing on the Wall*, p. 140.
66. *The Economist*, 22 June 1974.
67. *The Times*, 1 August 1974.
68. *The Economist*, 16 November 1974.
69. *Labour Weekly*, 25 October 1974; and *Bank of England Quarterly Bulletin*, 14 (1974), pp. 435–6.
70. Michael Foot, *Loners and Loyalists* (London, Collins, 1986), p. 49. See also B. Castle, *The Castle Diaries 1974–76*, pp. 11 and 531.
71. Peter Shore, *Leading the Left* (London, Weidenfield and Nicolson, 1993), p. 123.
72. Interview, September 1993.
73. See John Hughes, 'Those Company Profits', *Workers' Control Bulletin*, 22 (December 1974), pp. 7–9. *The Economist* reported Jack Jones as holding a similar view, 6 September 1975.
74. Stuart Holland, *The Socialist Challenge* (London, Quartet, 1975), p. 57.

75. 'Current Economic Developments, July 1975', RE: 232/July 1975, p. 28.
76. 'The Alleged Profits Crisis and Labour Policies', Tribune group papers; and Stuart Holland, 'An Alternative Economic Strategy', in M. Barratt Brown et al (eds), *Full Employment Priority* (Nottingham, Spokesman, 1978), pp. 133–6.
77. *Tribune*, 18 October 1974. See also Brian Sedgemore, *Tribune*, 8 November 1974.
78. M. Meacher, 'Interview', p. 9. A point also made by Labour's research department, 'Economic Report', RE: 336/November 1975.
79. IPSC minutes, 21 June 1975. Others on the committee were pessimistic.
80. Stuart Holland and Paul Ormerod, 'Corporation Tax and Economic Policy Issues', RD: 434/June 1980, written in 1978; and J. Hughes, 'A Programme for Industrial Development' (unpublished paper, 1975), p. 1.
81. See the discussion in W. Martin (ed.), *The Economics of the Profits Crisis* (London, HMSO, 1981).
82. T. Benn, *Parliament, People and Power*, p. 29. Donoughue makes a similar point, *Prime Minister*, p. 60.
83. Lewis Minkin, *The Labour Party Conference* (Manchester, Manchester University Press, 1980), pp. 349 and 359.
84. See T. Benn, *Against the Tide*, p. 445; B. Castle, *The Castle Diaries 1974–76*, pp. 511–2; and Jack Jones, *Union Man* (London, Collins, 1986), pp. 300–1.
85. IPSC minutes, 25 March 1975, 8 April 1975 and 22 April 1975;
86. Tony Benn, Frances Morrell and Francis Cripps, 'A Ten Year Industrial Strategy for Britain', RE: 126 April 1975, p. 16. It was reproduced as T. Benn, F. Morrell and F. Cripps, *A Ten Year Industrial Strategy for Britain* (IWC pamphlet 49, 1975).
87. IPSC minutes, 21 June 1975. See also 'Economic and Industrial Planning'; RE: 144/May 1975 and RE: 144a/May 1975; and Labour party, *Labour and Industry* (1975).
88. B. Castle, *The Castle Diaries 1974–76*, p. 493.
89. IPSC minutes, 27 June 1975.
90. RE: 599/April 1976; and *The Times*, 13 April 1976.
91. NEC minutes, 12 May 1976.
92. NEC minutes, 19 May 1976.
93. Labour party, *Labour's Programme 1976* (1976), p. 6.
94. *The Times*, 28 May 1976. See also Eric Varley, 'Comments on Labour's Programme 1976', RE: 647/May 1976.
95. P. Shore, *Leading the Left*, p. 123.
96. Report of the NEC Delegation on Industrial Policy, minutes, 4 February 1976, RE: 511/March 1976. Other meetings are detailed in RE: 728/July 1976 and RE: 1946/December 1978.
97. See 'Economic and Industrial Policy', RE: 521/March 1976; 'Alternative Economic Strategies', RE: 900/December 1976; 'A Summary of Labour's Industrial Policy', RE: 1341/October 1977; 'Planning Agreements and Industrial Policy Under Current Legislation', RE:

1427/December 1977; and 'Proposals for the 1978 Budget', RE: 1529.

98. 'An Agenda for Agreement', RE: 966/February 1977, p. 4. See also D. Healey and E. Varley, 'Industrial Strategy', RE: 1532/February 1978, p. 7; R. Liddle, 'The Government's Policy and Labour Party Programme', RE: 1383/November 1977; and Department of Industry, 'The Strengths and Weaknesses of the Sectoral Approach', RE: 1533/February 1978.

99. See G. Bish, 'Working Relations Between Government and Party', in K. Coates (ed.), *What Went Wrong*, pp. 163–9.

100. HPC minutes, 6 February 1978 and 13 February 1978; IPSC minutes, 29 June 1978; and NEC minutes, 22 February 1978.

101. 'The Crisis and the Only Way in which the Labour Government Can Solve It!', *Tribune*, 1 January 1975. Members of the PLP frequently criticised the government's policy trajectory – they were equally aware of the limitations as to what they could do to secure a more favourable economic policy. See PLP minutes, 21 November 1974, 16 April 1975, 8 July 1975 and 11 November 1975; and Tribune group minutes, 14 July 1975.

102. M. Foot, *Loners and Loyalists*, p. 114.

103. J. Jones, *Union Man*, p. 309.

104. *The Times*, 13 March 1976.

105. *The Trade Union Role in Industrial Policy*, pp. 83–4; and TUC, *Industrial Strategy: Action at Company and Plant Levels* (1979), p. 1. See also LC minutes, 31 January 1977.

106. TUC, *Economic Review* (1977), p. 36.

107. For example, Len Murray called for import controls, planning agreements and a strong NEB at the 1975 Congress. Jack Jones supported industrial democracy, import controls, planning agreements, and price controls at various times. See *Tribune*, 5 April 1974, 4 July 1975, 21 November 1975 and 5 March 1976. David Basnett endorsed capital and import controls, price controls, and increased investment. See TUC, *Annual Report* (1976), pp. 528–9, and TUC, *Annual Report* (1978), p. 443. Hugh Scanlon moved to the right after 1974 and supported Labour's pay policy. However he still called for an industrial strategy, TUC, *Annual Report* (1978), pp. 523–5. See also *The Social Contract 1976–77*, pp. 23–39; and *The Trade Union Contribution to Industrial Policy*, pp. 17–33.

108. Lewis Minkin, *The Contentious Alliance Trade Unions and the Labour Party* (Edinburgh, Edinburgh University Press, 1991), p. 170.

109. J. Jones, *Union Man*, p. 304.

110. Interview, TUC Official, August 1993. See also Jack Jones, *Union Man*, pp. 261 and 282; and quoted in Coventry Trades Council et al, *State Intervention in Industry*, p. 121.

111. Stephen Bornstein and Peter Gourevitch, 'Unions in a Declining Economy: The Case of the British TUC', in P. Gourevitch et al, *Unions and Economic Crisis* (London, George Allen and Unwin, 1984), pp. 13–88, p. 51.

112. J. Jones, *Union Man*, pp. 296–8.

113. Interview, July 1989.
114. Those that did included: ASTMS, *The Crisis in British Economic Planning* (1975); NUPE, *Inflation Attack or Retreat?* (1975); and NUPE, *Time to Change Course* (1976).
115. Jack Jones, *Union Man*, p. 308.
116. TUC-Labour Party Liaison Committee, *The Next Three Years and The Problem of Priorities* (1976), p. 8.
117. TUC-Labour Party Liaison Committee, *The Next Three Years and into the Eighties* (1977); and, TUC-Labour Party Liaison Committee, *Into the Eighties: An Agreement* (1978).
118. NEC minutes, 23 June 1976; and 28 July 1976.
119. Stuart Holland, 'Planning Disagreements', in Stuart Holland (ed.), *Beyond Capitalist Planning* (Oxford, Blackwell, 1978), pp. 137–64, p. 145.
120. B. Castle, *Fighting All the Way* (London, Macmillan, 1993), p. 478.
121. 'Economic and Industrial Policy', RE: 521/March 1976, p. 5.
122. G. Hodgson, *Labour at the Crossroads* (Oxford, Martin Robertson, 1981), p. 129; and D. Hoyle, 'Labour Party and Nationalisation', *Labour Monthly* (March 1976), pp. 111–5, p. 114.
123. 'The NEB and the Industrial Strategy', RE: 962/February 1977, p. 3.
124. IPSC minutes, 22 June 1976 and 29 June 1978.
125. Quoted by Coventry Trades Council et al, *State Intervention in Industry*, p. 80.
126. T. Benn, *Parliament, People and Power* (London, Verso, 1982), p. 30.
127. M. Meacher, 'Interview', p. 7.
128. Quoted by Geoff Hodgson, *Labour at the Crossroads*, p. 134. Holland had called for grass roots support earlier; 'Shop Floor Action To Force Through Labour's Programme', *Workers' Control Bulletin* (December 1973), p. 2.
129. Interview, September 1993.
130. Quoted by Coventry Trades Council et al, *State Intervention in Industry*, p. 121.
131. In this sense the government's abandonment of the industrial strategy did not represent, for the most part, a betrayal as many leftwingers alleged subsequently. Ministers had made no secret of their hostility to the AES before 1974. In office they attempted simply to implement the measures they had defended in opposition. Wilson's rhetoric, however, was characteristically ambiguous in this regard.
132. B. Sedgemore, *The Secret Constitution*, p. 136.
133. B. Castle, *The Castle Diaries 1974–76*, p. 675.
134. 'Industrial Strategy: Government and Party', p. 12.
135. T. Benn, *Parliament, People and Power*, p. 28; and S. Holland, 'New Public Enterprise and Economic Planning', in K. Coates, *How to Win?* (Nottingham, Spokesman, 1981), pp. 111–46, p. 118.
136. RD: 6/June 1979, p. 2.

CHAPTER 7: POLITICS AND POLICY-MAKING IN THE LABOUR
PARTY AFTER 1979

1. Denis Healey, *The Time of My Life* (London, Michael Joseph, 1989),
   p. 466.
2. Peter Shore, *Leading the Left* (London, Weidenfield and Nicolson,
   1993), p. 119.
3. The pressure to alter the structure of the party was not new. The
   Campaign for Labour Party Democracy had been set up in 1973 as
   a result of Harold Wilson's rejection of the proposal to nationalise
   25 top companies. See Chris Mullin, *How to Reselect Your MP* (CLPD
   and IWC pamphlet 77, 1981), p. 19; and *Workers' Control Bulletin*,
   1 (October 1973), p. 5.
4. *Tribune*, 11 May 1979.
5. *Labour Weekly*, 10 August 1979.
6. See Patrick Seyd, *The Rise and Fall of the Labour Left* (London,
   Macmillan, 1987), especially pp. 74–5, 83–9, 97–100.
7. Anthony King, 'Mrs Thatcher's First Term', in Austin Ranney (ed.),
   Britain at the Polls, 1983 (Durham, Duke University Press, 1985),
   pp. 1–38, p. 16.
8. David Kogan and Maurice Kogan, *The Battle for the Labour Party* (London, Kogan Page, 1983).
9. *The Times*, 3 October 1979. By 1980 *The Times* reported that moderates could count on only seven votes; 1 October 1980.
10. *The Times*, 30 September 1981.
11. *The Times*, 29 September 1982.
12. David Owen, *Time to Declare* (London, Michael Joseph, 1991),
    p. 418.
13. Giles Radice, *Labour's Path to Power* (London, Macmillan, 1989),
    p. 24.
14. *The Daily Telegraph*, 15 January 1979.
15. See RD: 23/July 1979, reproduced as Geoff Bish, 'Drafting the Manifesto', in Ken Coates (ed.) *What Went Wrong* (Nottingham, Spokesman, 1979), pp. 187–206; IWC Briefing, 'Labour's Manifesto: What Got Left Out', *Workers' Control*, 5 (1979), pp. 14–16; and David Butler and Dennis Kavanagh, *The British General Election of 1979* (London, Macmillan, 1980), pp. 144–53.
16. They were: 'NEC Proposals for the Manifesto: Keep Britain Labour',
    RE: 1898; 'Minutes of the Cabinet/NEC working group on the manifesto, RE: 2129/March 1979; and 'NEC Proposals', RE: 2138/April 1979. NEC minutes, 2 April 1979.
17. G. Bish, 'Drafting the Manifesto', p. 197.
18. Under Clause V (2) of Labour's constitution the drafting of the manifesto should be carried out jointly by the NEC and the shadow cabinet (or cabinet) drawing from conference decisions.
19. Unsurprisingly rightwingers did not view the production of the manifesto in the same terms as leftwingers. They claimed that Callaghan went to considerable trouble to preserve the wording of the NEC version, which was an unworkable draft because of its length and

pedantry. The NEC, however, was uninterested in compromise and Callaghan's patience ran out in the rush to produce the manifesto. Even then the Prime Minister's draft was shown to at least one leftwinger.

20. G. Bish, 'Drafting the Manifesto', p. 201.
21. Eric Heffer, *Never a Yes Man* (London, Verso, 1991), p. 172.
22. See HPC minutes, 11 June 1979 and 16 July 1979, p. 3; and *The Daily Telegraph*, 17 July 1979.
23. *The Daily Telegraph*, 8 May 1979 and 11 May 1979.
24. *The Daily Telegraph*, 21 June 1979. Reproduced in E. Heffer, *Never a Yes Man*, p. 184.
25. *Tribune*, 29 June 1979.
26. *Tribune*, 28 September 1979.
27. *Observer*, 15 July 1979.
28. See, for example, Tribune group minutes, 12 June 1979: 'Dennis Skinner said that the only way of convincing the man in the street that the next Labour government will carry out our Labour party policy is to demonstrate that we are democratising our party'.
29. See P. Seyd, *The Rise and Fall of the Labour Left*, pp. 103–24.
30. *The Daily Telegraph*, 12 June 1979.
31. *The Guardian*, 4 July 1979; and *The Daily Telegraph*, 5 July 1979 and 26 July 1979.
32. For example, Tony Benn's collection *Arguments for Socialism* (Harmondsworth, Penguin, 1980, originally 1979) summarised previous speeches, some over six years old.
33. PC minutes, 18 July 1979. See also PC minutes, 25 July 1979 and 13 February 1980 and PLP minutes, 15 April 1980.
34. *LPACR* (1979), p. 167.
35. *LPACR* (1979), p. 287.
36. *LPACR* (1979), p. 186. Litterick had lost his seat in the election.
37. *LPACR* (1979), p. 189.
38. Although passed, the amendment for shifting control of the manifesto was delayed for a year.
39. *LPACR* (1980), p. 148.
40. See Ivor Crewe and Anthony King, *The SDP* (Oxford, Oxford University Press, 1995), p. 75.
41. See Noel Tracey, *The Origins of the Social Democratic Party* (London, Croom Helm, 1983), pp. 37–9. In all 29 MPs left Labour.
42. *The Sunday Times*, 5 April 1981 and 12 April 1981; and Phillip Whitehead, *The Writing on the Wall* (London, Michael Joseph, 1985), p. 404. The letter was organised by Jack Straw and Robin Cook.
43. *The Times*, 3 April 1981; and T. Benn, 'Statement of Candidature' (Benn archive).
44. Benn diary, 11 May 1981.
45. *The Daily Telegraph*, 28 September 1981.
46. Judith Hart, 'Open letter', 2 April 1981 (Benn archive).
47. Eric Heffer, paper to the Tribune Group, 10 April 1981 (Benn archive). Similar points were made by John Prescott and Jack Straw at the Tribune group meeting, 13 April 1981.

48. Tony Benn, *The End of an Era* (London, Hutchinson, 1992), pp. 120–2.
49. Judith Hart, 'Open letter'.
50. Neil Kinnock, 'Personality, Policies and Democratic Socialism', *Tribune*, 18 September 1981.
51. *The Times*, 8 September 1981.
52. N. Kinnock, 'Personality, Politics and Democratic Socialism'.
53. P. Seyd, *The Rise and Fall of the Labour Left*, pp. 135–6.
54. N. Kinnock, 'Personality, Politics and Democratic Socialism'.
55. P. Seyd, *The Rise and Fall of the Labour Left*, p. 165.
56. PC minutes, 11 November 1981; and PLP minutes, 12 November 1981.
57. See Mervyn Jones, *Michael Foot* (London, Victor Gollancz, 1994), pp. 467–78.
58. See Michael Crick, *The March of Militant* (London, Faber and Faber, 1986); and Eric Shaw, *Discipline and Discord* (Manchester, Manchester University Press, 1988).
59. HPC minutes, 5 April 1982, 10 April 1982, and 10 May 1982. See Lewis Minkin, *The Contentious Alliance Trade Unions and the Labour Party* (Edinburgh, Edinburgh University Press, 1991), p. 399. The Home Policy Committee was responsible for producing the drafts of the domestic sections of, amongst other party documents, *Labour's Draft Manifesto* (1980) and *The Socialist Alternative* (1981), as well as *Labour's Programme 1982* (1982).
60. RD: 671/January 1981; and J. Hart, 'Party Work on Industry', RD: 2145/March 1982.
61. IPSC minutes, 16 March 1982, 23 March 1982, 6 April 1982, 21 April 1982, and 28 April 1982; and NEC, *Report* (1982), p. 60. Few changes, however, were made to the drafts produced by the planning and public ownership working groups. See RD: 2337/April 1982. The Industrial Policy Sub-Committee's satisfaction with Labour's existing industrial policy commitments after 1979 is indicated by the amount of time spent by the committee examining relatively peripheral issues such as new technology and co-operatives. Support for the party's central policies was re-affirmed.
62. RD: 178/December 1979.
63. NEC, *Report* (1982), p. 58.
64. See *LPACR* (1979) and NEC, *Reports* (1980–1982).
65. NEC, *Report* (1982), pp. 58 and 60.
66. Interview, August 1993.
67. BBC, *The Wilderness Years*, 12 December 1995.
68. NEC report, 27 July 1983.
69. 'Future Work of the Department', RD: 4/June 1979.
70. HPC minutes, 10 May 1982.
71. See, for example, HPC minutes, 16 January 1981, 7 December 1981; and FEASC minutes, 30 April 1980, 9 April 1981, and 18 May 1981.
72. *The Times*, 5 April 1980.
73. *The Times*, 21 March 1980.
74. T. Benn, *Conflicts of Interest* (London, Hutchinson, 1990), p. 601.

75. T. Benn and E. Heffer, 'Labour's Election Manifesto', RD: 39/September 1979, p. 3. See also RD: 145/November 1979; *The Daily Telegraph*, 11 September 1979; and T. Benn, *Conflicts of Interest*, pp. 532–3.
76. HPC minutes, 10 September 1979; and NEC minutes, 28 November 1979, p. 20.
77. 'The Draft Manifesto', RD: 325/April 1980, p. 4. See also HPC minutes, 3 December 1979 and 14 April 1980; *The Times*, 5–6 December 1979 and 11 April 1980. It was agreed by the NEC; minutes, 28 May 1980.
78. PC minutes, 30 January 1980 and 7 February 1980.
79. PC minutes, 4 June 1980, 5 June 1980 and 9 July 1980; PLP minutes, 12 June 1980; NEC minutes, 25 June 1980; and HPC minutes, 7 July 1980.
80. *Labour Weekly*, 11 July 1980.
81. *The Times*, 10 July 1980.
82. NEC minutes, 23 July 1980, p. 86; and *The Times*, 24 July 1980.
83. HPC minutes, 1 December 1980, p. 1. A campaign document was produced early in 1983 which provided the basis for the election manifesto.
84. HPC minutes, 10 November 1982; and NEC minutes, 27 October 1982, p. 2.
85. Austin Mitchell, *Four Years in the Death of the Labour Party* (London, Methuen, 1983), p. 64.
86. Benn diary, 10 January 1983.
87. Benn diary, 19 May 1982.
88. The shadow cabinet had wanted a shorter document. PC minutes, 4 May 1983 and 10 May 1983.
89. David Butler and Dennis Kavanagh, *The British General Election of 1983* (London, Macmillan, 1984), p. 64.
90. D. Butler and D. Kavanagh, *The British General Election of 1983*, p. 61.
91. Quoted by Hilary Wainwright, *Labour: A Tale of Two Parties* (London, Hogarth, 1987), p. 70.
92. *The Sunday Times*, 22 May 1983.
93. *LPACR* (1982), pp. 67, 106 and 171–2.
94. Conference rejected the advice of the NEC on 26 occasions between 1979 and 1982, but few of these defeats were directly related to economic issues; L. Minkin, *The Contentious Alliance*, p. 312.
95. PC minutes, 19 May 1982.
96. See Austin Mitchell, 'Labour's Response to Thatcher', *Political Quarterly*, 51 (1980), pp. 257–73.
97. L. Minkin, *The Contentious Alliance*, p. 423.
98. 'Programme of Work', RD: 6/June 1979, p. 5.
99. L. Minkin, *The Contentious Alliance*, p. 398.
100. Interview, August 1993.
101. RD: 4/June 1979 and RD: 6/June 1979.
102. 'Programme of Work 1980/81', RD: 576/November 1980, p. 2.
103. PCC minutes, 11 February 1981.
104. PCC minutes, 8 April 1981.

105. RD: 832/April 1981.
106. Benn diary, 8 April 1981.
107. PCC minutes, 25 May 1982; and *Labour Weekly*, 4 June 1982.
108. RD: 2407A/June 1982.
109. RD: 2410/June 1982, p. 2.
110. 'Policy Development', RD: 2902/November 1983, p. 4.
111. PC minutes, 12 May 1982, 19 May 1982 and 17 June 1982.
112. PC minutes, 26 May 1982.
113. PC minutes, 19 May 1982.
114. *Tribune*, 28 May 1982.
115. Unresolved tensions also emerged between Labour's regional poli-
     cies as expressed by John Prescott and the planning proposals of
     the AES. See L. Minkin, *The Contentious Alliance*, pp. 432–3.
116. Benn diary, 8 June 1982. *The Guardian* commented 'Mr Shore criti-
     cised the programme and suggested greater emphasis on fiscal mat-
     ters', 9 June 1982.
117. Benn diary, 10 June 1982.
118. 'A Note on Priorities', RD: 2522/October 1982, pp. 9–10.
119. RD: 2889/October 1983, p. 3.
120. LC minutes, 27 April 1981, p. 286.
121. LC minutes, 24 November 1980; and 'Planning and Industrial Democ-
     racy', RD: 561/November 1980.
122. NEC minutes, 27 October 1982, p. 4; and *The Times*, 28 October
     1982.
123. TUC-Labour Party Liaison Committee, *Partners in Rebuilding Britain*
     (1983).
124. L. Minkin, *The Contentious Alliance*, p. 407.
125. HPC minutes, 8 February 1982, p. 1.
126. Benn diary, 25 May 1982.
127. Benn diary, 16 April 1981, 26 October 1981, and 21 December 1981.
128. Benn diary, 21 September 1981.
129. Benn diary, 21 September 1981.
130. Benn diary, 26 October 1981.
131. PIDSC minutes, 21 September 1981, p. 2. A point also made at an
     earlier meeting; minutes, 16 April 1981.
132. PIDSC minutes, 26 January 1982, p. 4.
133. Benn diary, 26 January 1982.
134. LC minutes, 24 May 1982, p. 3.
135. Benn diary, 26 April 1982.
136. *Labour's Programme 1982*, p. 43; and TUC-Labour Party Liaison Com-
     mittee, *Economic Planning and Industrial Democracy* (1982), pp. 17–18.
137. PIDSC minutes, 26 January 1982, p. 3.
138. LC minutes, 24 May 1982, p. 4.
139. LCC, *Labour Activist*, 20 December 1982; and S. Holland, 'Economic
     Objectives', in J. Lansman and A. Meale (eds), *Beyond Thatcher The
     Real Alternative* (London, Junction Books, 1983), pp. 17–38, p. 30.
140. HPC minutes, 8 March 1982, p. 1.
141. HPC minutes, 10 June 1982.
142. *The Sunday Times*, 31 August 1980.

143. Interview, August 1993.
144. Interview, September 1993.
145. 'A Re-evaluation of the NEC's Policy for Car Imports', RD: 744/ February 1981, p. 1; and NEC minutes, 23 April 1980.
146. *Labour Weekly*, 2 May 1980.
147. *Economic Reviews* included: TUC, *Plan for Growth* (1981); TUC, *Programme for Recovery* (1982); and TUC, *The Battle for Jobs* (1983).
148. See, for example, TUC, 'Import Penetration' (May 1980) recording a meeting with the Conservative Trade Secretary, John Nott.
149. *Tribune*, 3 October 1980.
150. LC minutes, 21 January 1980, p. 4.
151. LC minutes, 21 July 1980, pp. 255–6.
152. See, for example, TUC, *Annual Report* (1979), pp. 513 and 544; *Annual Report* (1981), pp. 501 and 626; and *Annual Report* (1982), p. 543
153. *Tribune*, 5 September 1980.
154. 'Policies and Priorities for Labour's Programme', RD: 2356/May 1982, p. 6.
155. For support see AUEW-TASS, *Import Controls Now* (1980); AUEW-TASS, *Save British Industry* (no date); NALGO, *Alternative Economic Strategy* (1983); TGWU, *Control Imports Now!* (1980); GMWU, *Building Industry in Crisis* (1981) and *Building Materials in Crisis* (1981). For opposition see EETPU, *Political Bulletin*, 3 (1980) and 9 (1983).
156. For example, Alan Sapper outlined the AES in the first issue of *New Socialist*; 'Industry on the Scrapheap', *New Socialist*, 1 (September/October 1981), pp. 19–24.
157. L. Minkin, *The Contentious Alliance*, p. 423.
158. *LPACR* (1979), p. 240.
159. *LPACR* (1979), p. 187.
160. *Tribune*, 14 September 1979.
161. 'Policy Coordination Committee', RD: 719/February 1981, p. 4.

CHAPTER 8: CONCLUSIONS

1. This section draws heavily from articles in the *Socialist Economic Review* (London, Merlin, 1981–3), especially Adam Sharples, 'Alternative Economic Strategies: Labour Movement Responses to the Crisis', *Socialist Economic Review*, 1 (1981), pp. 71–92; *Economic Bulletin*; *Politics and Power*;and *New Socialist*. See also CSE London Working Group, *The Alternative Economic Strategy* (London, CSE Books and the LCC, 1980); Ken Coates (ed.), *How to Win* (Nottingham, Spokesman, 1981); Francis Cripps et al, *Manifesto* (London, Pan, 1981); Sam Aaronovitch, *The Road from Thatcherism* (London, Lawrence and Wishart, 1981); Mike Prior and David Purdy, *Out of the Ghetto* (Nottingham, Spokesman, 1979); Geoff Hodgson, *Socialist Economic Strategy* (ILP, 1979); and Mark Wickham-Jones, 'The Political Economy of the Alternative Economic Strategy' (University of Manchester PhD Thesis, 1994), pp. 521–32.

2. Stuart Holland (ed.), *Out of Crisis* (Nottingham, Spokesman, 1983).
3. RD: 2751/March 1983.
4. Richard Pryke, *The Nationalised Industries* (Oxford, Martin Robertson, 1981), p. 257.
5. Robert Dahl, 'Workers' Control of Industry and the British Labour Party', *American Political Science Review*, XLI (1947), pp. 875–900, p. 875.
6. CEPG, *Cambridge Economic Policy Review*, 8 (1982), pp. 1–3.
7. See Tony Topham (ed.), *Planning the Planners* (Nottingham, Spokesman, 1983).
8. David Lipsey, 'A "Right" Critique of the Alternative Economic Strategy', *Socialist Economic Review*, 2 (1982), pp. 109–17.
9. Barry Hindess, *Parliamentary Democracy and Socialist Politics* (London, Routledge and Kegan Paul, 1983), p. 88.
10. Patrick Seyd, *The Rise and Fall of the Labour Left* (London, Macmillan, 1987), p. 30; and J. Tomlinson, *The Unequal Struggle?* (London, Methuen, 1982), pp. 2–4.
11. Anna Coote, 'The AES: A New Starting Point', *New Socialist* (November/December 1981), pp. 4–7.
12. Jean Gardiner and Sheila Smith, 'Feminism and the Alternative Economic Strategy' *Socialist Economic Review*, 2 (1982), pp. 31–46, p. 31.
13. He echoed many points made earlier by Crosland and others; Jim Tomlinson, *The Unequal Struggle*, pp. 99–122.
14. See S. Holland (ed.), *Out of Crisis*, p. 29.
15. Interview, Labour research official, August 1993.
16. Anthony Downs, *An Economic Theory of Democracy* (New York, Harper and Row, 1957), p. 28.
17. Ivor Crewe, 'Why the Conservatives Won', in Howard Penniman (ed.), *Britain at the Polls* (Washington, AEI, 1981), pp. 263–306; and Ivor Crewe, 'The Labour Party and the Electorate', in Dennis Kavanagh (ed.), *The Politics of the Labour Party* (London, George Allen and Unwin, 1982), pp. 9–49.
18. Gallup Political Index (July 1972), p. 113.
19. On import controls see Gallup Political Index, (September 1977, and July 1980). On industrial democracy see Gallup Political Index (September 1973), p. 160 and (September 1975), p. 8. For support for leaving the EEC, reflation, import controls and a Labour-union agreement on economic policy see Gallup Political Index (October 1981 and October 1982).
20. See, for example, RD: 2798/May 1983, p. 1.
21. Gallup Political Index (November 1974).
22. A. Heath, R. Jowell and J. Curtice, *How Britain Votes* (Oxford, Pergamon, 1985), p. 89.
23. Patrick Dunleavy and Christopher Husbands, *British Democracy at the Crossroads* (London, George Allen and Unwin, 1986), pp. 51–2; and Patrick Dunleavy, *Democracy, Bureaucracy and Public Choice* (London, Harvester Wheatsheaf, 1991), pp. 100–4 and 112–44.
24. 'The General Election Campaign A Note On Priorities', RD: 2522/October 1982, p. 2.

25. RD: 576/November 1980.
26. See Gallup Political Index (March 1974–June 1975).
27. A. Downs, *An Economic Theory of Democracy*, pp. 55–60.
28. RD: 716/February 1981, p. 2.
29. See Patrick Seyd, *The Rise and Fall of the Labour Left* (London, Macmillan, 1987), pp. 180–1.
30. For a theoretical account stressing the role of institutions see K. Thelen and S. Steinmo, 'Historical Institutionalism in Comparative Politics', in S. Steinmo, K. Thelen and F. Longstreth (eds), *Structuring Politics* (Cambridge, Cambridge University Press, 1992), pp. 1–32.
31. Jonas Pontusson, *The Limits of Social Democracy* (Cornell, Cornell University Press, 1992), p. 2.
32. See David Coates, *Labour in Power* (London, Longman, 1980), pp. 246–51; and David Coates, 'The Labour Party and the Transition to Socialism', *New Left Review*, 129 (1981), pp. 3–22. See also Alan Freeman, 'The Alternative Economic Strategy: A Critique', *International* (1981), pp 15–24; and Coventry Trades Council et al, *State Intervention in Industry*, pp. 141–62.
33. David Howell, *British Social Democracy* (London, Croom Helm, 1976), p. 289.
34. David Coates, *The Labour Party and the Struggle for Socialism* (Cambridge, Cambridge University Press, 1975), p. 211.
35. Leo Panitch, *Working Class Politics in Crisis* (London, Verso, 1986), p. 93. See also Leo Panitch, *Social Democracy and Industrial Militancy* (Cambridge, Cambridge University Press, 1976), pp. 229–30.
36. L. Panitch, *Working Class Politics in Crisis*, p. 101.
37. D. Coates, 'The Labour Party and the Transition to Socialism', pp. 5–7. See also David Coates, 'Space and Agency in the Transition to Socialism', *New Left Review*, 135 (1982), pp. 49–63.
38. L. Panitch, *Working Class Politics in Crisis*, p. 116.
39. See L. Panitch, *Working Class Politics in Crisis*, pp. 1–55; and L. Panitch 'Socialist Renewal and the Labour Party', *Socialist Register* (1988), pp. 319–65.
40. Bob Rowthorn, 'The Politics of the Alternative Economic Strategy', *Marxism Today* (January 1981), pp. 4–10; D. Coates, *Labour in Power*, p. 246; D. Coates, 'The Labour Party and the Transition to Socialism', pp. 9–11; and John Harrison, 'A "Left" Critique of the Alternative Economic Strategy', *Socialist Economic Review*, 2 (1982), pp. 117–26.
41. Ben Fine, 'Multinational Corporations, the British Economy and the Alternative Economic Strategy', *Economic Bulletin*, 10 (1983), pp. 10–35.
42. Andrew Glyn, *Capitalist Crisis Tribune's 'Alternative Strategy' or Socialist Plan* (Militant, 1983), pp. 37–9.
43. L. Panitch, 'Socialist Renewal and the Labour Party', p. 322.
44. See Ralph Miliband, *Parliamentary Socialism* (London, Merlin, 1972, originally, 1961), p. 376.
45. See D. S. King and M. Wickham-Jones, 'Social Democracy and Rational Workers', *British Journal of Political Science*, 20 (1990), pp. 387–413, pp. 406–412.

46. For example, A. Freeman, 'The Alternative Economic Strategy: A Critique', pp. 23–24.
47. D. Coates, *The Labour Party and the Struggle for Socialism*, p. 220.
48. S. Steinmo, 'Social Democracy versus Socialism: Goal Adaptation in Social Democratic Sweden', *Politics and Society*, 16 (1988), pp. 403–50, pp. 405 and 435.
49. J. Pontusson, *The Limits of Social Democracy*, p. 20.
50. L. Minkin, *The Labour Party Conference* (Manchester, Manchester University Press, 1980), pp. 239–42.
51. R. McKenzie, *British Political Parties* (London, Heinemann, 1967, originally 1955), p. 526.
52. RD: 2889/October 1983, p. 3.
53. Patrick Cosgrave, *The Spectator*, 17 February 1973.
54. 'An Agenda for Agreement', RE: 966/February 1977, p. 4.
55. P. Seyd, *The Rise and Fall of the Labour Left*, p. 159.
56. R. Crossman, *New Statesman*, 21 July 1961, p. 82.
57. Interview, November 1984.
58. NEC report, 27 July 1983.
59. N. Webb and R. Wybrow, *The Gallup Report* (London, Sphere, 1981), p. 24.
60. N. Webb and R. Wybrow, *The Gallup Report* (London, Sphere, 1982).
61. Gallup Political Index (May 1979–December 1981).
62. See Helmut Norpoth, *Confidence Regained* (Michigan, University of Michigan, 1992), p. 190; and Paul Whiteley, *The Labour Party in Crisis* (London, Methuen, 1983), pp. 46–50.
63. See Patrick Seyd and Paul Whiteley, *Labour's Grass Roots* (Oxford, Oxford University Press, 1992), p. 216.
64. See also P. Whiteley, *The Labour Party in Crisis*, p. 3.
65. Patrick Seyd, 'Labour: The Great Transformation', in Anthony King et al, *Britain at the Polls, 1992* (Chatham, New Jersey, 1993), pp. 70–100, p. 72.

EPILOGUE

1. See Colin Hughes and Patrick Wintour, *Labour Rebuilt* (London, Fourth Estate 1990); Martin Smith and Joanna Spear (eds), *The Changing Labour Party* (London, Routledge, 1991); and Steven Fielding, *Labour: Decline and Renewal* (Manchester, Baseline Books, 1995).
2. See David Butler and Dennis Kavanagh, *The British General Election of 1983* (London, Macmillan, 1984); Austin Ranney (ed.), *Britain at the Polls, 1983* (Durham, Duke University Press, 1985); and Michael Foot, *Another Heart and Other Pulses* (London, Collins, 1984).
3. G. Bish, 'The Failures: And Some Lessons', RD: 2808/July 1983, p. 5.
4. See 'Campaign Strategy', RD: 2797/May 1983; RD: 2798/May 1983; and RD: 2805/July 1983.
5. G. Bish 'Future Policy Development', RD: 2806/July 1983, p. 5.
6. 'The Failures: And Some Lessons', p. 5.
7. 'Programme of Work 1983–84', RD: 2889/October 1983, p. 1.
8. 'Future Policy Development', p. 1.

9. Neil Kinnock, 'Reforming the Labour Party', *Contemporary Record*, vol. 8, no 4 (1994), pp. 535–554, p. 536.
10. D. Butler and P. Jowett, *Party Strategies in Britain* (London, Macmillan, 1985), pp. 57–70; and D. Butler and D. Kavanagh, *The British General Election of 1987* (London, Macmillan, 1988), pp. 47–73.
11. See Lewis Minkin, *The Contentious Alliance Trade Unions and the Labour Party* (Edinburgh, Edinburgh University Press, 1991), pp. 395–484; Patrick Seyd, 'Labour: The Great Transformation', in Antony King et al, *Britain at the Polls 1992* (Chatham, New Jersey, Chatham House, 1993), pp. 70–100; and Eric Shaw, *The Labour Party since 1979* (London, Routledge, 1994), pp. 117–23.
12. Neil Kinnock, 'Reforming the Labour Party', p. 536.
13. Patrick Seyd, 'Benn without Bennism', *New Socialist*, 27 (May 1985), pp. 5–10; and Patrick Seyd, *The Rise and Fall of the Labour Left* (London, Macmillan, 1987), p. 170.
14. Patrick Seyd and Paul Whiteley, *Labour's Grass Roots* (Oxford, Oxford University Press, pp. 152 and 161.
15. Neil Kinnock, 'Reforming the Labour Party', p. 536.
16. RD: 2889/October 1983, p. 2.
17. Neil Kinnock, 'Reforming the Labour Party', p. 538 and p. 539.
18. RD: 2889/October 1983, p. 5.
19. NEC, *Report* (1984), p. 70; D. Butler and D. Kavanagh, *The British General Election of 1987*, p. 54; Richard Heffernan and Mike Marqusee, *Defeat from the Jaws of Victory* (London, Verso, 1992) pp. 46–7; and M. Van Hattem, 'The Labour Party's Second Term of Opposition', *Political Quarterly*, 55 (1984), pp. 364–8, p. 368.
20. RD: 2951/March 1984, p. 2.
21. G. Bish, 'Future Policy Development', p. 3.
22. R. Hattersley, *A Duty to Win* (London, 1983), p. 53.
23. *The Economist*, 8 October 1983.
24. Interview, TUC Official, August 1993
25. Interview, TUC Official, September 1993.
26. John Eatwell, 'The Development of Labour Policy, 1979–1992', in J. Michie (ed.), *The Economic Legacy* (London, Academic Press, 1992), pp. 333–9, p. 336.
27. RD: 2798/May 1983, p. 4.
28. RD: 2805/July 1983, p. 3.
29. Labour party, *Britain Will Win* (1987).
30. J. Eatwell, 'The Development of Labour Policy, 1979–1992', pp. 334–335.
31. A. Glyn, *A Million Jobs a Year* (London, Verso, 1985).
32. Interview, March 1992.
33. See the discussion in M. Mackintosh and H. Wainwright (eds), *A Taste of Power* (London, Verso, 1987).
34. Sam Aaronovitch, 'Goodbye to All That?', *Marxism Today* (February 1986), pp. 20–26.
35. Patrick Seyd and Paul Whiteley, *Labour's Grass Roots*, pp. 89–90.
36. P. Seyd, Labour: the Great Transformation', p. 97.
37. Paul Whiteley and Patrick Seyd, 'Labours Vote and Local Activism', *Parliamentary Affairs*, 45 (1992), pp. 582–595.

Index